Build

Web Applications

With

Java

Learn every aspect to build web applications from scratch

Yousuf Baig

Build Web Applications with Java

ISBN-13: 978-1514668078

ISBN-10: 1514668076

In loving memory of my mother late Anees Ayesha

CONTENTS

PREFACE xvii

1 INTRODUCTION 1

What are we building? 1

Why are we building? 1

How are we building? 1

The Outline 2

Step 1: Compose Requirements Specifications. 2

Step 2: Create Prototype of the Application. 2

Step 3: Blueprint the Architecture and High Level Design. 2

Step 4: Design the Database. 2

Step 5: Build the Java Framework. 3

Step 6: Build the Shared Components. 3

Step 7: Build the Individual Use Cases. 3

Step 8: Testing. 3

Step 9: Deployment. 4

2 PREPARING THE ENVIRONMENT 5

Hardware Requirements 5

Software Requirements 5

Installing Oracle XE Database 6

Installing Oracle jdeveloper 11g 14

Installing Apache Tomcat 8 23

3 SDLC, OOAD AND UML **27**

Software Development Life Cycle (SDLC) 27

Object Oriented Analysis and Design (OOAD) 30

Unified Modeling Language (UML) 30

Use Case Diagram 30

Class Diagram 31

Sequence Diagram 31

Activity Diagram 31

4 REQUIREMENTS **33**

The Requirements Phase 33

Requirements Specifications 33

Application Title 34

Executive Summary 34

Detailed Requirements Specification 34

Authentication and Authorization Module 35

R1: The Authentication. 35

R2: The Authorization 35

The Student Module 36

R3: Load Student 36

R4: Unique Student Identifier. 37

R5: Student Details. 37

R6: Student Academics. 38

Scholastic Performance - Core Curriculum - Assessment 39

Co – Scholastic Activities 39

Scholastic Performance - Co Curriculum - Assessment 40

Synthesis and Recommendations 41

R7: Show Student Attendance. 41

R8: Student Fees. 42

The Administration Module 43

R9: Manage Student Attendance. 43

R10: Add Student. 45

R11: Report by Class. 48

Report Criteria 49

Report Results 49

The Help and Miscellaneous Module 49

R12: Help Pages. 49

R13: Header and Footer. 50

R14: The Menu. 50

5 PROTOTYPING 53

Page layout and template 54

Prototype 1: Login Page. 57

Prototype 2: Dashboard/Home Page 58

Prototype 3: Load Student. 59

Prototype 4: Student Details Page.......60

Prototype 5: Student Results Page for Semester 1. 61

Prototype 5: Student Results Page for Semester 2. 62

Prototype 6: Student Attendance Page for Semester 1.......63

Prototype 6: Student Attendance Page for Semester 2.......64

Prototype 7: Fees Status Page.......65

Prototype 8: Manage Attendance Page. 66

Prototype 9: Add Student Page.......67

Prototype 10: Report by class page with report criteria options. 68

Prototype 10: Report by class page with report data.......69

Prototype 11: Help pages, results legend page. 70

6 THE CLIENT SIDE 71

JavaScript.......71

BisScript.js.......72

Cascaded Style Sheet 73

BISStyle.css 74

7 THE PATTERNS 79

Architectural Patterns.......80

MVC 80

Design Patterns.......80

Command Pattern.......80

Front Controller Design Patten 81

Value Object Design Pattern ... 81

8 THE ARCHITECTURE ... **83**

The BIS-SMS Application Architecture ... 84

9 DATABASE DESIGN ... **87**

BisSecurityRealm Schema ... 87

Users Table ... 88

User Roles Table ... 88

Bis Schema ... 88

Student Details Table ... 88

Parent Details Table ... 88

Employee Details Table ... 89

Transportation Details Table ... 89

Class Teacher Mapping Table ... 89

Student Attendance Table ... 89

Student Fees Table ... 89

Scholastic Results/Co Scholastic Results Tables ... 90

BIS Constants Table ... 90

10 THE FRAMEWORK ... **93**

The MVC Based Java Framework ... 93

View Layer ... 94

Model Layer ... 94

Controller Layer ... 94

BisFramework ... 95

The BisFramework Architecture ... 96

Client Tier 96
Database Tier 96
Web Server Tier 97
View Layer 97
Controller Layer 97
Model Layer 97
Command Processor 98
The Control Flow 98

11 THE LOGGING 101

What is logging and why it is needed? 101

Logging Levels 101

Using Log4j in jdeveloper 102

The log4j.properties file 105

12 SESSION MANAGEMENT 107

Understanding Session 107

Leveraging Http Session 108

13 INTERACTING WITH THE DATABASE 111

The approaches for database connectivity 111

Using Data Sources 112

14 THE BIS-SMS PROJECT COMPONENTS 113

Java Servlets 113

ControllerServlet.java 115

AjaxControllerServlet.java....117

The Command Processors....119

BisCP.java....121

BisCommand.java....121

The Service Classes....122

BisService.java....124

The Java Beans....124

StudentBean.java....126

BisBean.java....127

The Utility Classes....128

Bisutility.java....128

DatabaseService.java....132

BisConstants.java....134

The Java Server Pages....135

BisHome.jsp....137

Log4j....142

15 IMPLEMENTING USE CASES....143

Use Case: Authentication....144

BisLogin.jsp....145

Use Case: Authorization....149

BisDashboard.jsp....149

BisHome.jsp....157

Use Case: Load Student....158

LoadStudentCP.java....162

StudentDetailsService.java 163
BisDashboard.jsp 165
BisScript.js 166

Use Case: Get student details. 167
GetStudentDetailsCP.java 173
StudentDetailsService.java 174
StudentDetailsBean.java 182
StudentDetails.jsp 187

Use Case: Get student attendance. 196
GetStudentAttendanceCP.java 198
StudentAttendanceService.java 199
StudentAttendanceBean.java 206
StudentAttendance.jsp 207

Use Case: Get student fees. 211
GetStudentFeesCP.java 213
StudentFeesService.java 214
StudentFeesBean.java 217
StudentFees.jsp 222

Use Case: Get student results. 230
GetStudentAcademicsCP.java 232
StudentAcademicsService.java 234
StudentResultsBean.java 238
StudentAcademics.jsp 246

Use Case: Help pages. 256
ResultsLegend.html 257

Use Case: Report by class. 263
GetReportByClassCP.java 267
ReportByClassService.java 268
ReportByClassBean.java 272
ReportByClass.jsp 273
Use Case: Add Student. 277
AddStudentCP.java 281
AddStudentService.java 283
StudentDetailsBean.java 291
AddStudent.jsp 291
Use Case: Manage Student Attendance. 297
ManageAttendanceCP.java 301
StudentAttendanceService.java 303
StudentAttendanceBean.java 304
ManageAttendance.jsp 304
16 SECURING APPLICATION 311
Configuring data source security realm for Apache Tomcat 8 311
Enabling Security for BIS-SMS 314
BIS-SMS Users and Roles 315
17 BUILD AND DEPLOYMENT 317
The Web Application Archive 317
Building the Bis.war file 318
Deploying the .war file 321
Deploying Bis.war to Apache Tomcat 322

18 TESTING **325**

Unit Testing 325

System Testing 325

User Acceptance Testing (UAT) 326

19 DEBUGGING **327**

What is a bug? 327

Steps to resolve a bug 327

Describe the bug 327

Reproduce the bug 327

Diagnosis and resolution 328

Verifying the fix 330

Applying the patch 330

20 OTHER IMPORTANT TOPICS **331**

AJAX 331

Performance tuning and best practices 332

Scalability 333

21 IMPORTANT FILES **335**

web.xml 335

Context.xml 337

22 APPENDIX **339**

Database scripts 339

Schema: BisSecurityRealm 339

Schema: bis 339

Index **343**

PREFACE

Software engineering is a very vast and complex field. There are many programming languages, technologies, platforms, frameworks and methodologies available to build software solutions. To build software solutions a team with various roles is required. Each member of the team is required to have skills and experience for a particular role and responsibilities. For technical roles like developer, technical lead and solutions architect the umbrella of technical skills requirement is vast. Such roles demand knowledge, skills and understanding of programming languages, frameworks, patterns and other technologies.

The most popular programming language for building web based applications is Java. Java provides the standard edition which provides the core object oriented programming language capabilities. It also provides the enterprise edition using which enterprise applications can be built. There are many open source and paid frameworks available in the market built using Java programming language. These frameworks provide an option to quickly build web and enterprise applications. The popular frameworks for building web applications using Java provide lots of reusable components and many configurable solutions that help organizations save time, money and effort.

To be successful on a technical role in an organization or to build web applications using Java as an independent freelancer or to start a career in Java as a web programmer/developer it demands:

- To have expertise knowledge of Java programming language.
- Hands on experience of one or more popular frameworks like Spring, Struts and Oracle ADF.

- At least intermediate skill level of pl/sql and popular databases like Oracle and DB2.
- Knowledge of web tier technologies like Servlet, JSPs, HTML, CSS and JavaScript.
- Knowledge of web server, servlet containers and application servers.
- Fundamental knowledge of various security threats and their solutions.

That is the minimum list of requirement for skills, experience and knowledge besides the logical ability, intelligence quotient and other human intellectual parameters.

There are many good books available in the market which **independently** teach Java, Web Servers, MVC based Frameworks, JSP, PL/SQL, AJAX, JavaScript, CSS, HTML5, UML, SDLC etc. This book covers all of these things plus other aspects **together** while building an actual web application from inception till completion. This books takes a sample web application and builds it from scratch. Each aspect is explained at micro level with real time examples along with the uml diagrams and working code. The fundamental concepts of software engineering and programming web applications are covered with high importance. ***To get maximum benefit out of this book, it is strongly recommended to build the sample web application while going through the book.***

Objective

The objective of this book is to teach building modern day business web applications using java programming language and relevant technologies. This book teaches everything about building web applications with medium to high level of complexity in detail and in simpler way. This book also covers various software engineering concepts that are required for building software solutions.

The book takes you through each and every step of building a web application from scratch. The objective is to teach the reader every single aspect of software engineering required for building web applications from inception till deployment and support. In order to achieve the objective, a real life business requirement is taken and the sample project is built step by step from requirements gathering till deployment and support.

The book includes building a light weight MVC based Java framework and building the sample web application using it. During the course architecture, SDLC, UML, security, ajax, various patterns, best practices and other related topics are explained.

Prerequisite

Beginners level knowledge of Java programming language, database and web related technologies is required.

Audience

Anyone who wants to learn building web applications with Java programming language. This book is primarily intended for beginners who wants to learn various aspects of software engineering and building web applications using Java programming language. This book is not limited for the said audience, it can be used for reference by the architects, project managers and other stakeholders who are involved in a web based application project.

Disclaimer

The objective of this book is to teach the reader the various aspects of building web applications using Java programming language and related technologies. The sample application that is build as a part of learning is not meant for any real business purpose in as is condition. Neither the author nor the publisher holds any responsibility or legal liability in any such case.

Errors

Though every care is taken to make sure that the content of the book is of highest quality. Yet, human errors and mistakes do happen. In any such case, please notify the author at yousuf.baig@gmail.com. This will help the author in fixing any slipped errors or mistakes.

Questions and Feedback

The author is available on most of the popular social networking sites including facebook, linkedin and twitter. In case of any questions or feedback, the author can also be contacted at yousuf.baig@gmail.com.

Acknowledgements

First, thanks to my parents for everything. Thanks to my wife Asiya Baig for her love and support for my first book project. Many thanks to my sister Nazia Meraj and friend Shoukat Ali for always being there for me. Special thanks to my colleagues and friends for encouraging and supporting this book project. Thanks for motivating me and helping me with the suggestions and reviews. Big thanks to my children Myiesha, Zain and Zaid for their love and for being my inspiration in life.

1

INTRODUCTION

What are we building?

Through out the book we will be building a web based student management system (SMS) for a hypothetical school called "Baig International School" (BIS). The sample web application is abbreviated as BIS-SMS.

Why are we building?

The best way to learn anything in programming world is by getting the hands dirty. When a developer starts building any software solution, he/she gets lots of doubts and questions **while** actually doing it. We are building the sample BIS-SMS web application in order to learn various aspects of building web applications from scratch. When the reader architects, designs and does the coding hands on, the reader learns every aspect practically. When the reader builds the working application step by step, the confidence of the reader as a developer is boosted.

How are we building?

We are building the BIS-SMS web application following the water fall software development life cycle (SDLC) model. The approach for building the application using this model is detailed in the outline below.

The Outline

Here is the outline of the sample web application we will be building. We will follow waterfall model for the development of sample application. Hence, the below mentioned steps will strictly go in order. For. e.g. step 3 will not be touched before completion of step 2 which in turn is dependent on step 1.

Step 1: Compose Requirements Specifications.

Here we will pen down what the application will provide in detail. This will also draw the scope of our project. The requirements specifications needs to be clear, concise and specific.

Step 2: Create Prototype of the Application.

Here we will create plain HTML pages for each web page of the BIS-SMS application. We will also add navigation links between pages. This should clearly demonstrate how the application will look like and how it will behave upon user interaction. In short, this is referred to as UI (user interface) and UX (user experience). This should virtually represent the complete application with every single page and functionality mocked up in the prototype.

Step 3: Blueprint the Architecture and High Level Design.

Here we will create the ariel view of the application. This will show case the bigger picture which provides the quick understanding of functionalities, distribution and interaction of various modules, tiers and technologies. The best analogy is a house building plan which show cases the number of rooms, living area, utilities etc. The outcome of this exercise will be the software architecture diagram with details of each entity in it.

Step 4: Design the Database.

This is one of the most important activity. The database design has to be done very diligently living zero (ideally) or minimum scope for changes or modification in the future. A change in database entities like tables will have ripple effect on the design and code. For example, adding or removing a column even in a single database table after coding will have an impact everywhere including design, code and test cases, potentially the database queries may break.

Step 5: Build the Java Framework.

We will be building our own light weight MVC based framework. Once the framework is ready, it will help us focusing more on implementing business logic for individual use cases. The framework will provide us all the basic services. Remember, the framework we will be building is ***reusable***. The same can be used for building other web applications.

Step 6: Build the Shared Components.

We will identify and build all the shared components. Shared components are the reusable components which will be used throughout the application. Utility classes are the best example for shared components. For example a utility class for getting and releasing database connection can be built before the actual use cases implementation. To get a database connection, we will only be importing this class and making a method call which returns us a database connection.

Step 7: Build the Individual Use Cases.

We will list down all the use cases and start build one by one. Each use case will leverage the framework and the shared libraries to achieve the business logic it requires. Here we will detail the objective, flow and state of various entities via various diagrams. This will serve as low level design. This has to be very clear and complete. Looking at the low level design the developer should be able to code the use case.

Step 8: Testing.

We will finally test the application from end to end. This is referred to as system testing where we will integrate and test all the use cases together. We will also test all the use cases individually before integration, this is called unit testing. Post integration, the whole application will behave as single system for the end user. This testing will show us the end users perspective. This is referred to as User Acceptance Testing (UAT). We will perform unit testing, module testing, system testing and UAT in the order mentioned.

Step 9: Deployment.

This is the final step where we will bundle the application and deploy it to the server. Here we will build and deploy our application to the server. Prior to deployment we need to create dependencies like Data Sources on the server. We will create such artifacts before deployment. We will also look into various options available to build and deploy our application to the server.

2

PREPARING THE ENVIRONMENT

In this chapter we will create the design time and run time environment which will be used to build and deploy the sample application. Below is the list of hardware and software requirements.

Hardware Requirements

A laptop or a desktop with the following minimum configuration is recommended.

Processor: i3 or higher

RAM: 4 Gb Minimum

Software Requirements

In order to build and deploy the sample application, we need to install the following software.

Operation System: Any UNIX flavor or windows OS. However, windows is strongly recommended as the book explains building the sample application on windows 7 OS specifically. Installing OS is outside the scope of this book. If non windows OS is used, the installation instructions for the particular OS needs to be followed. Ensure that the setup/installation is available for the OS used. It may be required to download a different version of the setup/installation files based on the OS and version.

Database: Oracle XE 10g.

Web Server: Apache Tomcat 8 is used for deploying the application. This provides both the web server as well as the servlet container.

IDE: Oracle jdeveloper 11g is the integrated development environment (IDE) used for developing the application.

Let us get started with the installation of Oracle XE database, Oracle jdeveloper 11g and Apache Tomcat 8 server. Note that, all the installation instructions below applies to Windows 7 OS. For other operating systems, the installation instructions may differ.

Installing Oracle XE Database

Step 1: Download Oracle XE 10g setup file from: http://www.oracle.com/technology/products/database/xe for windows.

Step 2: Log on to windows with a user that has administrative privileges. Right click OracleXE.exe file and click run as administrator. This will launch the installer as shown in the figure below.

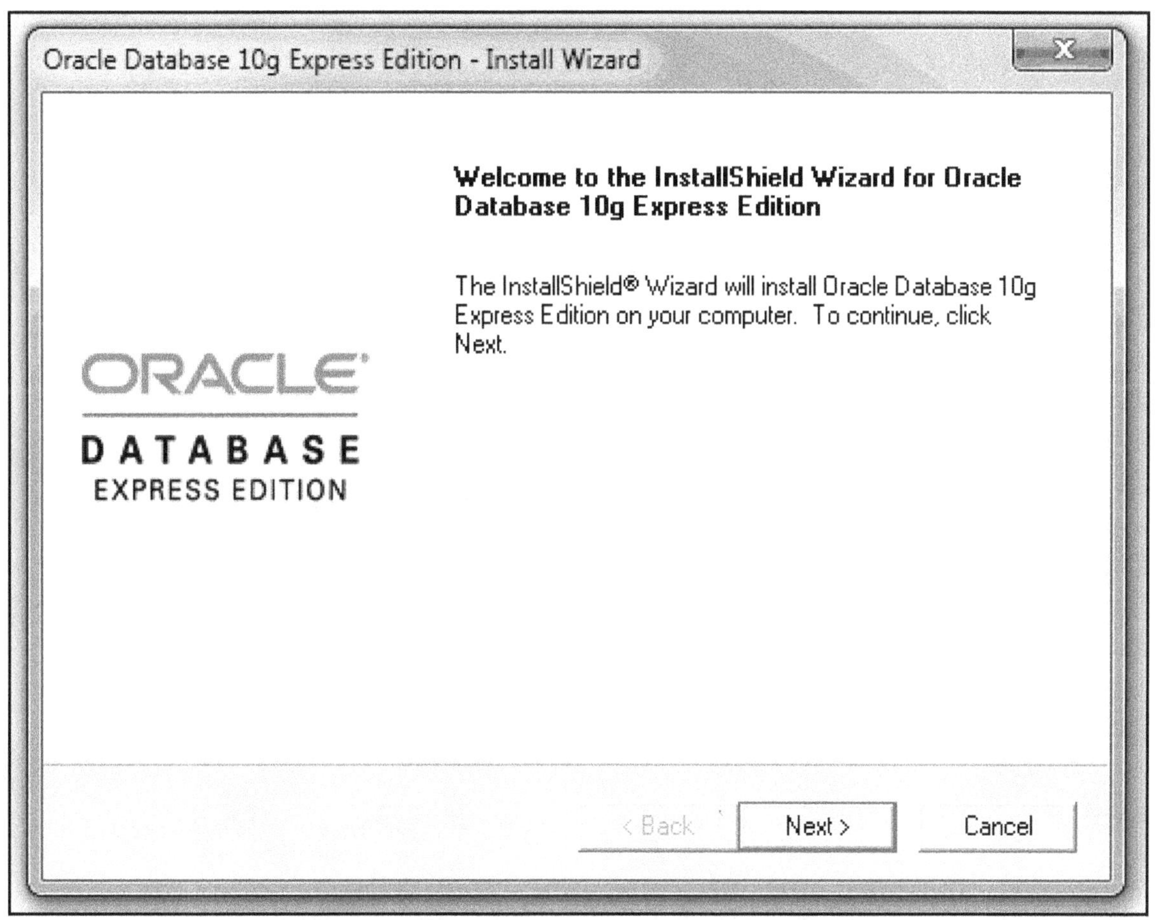

Step 3: Click next on the install wizard welcome window.

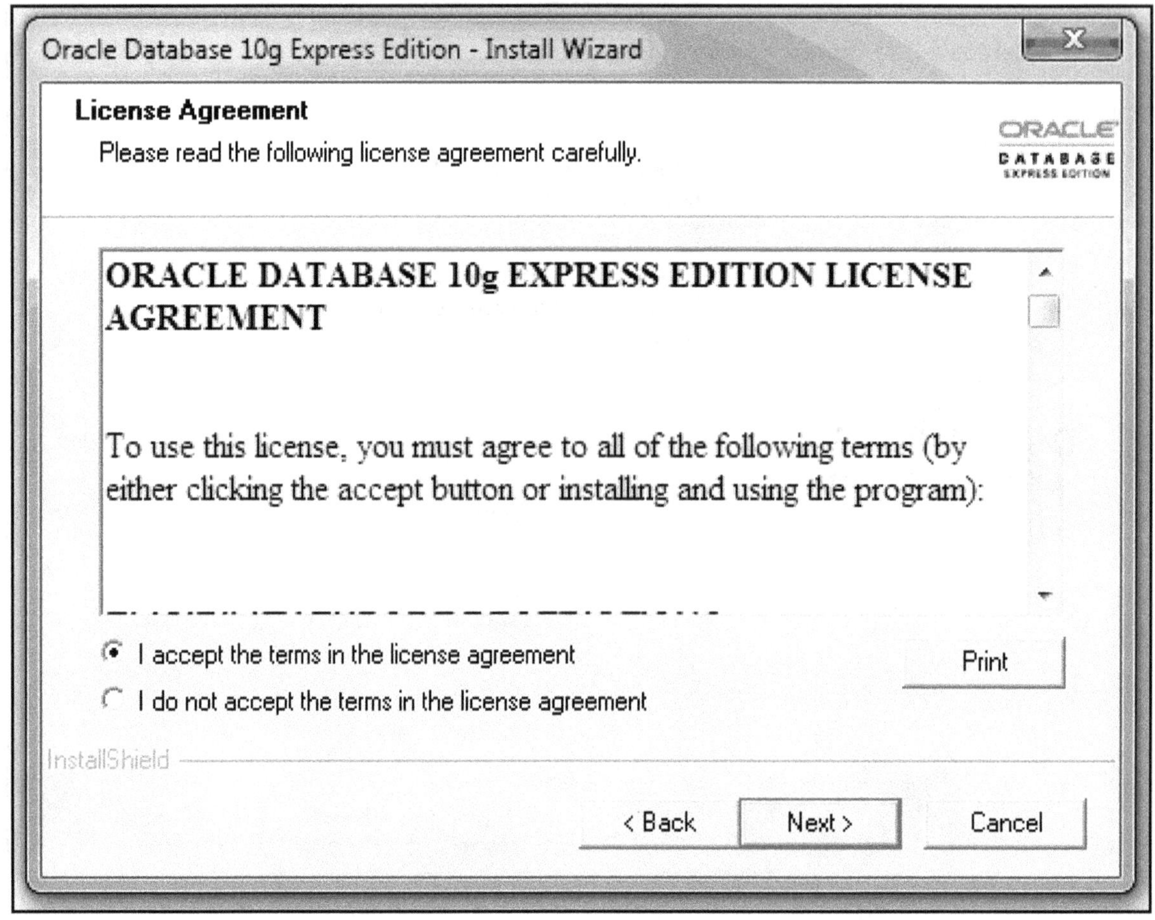

Step 4: You will be prompted with License Agreement details. Select "I Accept" and click next.

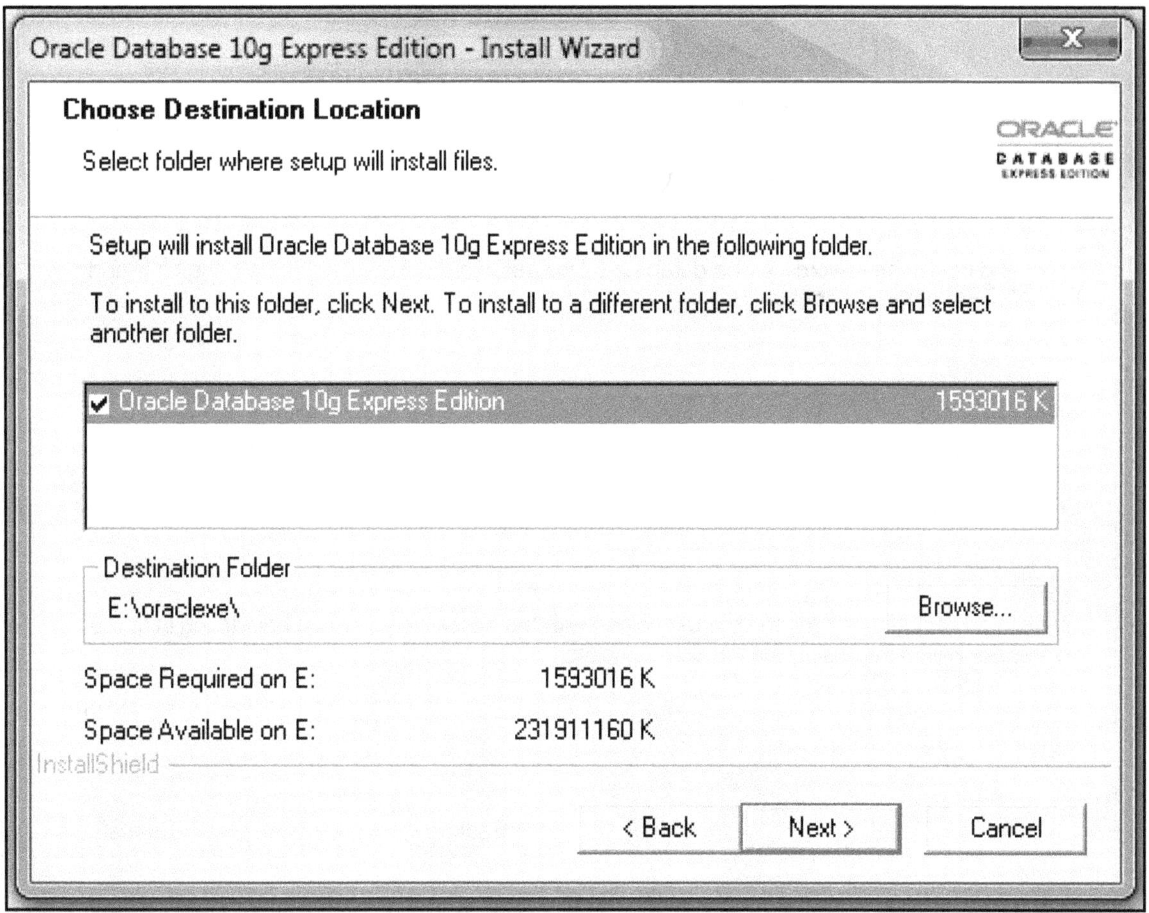

Step 5: Make sure that Oracle Database 10g Express Edition is selected. Specify a destination folder for the database installation and click next.

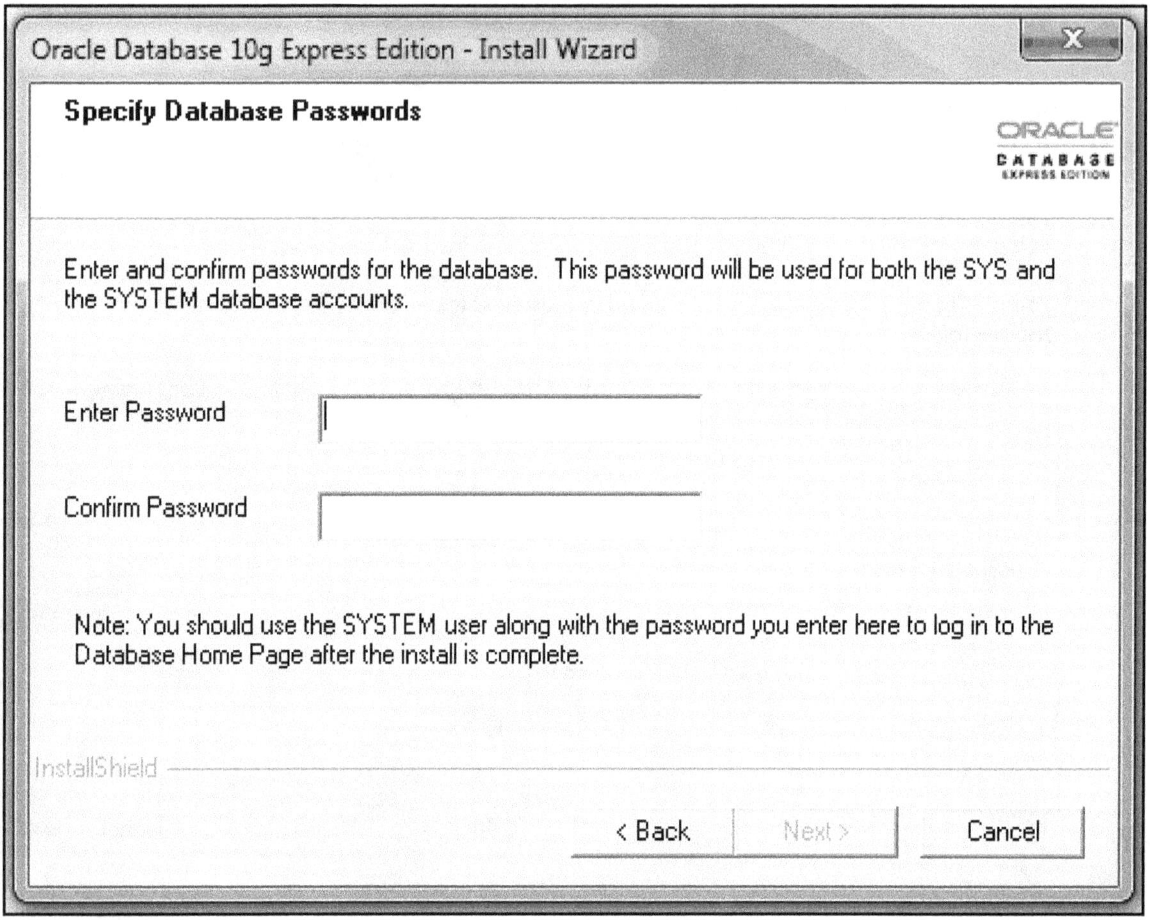

Oracle Database 10g Express Edition - Install Wizard

Specify Database Passwords

ORACLE DATABASE EXPRESS EDITION

Enter and confirm passwords for the database. This password will be used for both the SYS and the SYSTEM database accounts.

Enter Password

Confirm Password

Note: You should use the SYSTEM user along with the password you enter here to log in to the Database Home Page after the install is complete.

InstallShield

< Back Next > Cancel

Step 6: Specify the password for SYS and SYSTEM accounts and click next. Note that this password is required in later stages for administering the database.

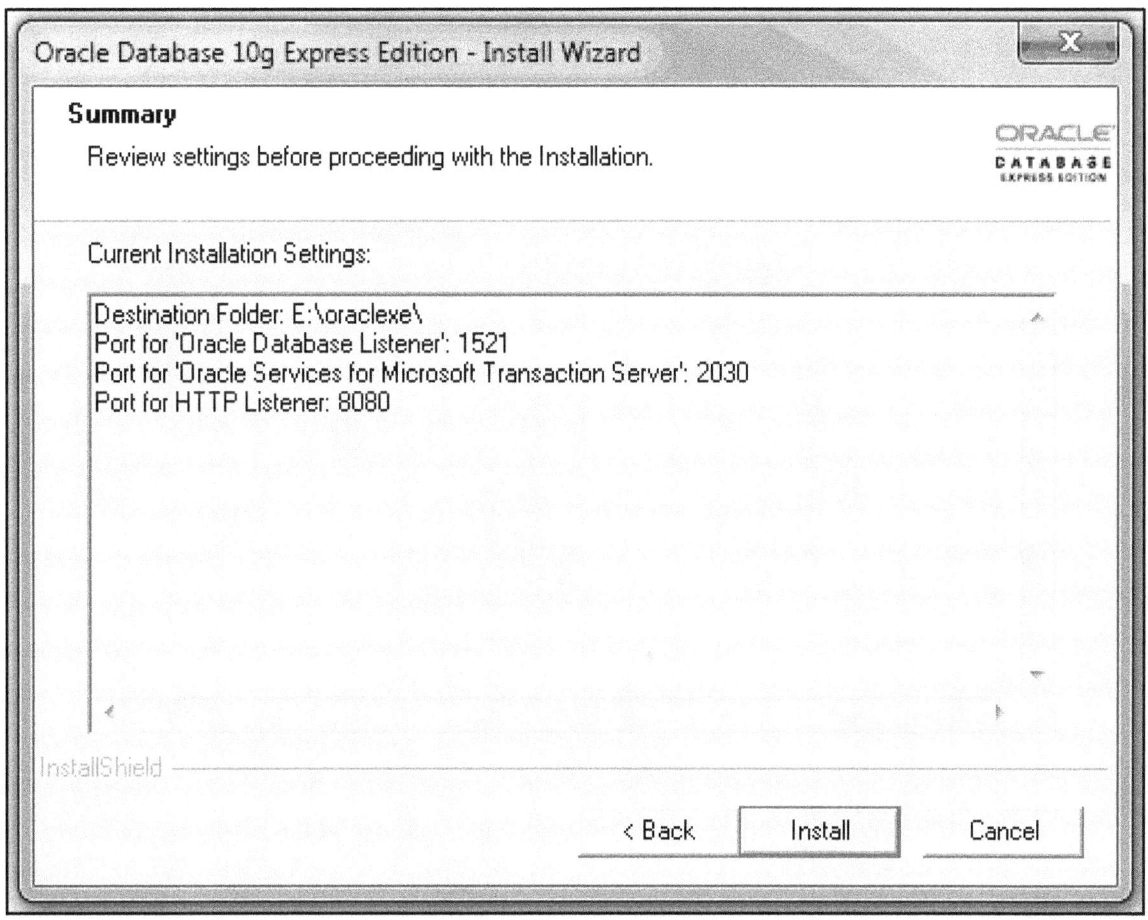

Step 7: The installation summary page is displayed. Click install to proceed.

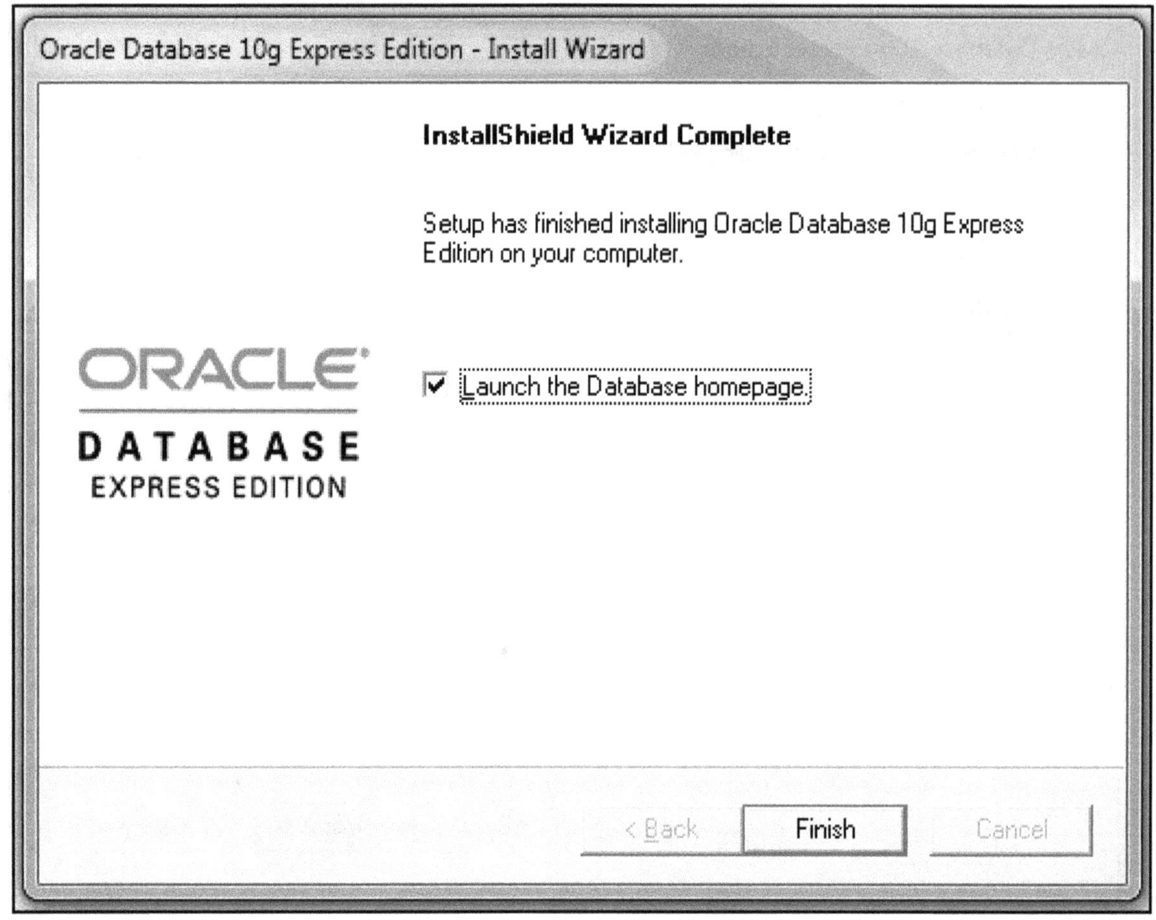

Step 8: The wizard displays the confirmation for the completion of the installation. Keep the Launch the Database homepage option checked and click finish.

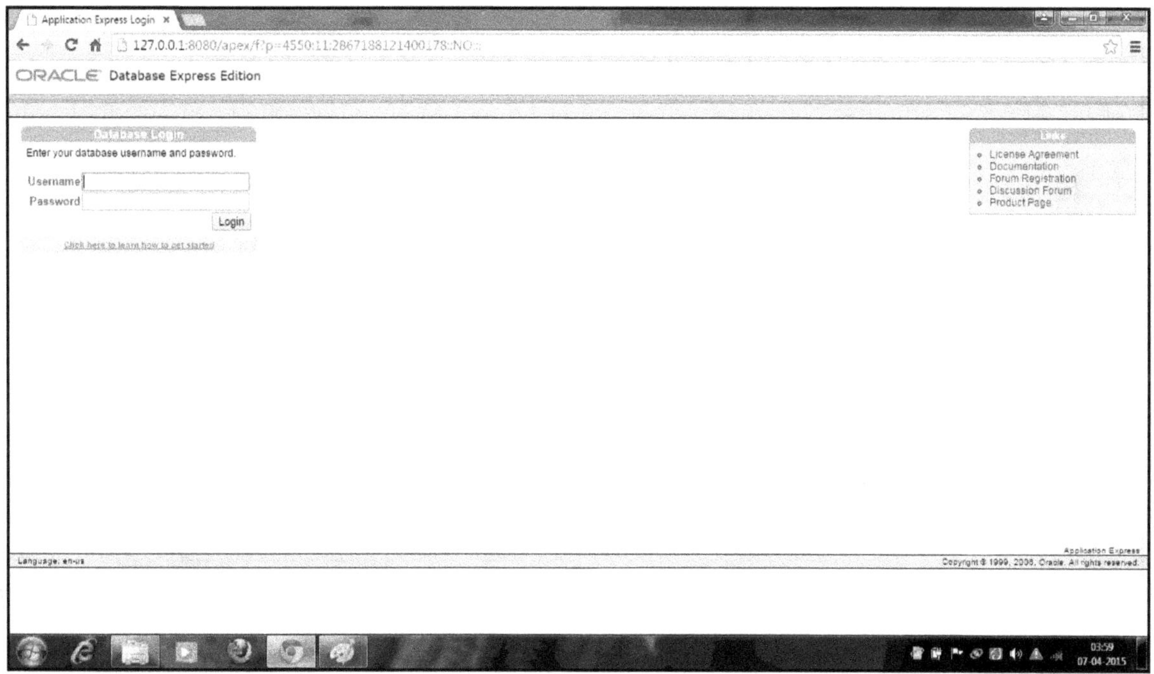

Step 9: This will launch the browser with the home page of the database just installed. Enter sys or system user with the password to login. Upon successful login, the following page is displayed.

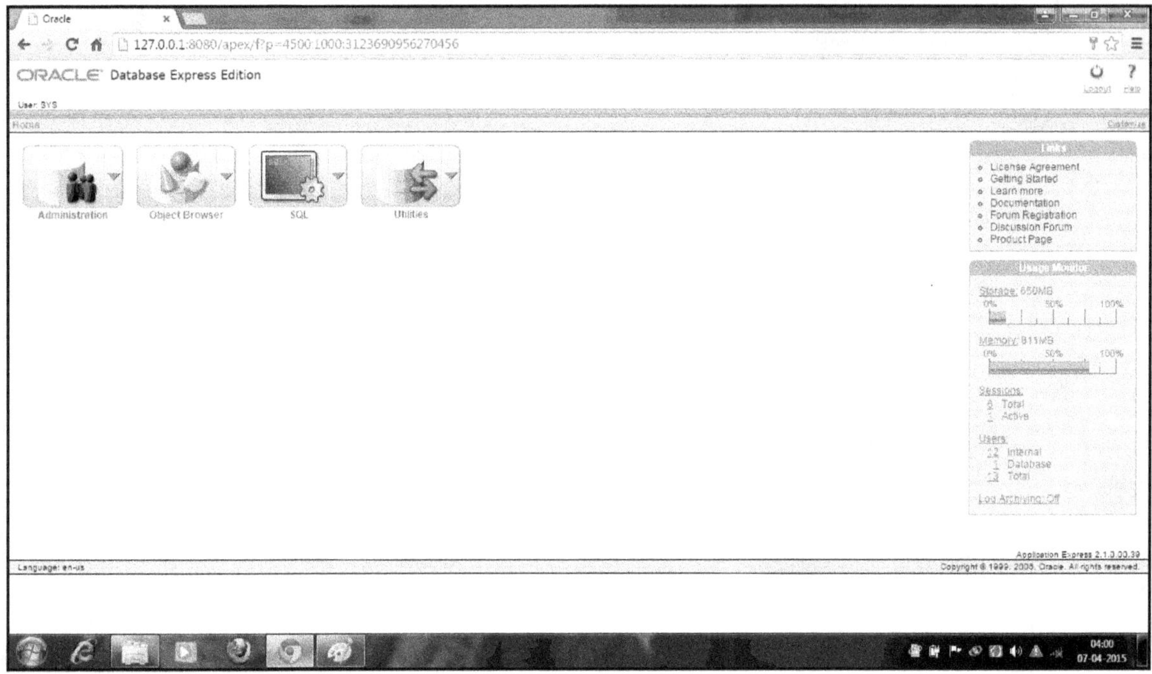

This concludes the installation of Oracle XE 10g database.

Installing Oracle jdeveloper 11g

Step 1: Download the installer for Oracle jdeveloper 11g from:
http://www.oracle.com/technetwork/developer-tools/jdev/downloads/index.html

Step 2: Log on to windows with a user that has administrative privileges. Right click jdevstudio11123install.exe file and click run as administrator.

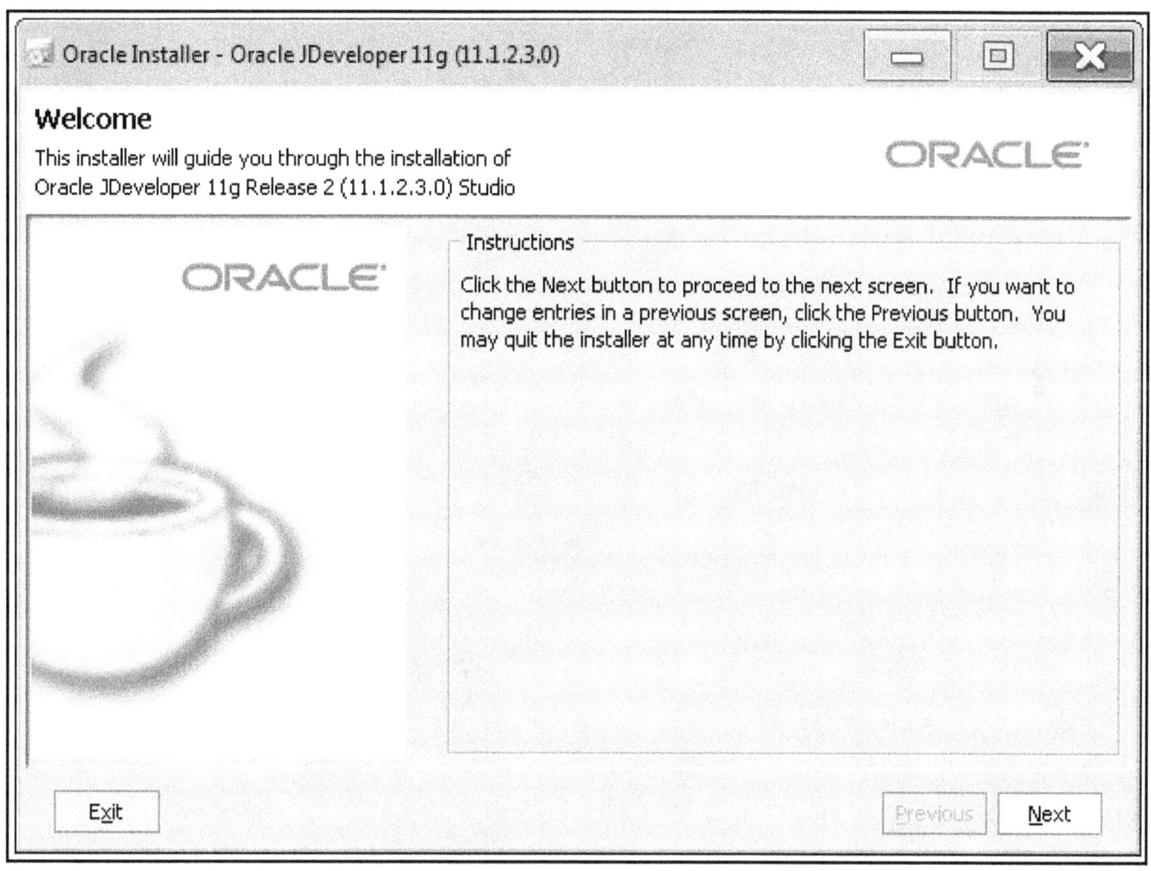

Step 3: This will launch the installer. Click next to proceed.

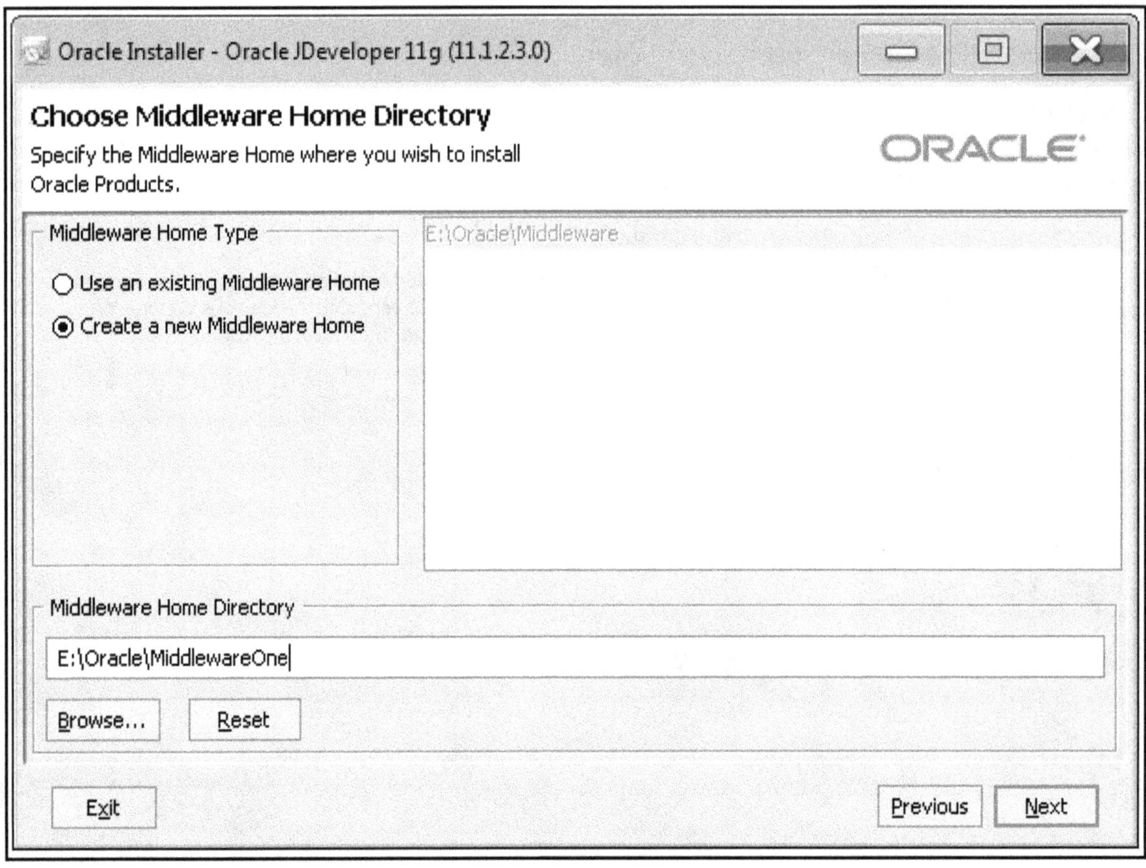

Step 4: Select "Create a new Middleware Home" radio and specify a home directory for the oracle middleware. This is the root directory where all the Oracle Middleware software will be installed. Click next to proceed.

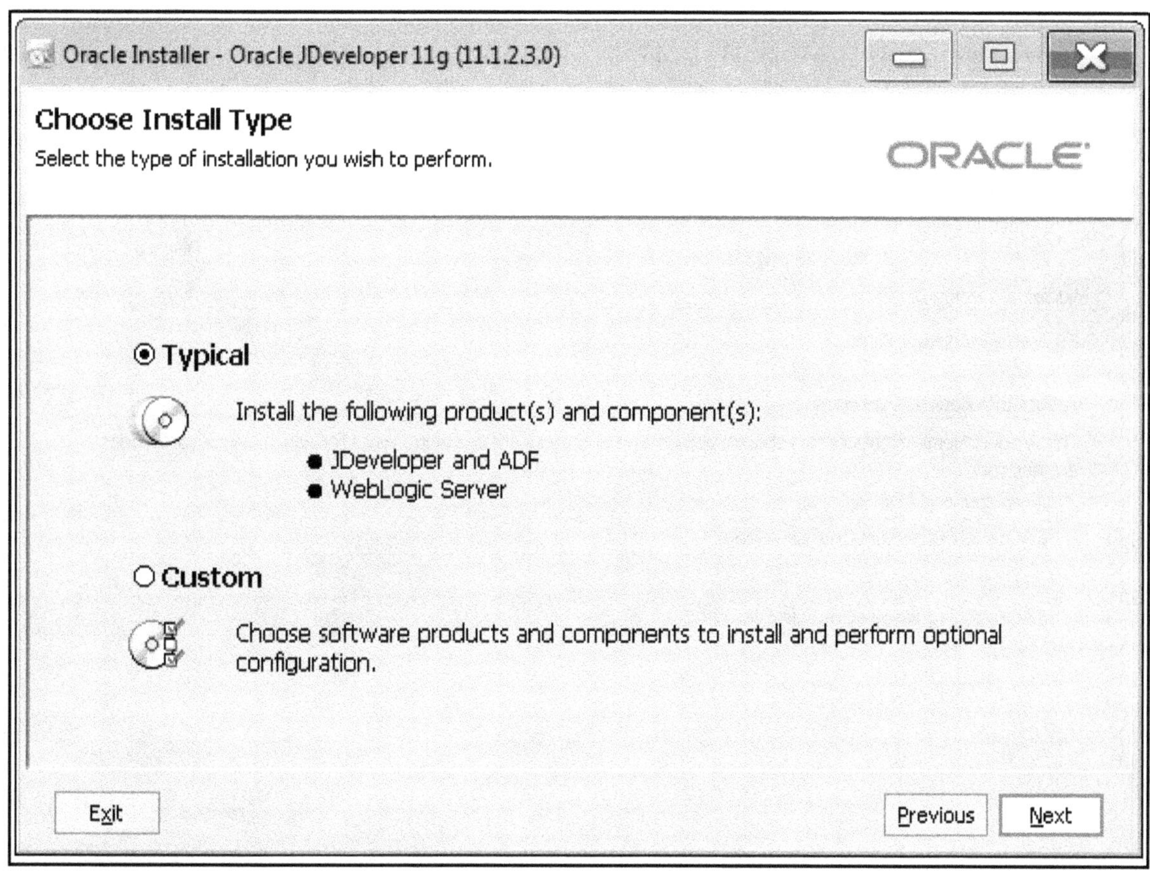

Step 5: Select Typical. This will install jdeveloper, ADF and Weblogic Server. Click next to proceed.

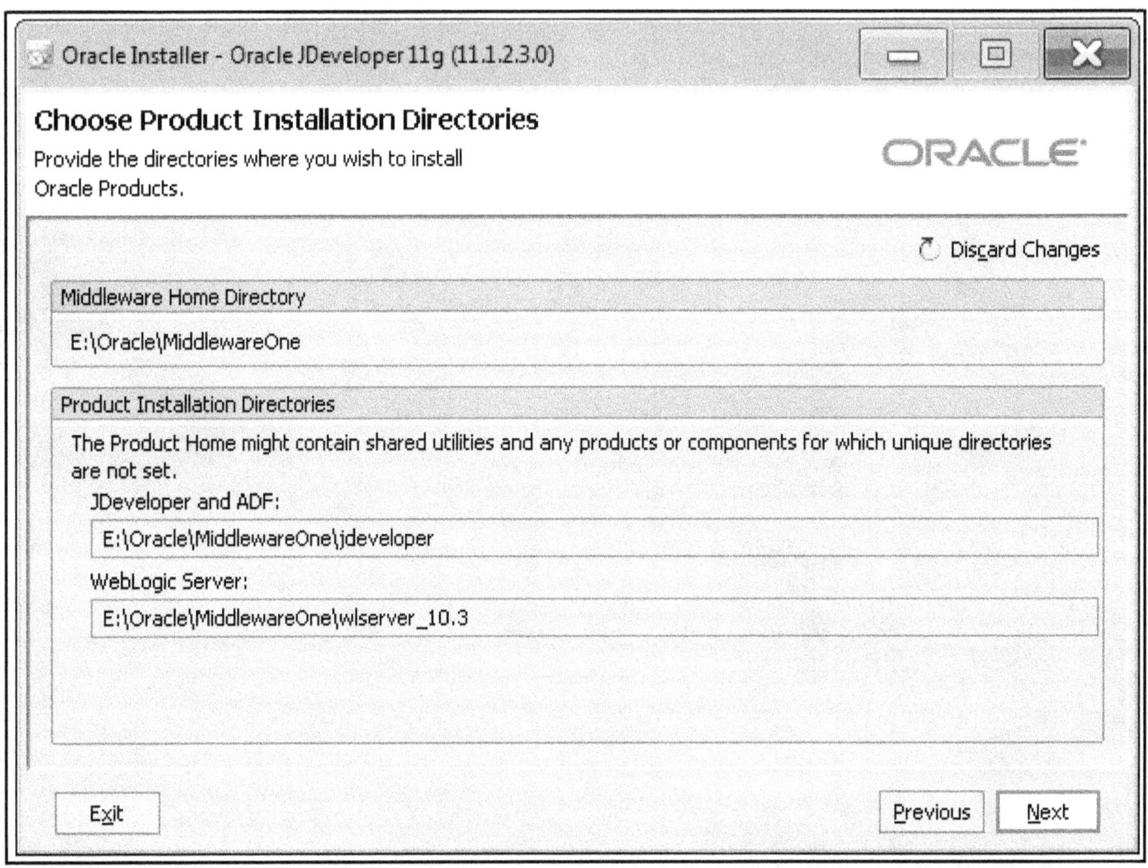

Step 6: The installer will display the installation directories for the server and IDE. Accept the default. Just click next on this screen and proceed further.

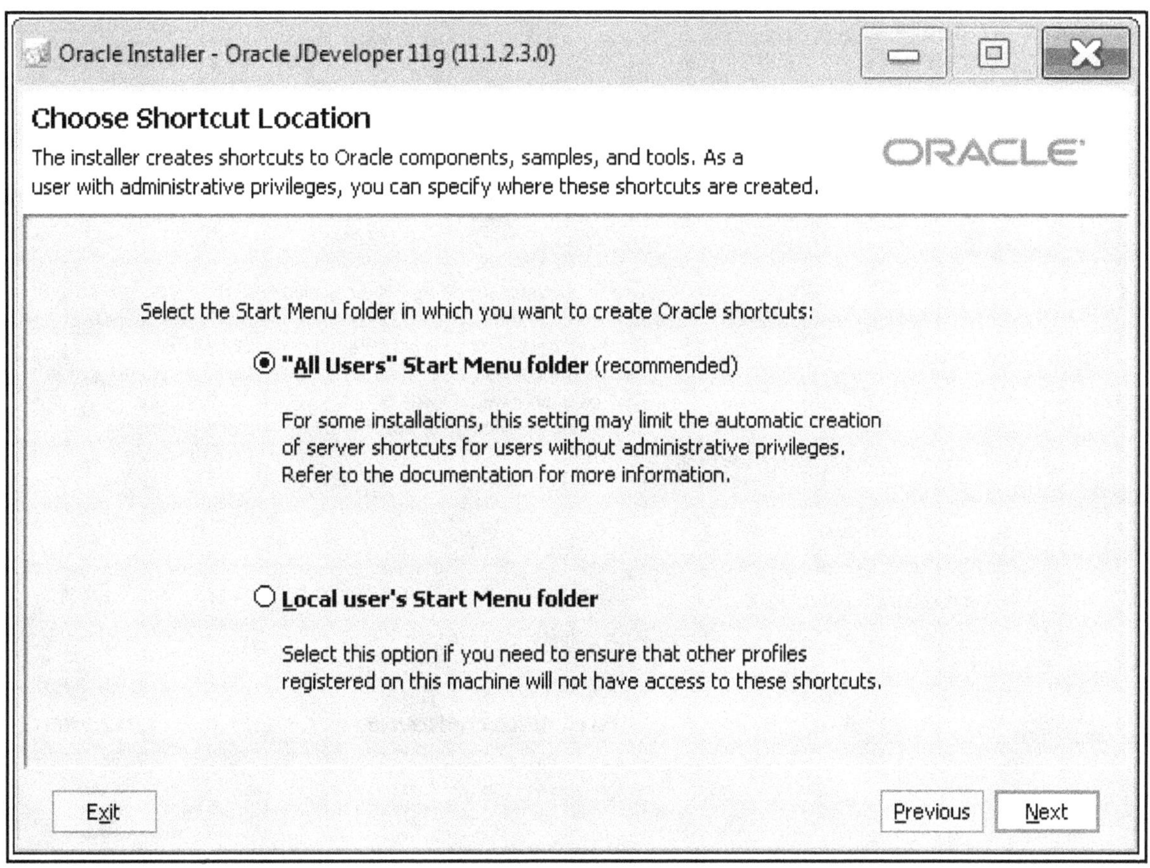

Step 7: Select All Users and click next.

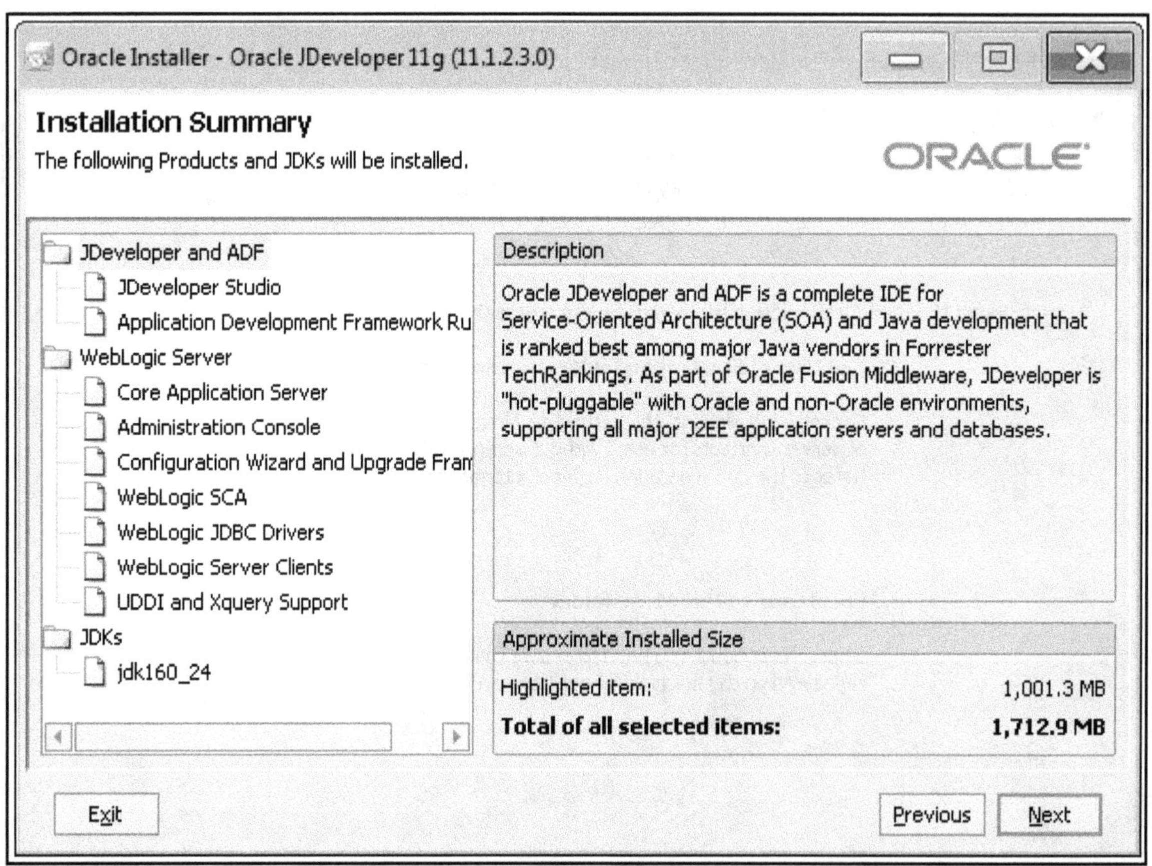

Step 8: Verify that the installation summary includes jdeveloper and ADF, Weblogic Server and JDK. Click next to proceed.

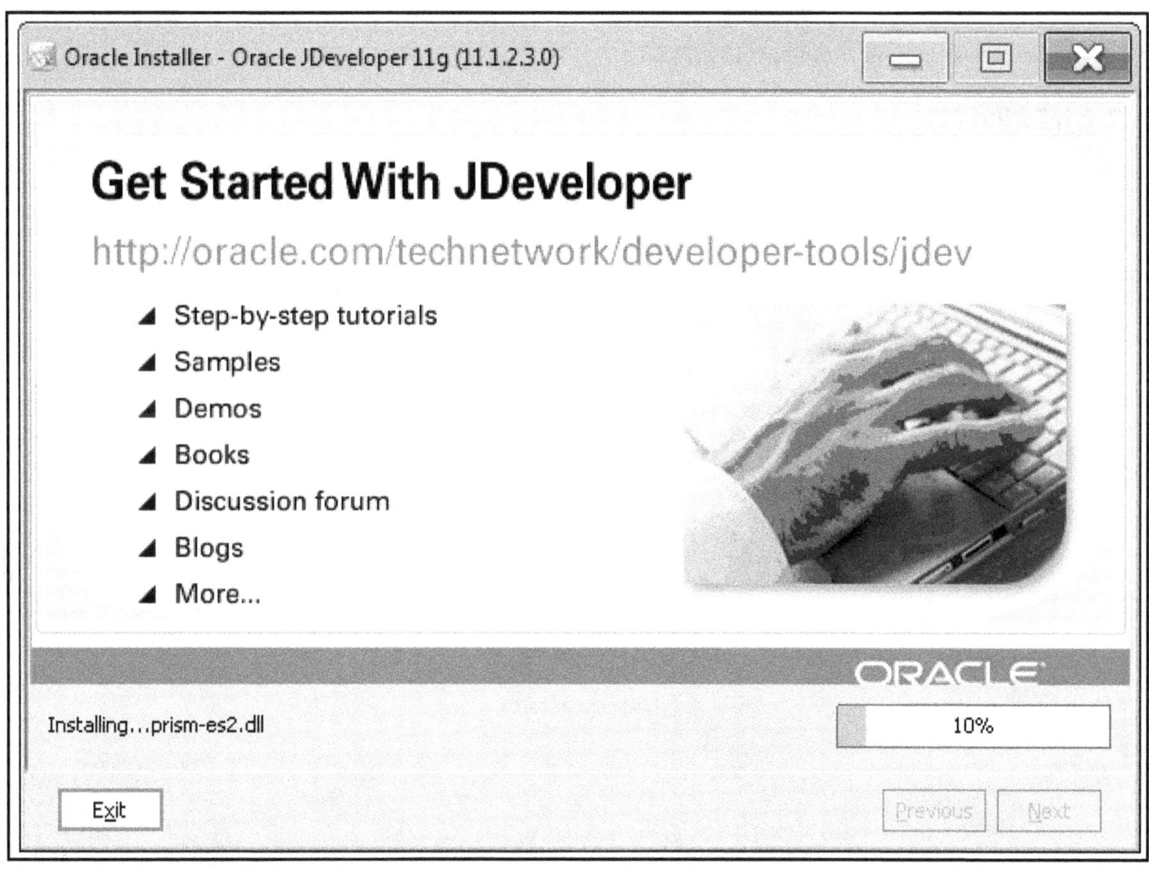

Step 9: This will start the installation.

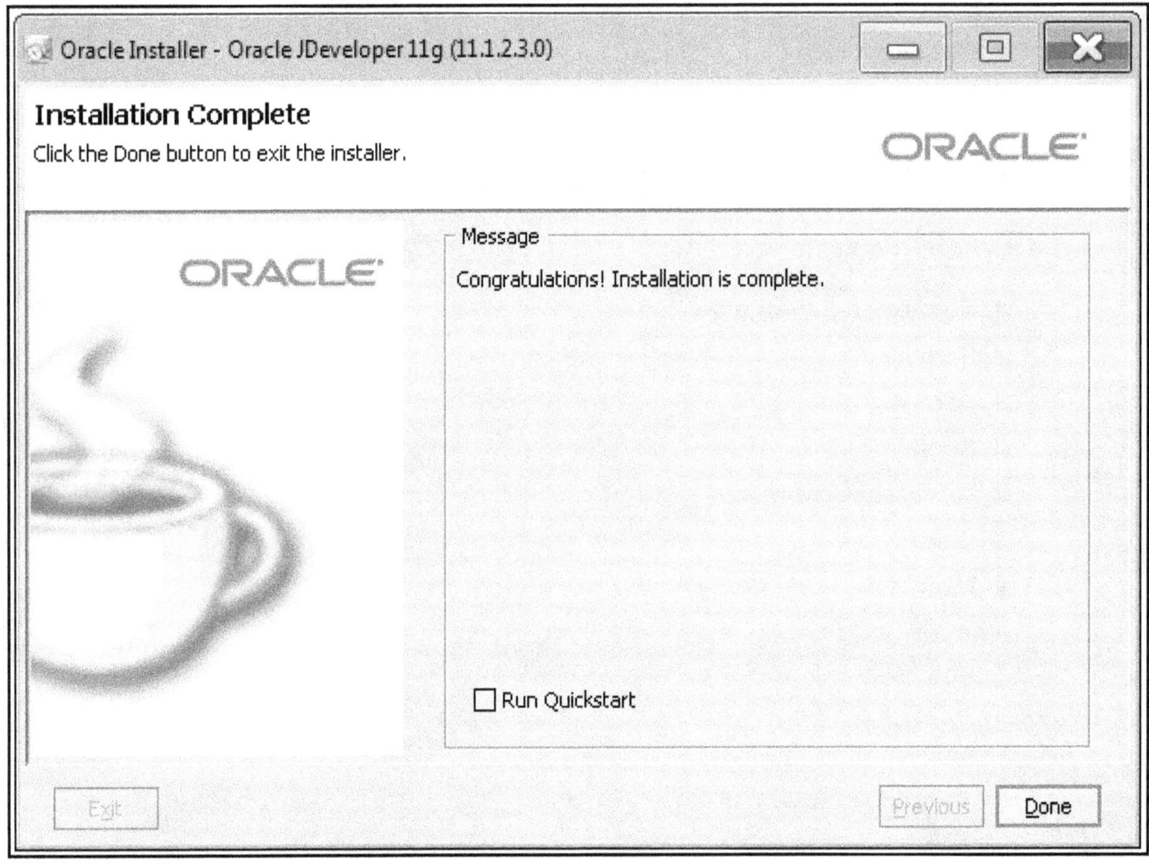

Step 10: Unselect the Run Quickstart checkbox and click done to finish the installation.

Step 11: Go to start menu and click JDeveloper Studio. This will launch Oracle jdeveloper.

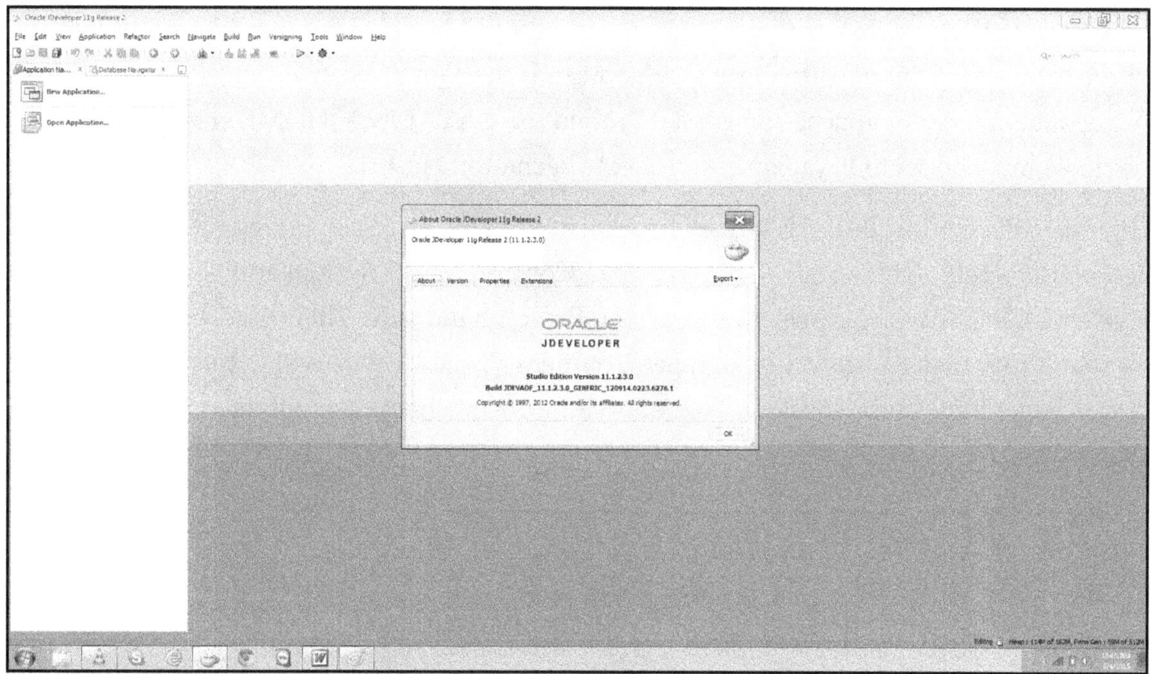

This concludes the installation of Oracle jdeveloper 11g.

Installing Apache Tomcat 8

Step 1: Download the zip installer file for Apache Tomcat 8 from:
https://tomcat.apache.org/download-80.cgi

Step 2: Unzip the file apache-tomcat-8.0.21-windows-x64.zip file to a local folder.

Step 3: Apache Tomcat 8.0 requires Java Standard Edition Runtime Environment (JRE) version 7 or later. If your system has a JRE version below this or if your system does not have JRE itself, please install JRE 7 or later before proceeding further.

We need the following environment variables for starting the Apache Tomcat 8.0 server: JRE_HOME and CATALINA_HOME.

The CATALINA_HOME environment variable should be set to the location of the root directory of the "binary" distribution of Tomcat. If the root directory is of the installation is E:\apache-tomcat-8\apache-tomcat-8.0.21 then the CATALINA_HOME environment variable must be set to E:\apache-tomcat-8\apache-tomcat-8.0.21.

To create the CATALINA_HOME environment variable go to start - right click on Computer - Select properties - This will open Control Panel - System and Security - System - Click Advanced system settings on the left hand side. This will open up the System Properties window. Click on Environment Variable. That will in turn open the Environment Variables window. The following picture show cases all these windows.

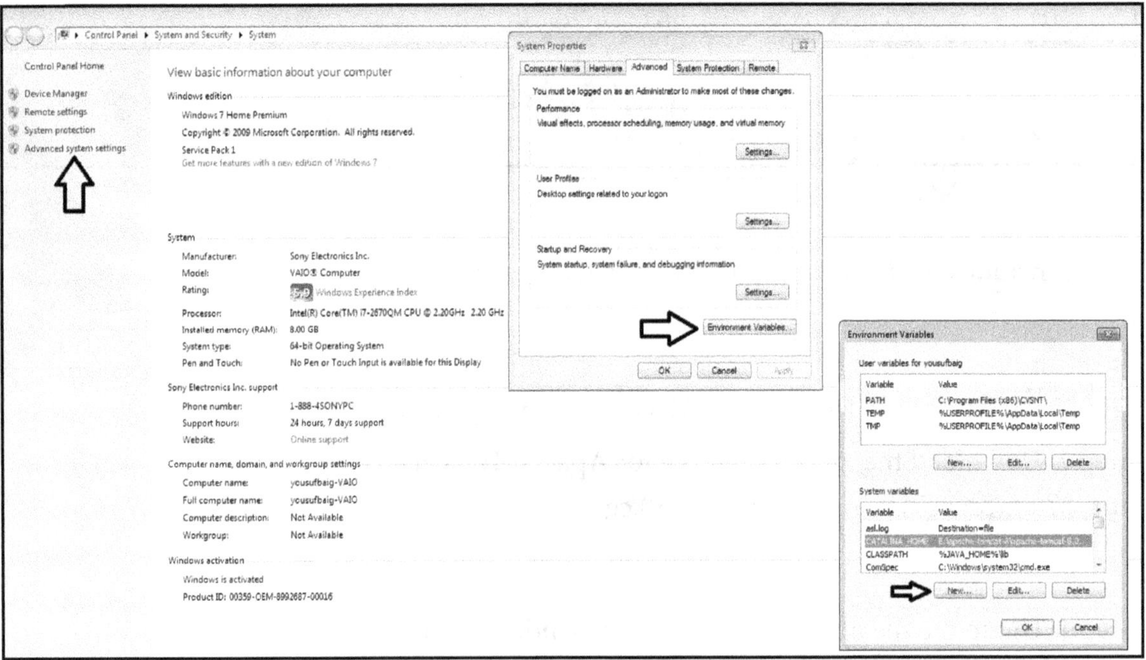

Click new and add variable name as CATALINA_HOME and variable value must be the home directory of the Apache Tomcat server as shown in the figure below.

Click OK to close all the windows.

Similarly create the JRE_HOME environment variable. The variable name must be JRE_HOME and the variable value must be the directory location of the JRE (which has the bin folder in it) as shown in the figure below.

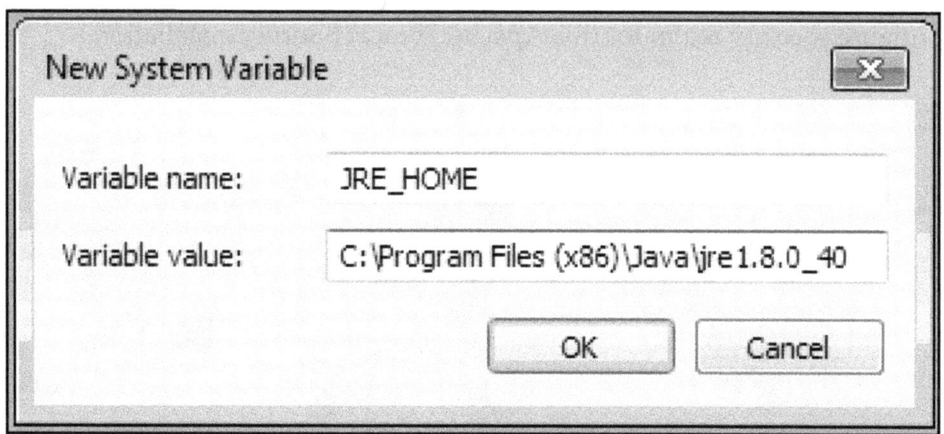

Click OK to close all the windows.

Step 4: Go to the bin folder and run the startup batch file. This will start the apache tomcat 8 server.

Step 5: Launch the browser and go to the following url: http://localhost:80. The database is already using port 8080. Hence, we will change the http port to 80 for Apache Tomcat 8 server.

To change the http port from default 8080 to 80:

Go to conf folder in the Apache Tomcat installation directory. Open the server.xml file to edit. Locate this tag <Connector port="8080" protocol="HTTP/1.1" connectionTimeout="20000" redirectPort="8443" /> and change the value for port from 8080 to 80. Save the file and restart the server. The Apache Tomcat 8 server will now listen for http requests on port 80.

If the installation is successful, the home page of Apache Tomcat server will be displayed.

This concludes the installation of Apache Tomcat 8 server. Please refer the section " Configuring data source security realm for Apache Tomcat " in chapter 16 Securing Application to configure security realm for this Apache Tomcat 8 server installation.

3

SDLC, OOAD AND UML

Software Development Life Cycle (SDLC)

From the very first thought of having a software solution for a situation till the actual deployment of the software, the software development goes through various phases. These phases form the building blocks of "*Software Development Life Cycle*" in short referred as SDLC. Some of these phases are interdependent on each other, while some are prerequisite for others. Some of them can be done in parallel while others may demand a particular order.

Various approaches can be taken to build a software solution from its inception till its completion. These approaches are referred to as SDLC methodologies. We will not go into details of these various methodologies. We will only focus on the SDLC methodology which we will be following to build our sample application.

The SDLC methodology we will be following is called water fall model. In this methodology, each phase of SDLC goes in a particular sequence. The major tangible phases of water fall SDLC are requirements analysis, design, implementation(coding), testing and maintenance. In water fall model, each phase has strict dependency on the previous phase(s). For. e.g. the design can not be started before the requirements are finalized. In water fall model, the following order for SDLC is followed.

1. Requirements Analysis
2. Design
3. Implementation

4. Testing
5. Deployment
6. Maintenance

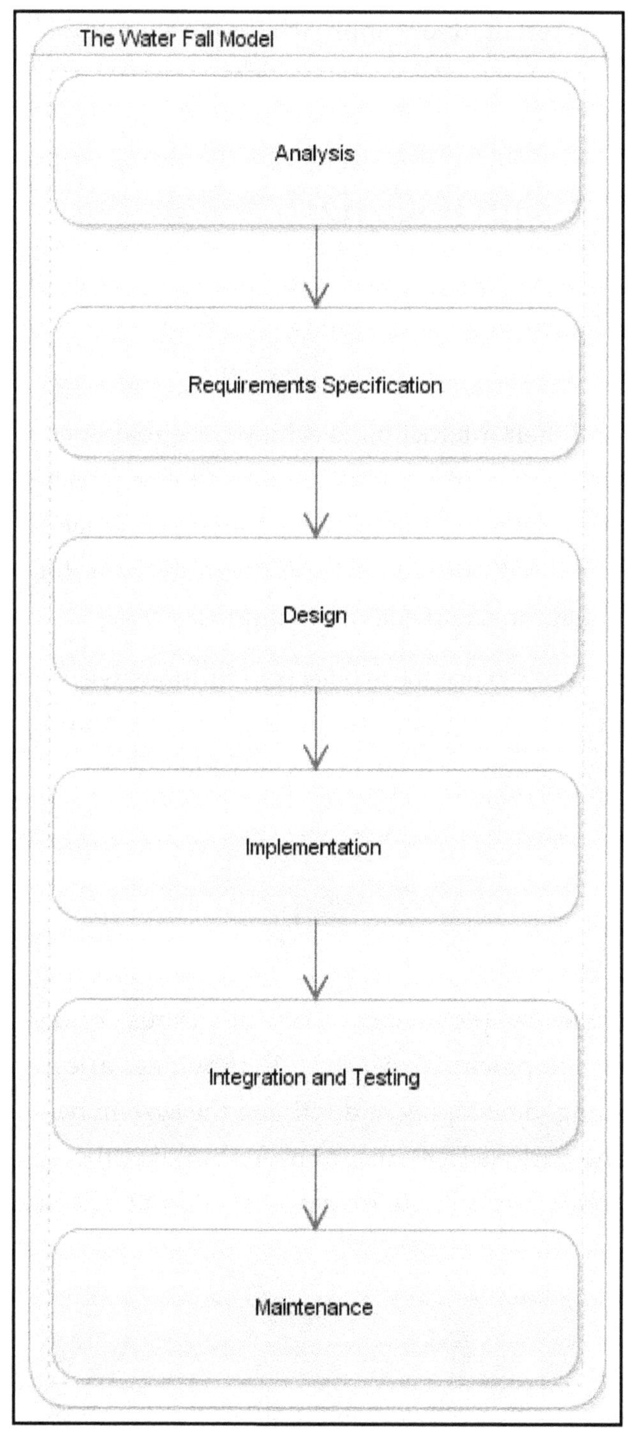
The Water Fall Model
Analysis
Requirements Specification
Design
Implementation
Integration and Testing
Maintenance

The outline section in chapter one describes waterfall model approach for the sample application we are building.

Object Oriented Analysis and Design (OOAD)

We are using Java programming language to build the sample web application. Java is an object oriented programming language and hence we will be dealing with many objects in the sample application.

OOAD is primarily identifying the objects and their interaction to achieve our goal. As a part of OOAD analysis and design we will come up with various classes and interfaces in the coming chapters. For each use case, we will see what objects are required and what interactions are required. These will be depicted with subjective UML diagrams including and not limited to class diagrams, sequence diagrams and activity diagrams.

The bottom line is, everything is an object in Java. To use these objects at runtime, we create classes with fields and methods. Hence, OOAD in our case drills down to planning and coming up with Java classes and interfaces and their interactions to achieve our requirements.

Unified Modeling Language (UML)

UML is a popular modeling language. It enables the pictorial depiction of various entities, interactions and activities through out the development life cycle. UML provides various types of diagrams which help in understanding, developing and refining the system being built. In the coming chapters we will be using various UML diagrams for building the sample web application. Here's a quick intro of various UML diagrams used in this book.

Use Case Diagram

A use case diagram is a visual representation of a user's interaction with a system. These can be different types of users of a system and also there can be different types of use cases for a given user. A use case pictorially depicts the interaction of a user with a specific role with the system.

Class Diagram

The class diagram is a static diagram and it describes the attributes and operations of a class. Class diagrams show case all the classes, interfaces, associations, collaborations and constraints in the application. These diagrams give a visual representation of the classes, interfaces and their relationships belonging to a particular system.

Sequence Diagram

As the name suggests, sequence diagrams pictorially depict the sequence of operations performed in a particular order to achieve a task. They depict the flow of various activities in a sequence. Sequence diagrams are basically interaction diagrams which depict the order and interactions between various software entities.

Activity Diagram

Activity diagrams depict the bigger picture of a system. They describe the flow from one activity to another and their conditions. Activity diagrams are commonly used to depict the algorithms. These are behavioral diagrams and have a finite number of steps, conditions and flows.

Various uml diagrams are used through out this book serving the very purpose of UML to understand things with more clarity.

4
REQUIREMENTS

The Requirements Phase

This is the first thing in any project. The client who wants a system to be built comes up with a document called requirements. This document details what exactly the client wants. The vendor who is building the system analyzes this document and goes back to the client with questions. The client provides answers and clarification for the vendor's queries and ambiguities. This phase is known as requirements analysis phase of the project. The outcome of requirements analysis phase is a requirements specification document.

Requirements Specifications

To put it simple, requirements specification details what needs to be built very specifically and clearly without any ambiguity. Requirements specifications is concise, specific, straight forward, detailed, clear and complete. Requirements specifications have to be clear, detailed enough and specific without any ambiguity. It includes detailed specifications of the requirements for the system to be built. This is generally a legally liable document.

For the client, the requirements specification is what exactly they want. For the implementers, the requirements specification is what they are going to build.

Let us take an example here: A person goes to a tailor for stitching a shirt. He provides the requirements by saying something like this: I need a shirt which needs to be full sleeved, white buttons, wide neck etc. The tailor gets specific, he pulls up his measurement tape and pens down the "requirements specifications" like 40.5 inch shoulder, 18 inch neck, 32 inch length, round white buttons etc.

Let us now pen down the ***requirements specification*** for the sample web application we are building.

Application Title

Baig International School Online Student Management System abbreviated as BIS-SMS.

Executive Summary

The online student management system provides a web based solution for management of student's information. This solution is aimed for students studying in a particular school from 1st grade to 10th grade. The various users of this application are students, teachers, non-teaching staff and school management. The solution serves as a single source of information for all the students of a given school. The information about a student include student's personal details, parent's details, attendance, results, performance, health and other attributes of a student.

The solution also provides reports, contact information for various non-teaching staff, charts for student's academic and non-academic performances and attendance.

Detailed Requirements Specification

The Online Student Management System application is divided into following modules.

- Authentication and Authorization
- Student
- Admin
- Reports

- Help
- Miscellaneous

Authentication and Authorization Module

The following requirements fall under this module.

R1: The Authentication.

The system shall provide a mechanism to authenticate the user. Upon first request to the application, the application must redirect the user to a login page.

Once the user submits the user id and password, the system shall perform authentication. If the user id and the password does not match or the user does not exist, the system shall provide an appropriate message and take the user back to the login page.

If the user is valid and provides valid password, the authenticated user must be taken to the dashboard page.

R2: The Authorization.

The system shall provide a mechanism to authorize the user based on a role. The menus and the dashboard should be rendered based on the role of the user. Only those links shall be displayed which the role has privilege. The user privileges and the role shall be as per the following table.

Role/Access	BisAdmin	BisTeacher	BisClerk
Student details view	✓	✓	✓
Results view	✓	✓	✗
Attendance view	✓	✓	✗
Fees view	✓	✗	✓
Add Student	✓	✗	✓
Edit Student	✓	✗	✓
Manage Result	✓	✓	✗
Manage Attendance	✓	✓	✗
Manage Fees	✓	✗	✓
Report by Bus	✓	✗	✓
Report by Fees	✓	✗	✓
Report by Class	✓	✓	✗
Help Pages	✓	✓	✓

The Student Module

This module must provide the following functional requirements.

R3: Load Student.

The system shall allow the user to load a student based on his/her student Id. The system shall have client side validations for student id with appropriate error messages.

R4: Unique Student Identifier.

On the pages where ever applicable, the system shall display the student name, semester, class, section and student id as a unique identifier for a given student and that should be referred to as "student in context". This shall be displayed in centered position just below the menus. This shall serve as an identification of a student in question. This student in context strip must be displayed for all the student related pages once load student activity is performed by the user.

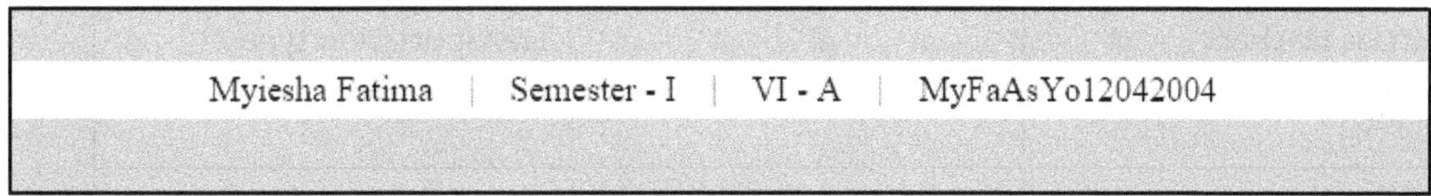

R5: Student Details.

Prerequisite: The student has to be loaded into context first.

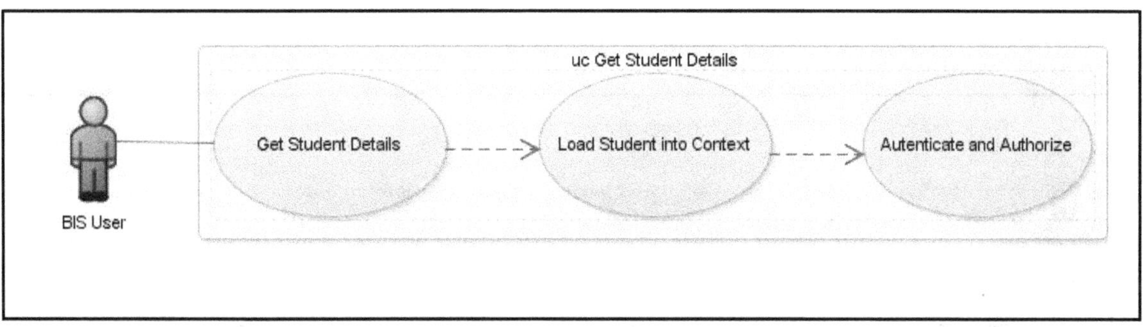

The system shall display the following information for a given student in a single page view.

Student	Parents	Bus
Student Id	Father	Bus Id
Name	Mother	Driver
Gender	Father's mobile	Driver's mobile
Date of birth	Mother's mobile	Helper
Grade	Address	Helper's mobile
Section		Bus number
Class teacher		Transportation type
Height		
Weight		
Blood group		

R6: Student Academics.

Prerequisite: The student has to be loaded into context first.

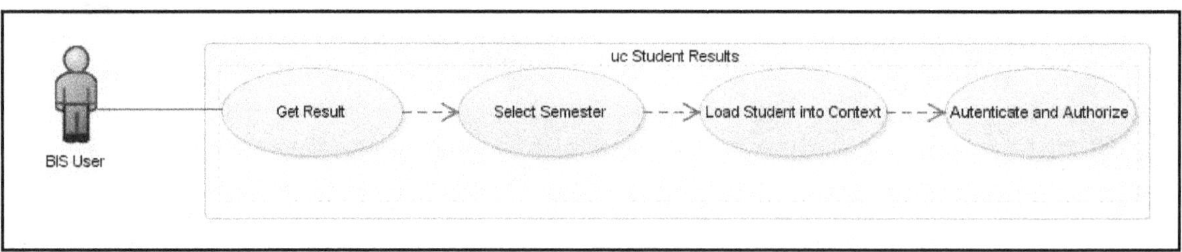

For a given semester and student, the system shall display the academic results information as per the tables below.

Scholastic Performance - Core Curriculum - Assessment

The system shall display the grades for the following subjects: English, Mathematics, Science, Social Science, Computer Science, Language II and Language III. The grades shall be A, B and C.

Subject vise grades for a given Semester and Remarks option under the table heading "Scholastic Performance - Core Curriculum – Assessment".

Scholastic Performance - Core Curriculum - Assessment		
Subject	Grade	Remarks
English	A	She needs to focus on spelling.
Mathematics	A	Sometimes, she needs to apply the concepts understood.
Science	C	She is not consistent in her studies
Social Science	B	She needs to show more interest
Language II	B	She needs to improve both in oral and written work
Language III	A	She needs to imporve in written work
Computer Science	A	She shows good interest in the subject

Co – Scholastic Activities

For a given semester and student, the system shall display the following academics information.

Subject vise grades for Critical Thinking, Creative Thinking, Collaborative Learning, Communication Skill, Comprehensive Growth, Intelligence Quotient, Emotional Quotient, Social Quotient, Health Quotient and Community Consciousness under the table heading "Co – Scholastic Activities". The grades shall be Latent, Developing, Emerging and Outstanding.

Co - Scholastic Activities	
Critical Thinking	Emerging
Creative Thinking	Emerging
Collaborative Learning	Latent
Communication Skills	Outstanding
Comprehensive Growth	Developing
IQ - Intelligence Quotient	Emerging
EQ - Emotional Quotient	Latent
EQ - Social Quotient	Developing
EQ - Health Quotient	Outstanding
EQ - Community Consciousness	Outstanding

Scholastic Performance - Co Curriculum - Assessment

For a given semester and student, the system shall display the following academics information.

The system shall display the grades for the following subjects: Arts, Music, Dance, Physical Education, Value Education and School Project. The grades shall be A, B and C.

Subject vise grades for a given Semester and Remarks option under the table heading "Scholastic Performance - Co Curriculum – Assessment".

Scholastic Performance - Co Curriculum - Assessment		
Subject	Grade	Remarks
Arts	A	Very innovative
Music	B	She is a good listener
Dance	A	She is a good dancer
Physical Education	C	Tries to follow school rules
Value Education	A	Willingly works and shares with others
School Project	A	Shows high degree of enthusiasm and works deligently
Other	-	-

Synthesis and Recommendations

For a given semester and student, the system shall display the following academics information. Scholastic Performance and Co – Scholastic Performance under the table heading "Synthesis and Recommendations". The system shall display the detailed remarks as per the table below.

Synthesis and Recommendations	
Scholastic Performance	She is trying to put efforst to improve her academics. Hardwork will lead to colourful results.
Co - Scholastic Performance	She is very cheerful and has a yearning to be a part of cultural activities.

R7: Show Student Attendance.

Prerequisite: The student has to be loaded into context first.

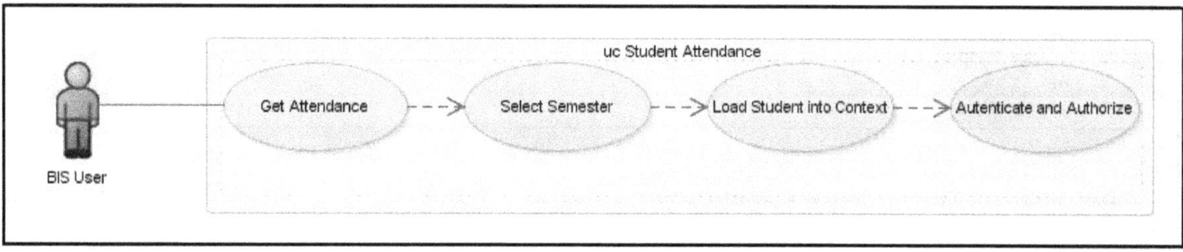

The system shall display the attendance for a given student and for a given semester in a single page view. The page shall display the total number of working days in a semester, the number of days the student was present and the number of days the student was absent. This should be displayed in numerical values, percentages and with a bar graph as per the figure below.

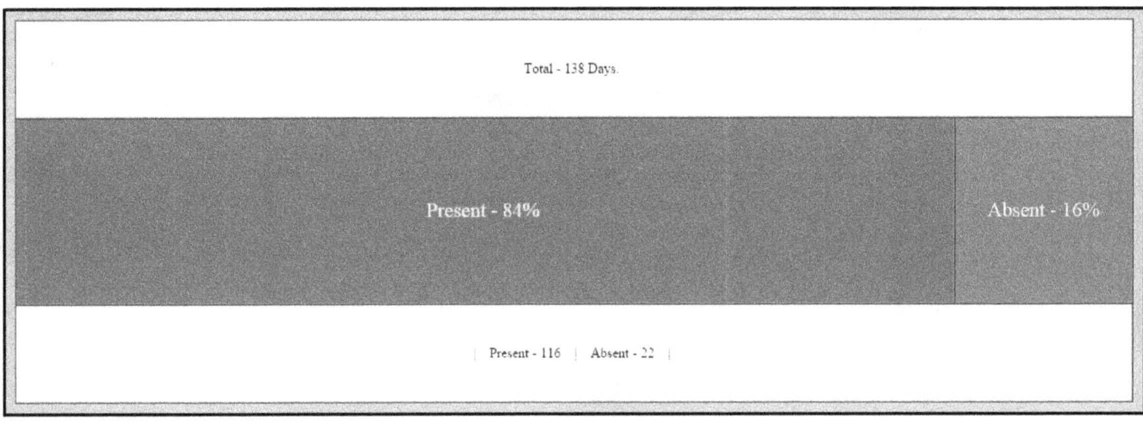

R8: Student Fees.

Prerequisite: The student has to be loaded into context first.

For a given student the system shall display the monthly fees status. This fees to be displayed includes the tuition fees and the bus fees. This shall be shown monthly for each quarter of the year. The fees status for tuition and bus shall be displayed as per the tables below.

Academic Fees											
Term One			Term Two			Term Three			Term Four		
April	May	June	July	August	September	October	November	December	January	February	March
Y	Y	Y	Y	Y	Y	Y	Y	Y	N	N	N

Bus Fees											
April	May	June	July	August	September	October	November	December	January	February	March
Y	Y	Y	Y	Y	Y	Y	Y	Y	N	N	N

The Administration Module

R9: Manage Student Attendance.

Prerequisite: The student has to be loaded into context first.

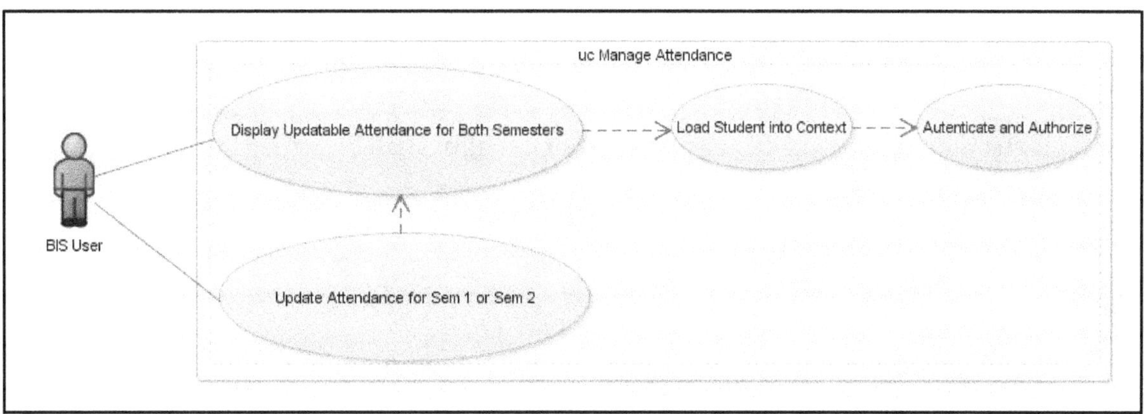

For a given student, the system shall display the attendance of both the semesters in a single page. Under a separate heading for each semester, the system shall display total working days, total number of days present and total number of days absent.

The present field shall be editable and shall be displaying the present value. The user shall be able to enter a numerical value and update it to the system. This applies to both the semesters. The page shall hold client side validations and must pose appropriate error messages for wrong values entered.

Upon successful update, the system shall display the updated values.

Example:

Before update:

Total working days : 150

Present: 140

Absent: 10

After update:

Total working days : 150

Present: 145

Absent: 5

For a given student, the update attendance functionality shall be as per the figures below for respective semester.

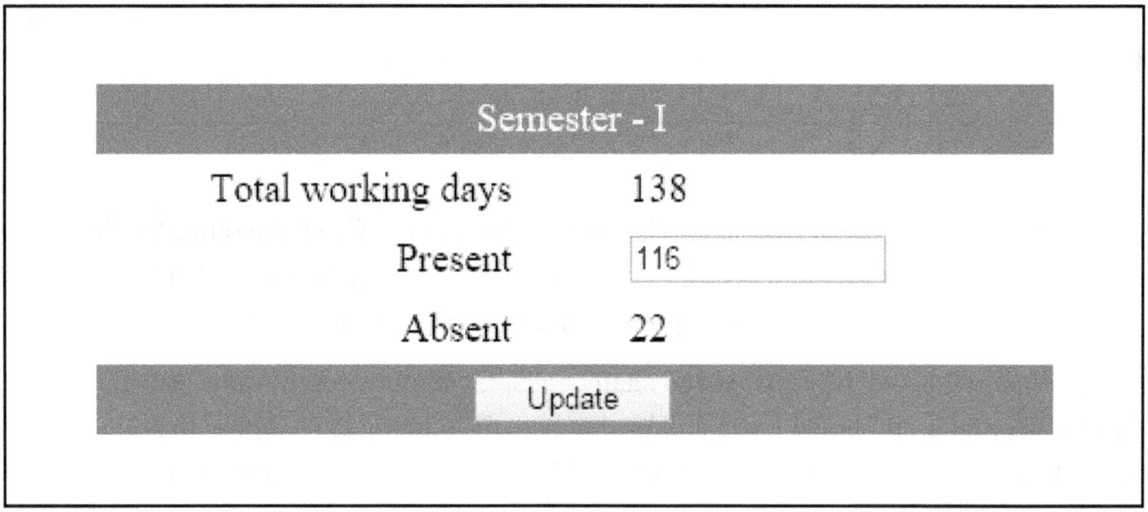

Semester - I	
Total working days	138
Present	116
Absent	22
Update	

Semester - II

Total working days	127
Present	98
Absent	29

Update

R10: Add Student.

Prerequisite: The logged in user must have the role privileges to add a student.

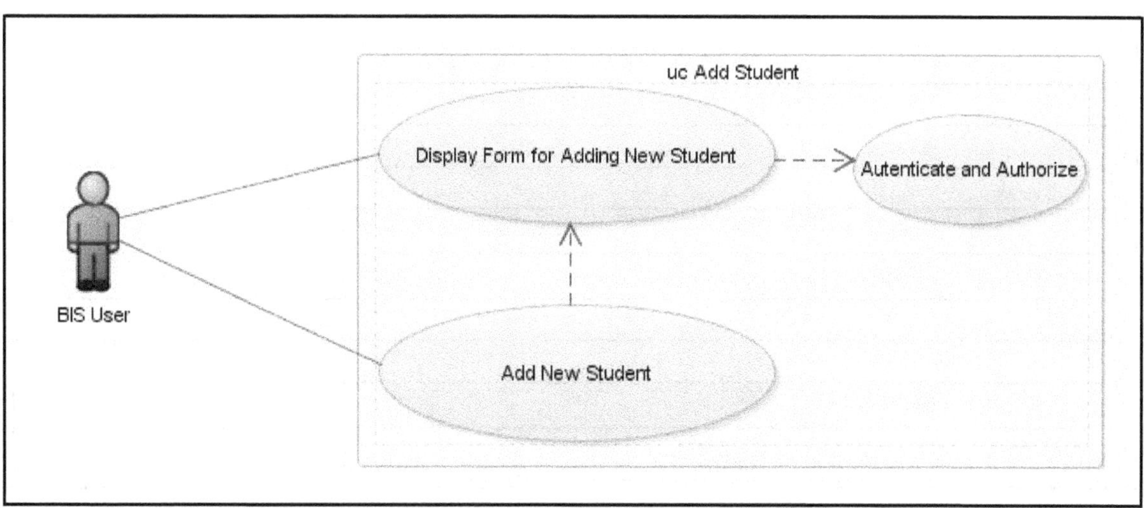

The system shall provide this functionality only for the roles as per role access mappings in requirements reference R2. The system shall provide a form with the following fields to add a new student to the system. The system shall perform all the required validations at client side for the values entered for each form element.

The system shall mandate few form fields as shown in the table below and other fields shall be allowed to be optional but recommended. The system shall auto generate a unique student id based on the student name, student birth date and parents name combination. And this student id shall be unique identifier for all the students belonging to the system.

The form shall have the fields as per the tables below.

First Name	
Middle Name	
Last Name	
Gender	Male Female
Date of birth	mm/dd/yyyy
Grade	L.K.G ▾
Section	A ▾
Height	Foot.Inches
Weight	KG
Blood Group	A +ve ▾
Siblings	

Father	
Mobile	
Mother	
Mobile	
Address	
Bus Number	01 ▼

The mandatory fields are marked with the "*" symbol. Following are the mandatory fields:

Student first name

Student last name

Mother's first name

Father's first name

Student's date of birth in mm/dd/yyyy format.

All other fields shall be optional but encouraged to be filled.

The Reporting Module

R11: Report by Class.

Prerequisite: The logged in user must have the role privileges for reports by class functionality.

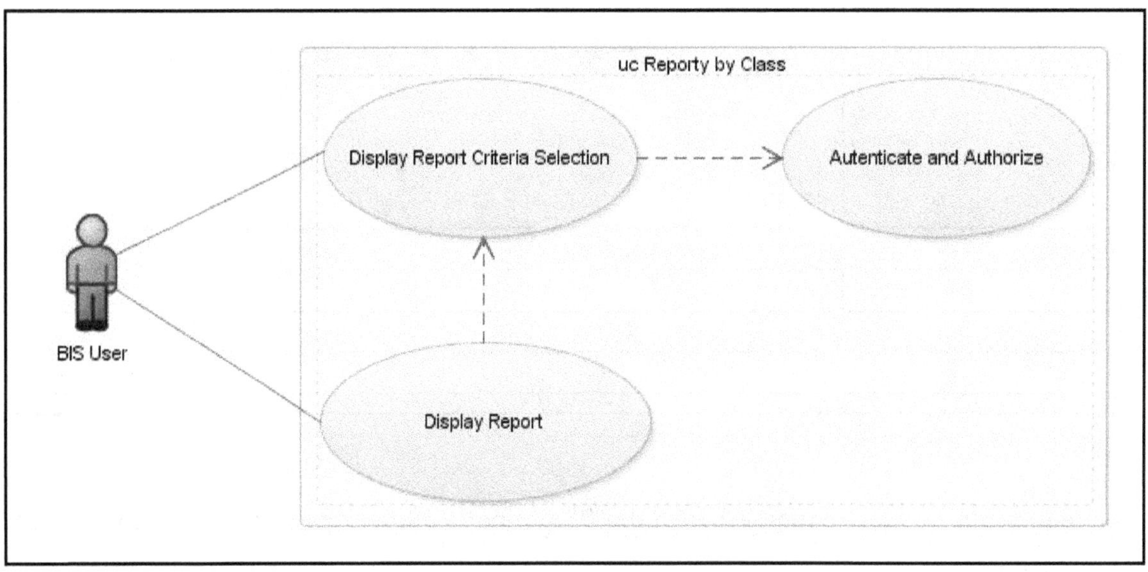

The system shall provide this functionality only for the roles as per role access mappings in requirements reference R2. For this functionality, the system shall provide a page with two regions. One for the report criteria and other for the report results.

The report criteria shall comprise of a drop down menu for class and a drop down menu for section. The user should be able to select a specific class and a section and upon clicking generate report button, the system shall query the database and provide the report as per the format given below.

Report Criteria

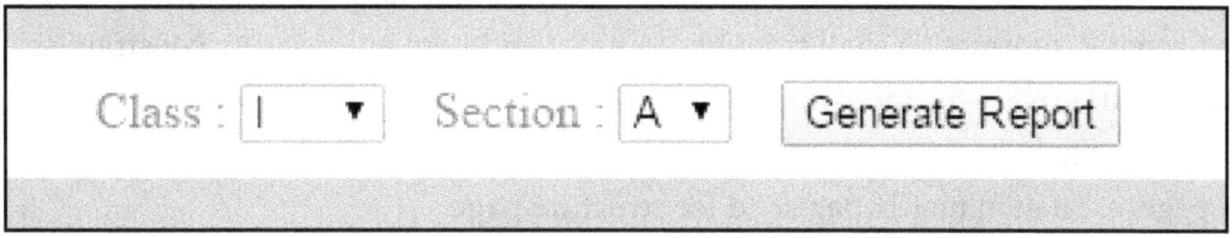

Class : I ▼ Section : A ▼ Generate Report

Report Results

Report: Class Wise | Class : VI | Section : A			
Name	**Student Id**	**Gender**	**Bus Id**
Myiesha Fatima	MyFaAsYo12042004	Female	18
Mohammed Zain	MoZaAsYo19062007	Male	18
Mohammed Zaid	MoZaAsYo30042009	Male	12
Mohammed Izaan	MoIzBuAs11122008	Female	18
Ibrahim Siddiqui Mohammed	IbMoAsIr31122010	Male	12
Zoha Mirza Fatima	ZoFaAlSh28022008	Female	12
Sattar Ali Khan	SaKhSiAh31122009	Male	12
Syed Khalid Pasha	SyPaShAz31122010	Male	18
Nisar Ahmed	NiAhSyZu30092002	Male	12
Momin Pasha	MoPaSaHa30112003	Male	12
Neetal H Shah	NeShAnRa10061976	Female	18
Yousuf Khan Pathan	YoPaRuMo02092000	Male	18

The report shall be displayed in tabular format as shown in the figure. It shall display the selected report criteria as a heading followed by the report results. The report must contain first name, middle name and last name in first column followed by student id, gender and bus id in the order mentioned. By default the report results must be sorted by first name of the student in alphabetical order.

The Help and Miscellaneous Module

R12: Help Pages.

Prerequisite: None

Security: Public pages

These pages shall be public and the access shall be granted to everyone i.e. for the logged in users as well as for the users who do not have an id. That is, these static pages providing general information shall be public in nature without any security constraints. The system shall provide the following static html pages under a separate menu heading titled "Help". The help pages shall include results legend page, FAQs page, holidays calendar page, escalation matrix page and fee structure page.

R13: Header and Footer.

Prerequisite: The user must be logged in.

Upon successful log in, the system shall display the consistent header and footer on all the pages. The header shall display the school name on the top in bigger fonts. The header shall also display the date and time, the logged in user name, the logout link and the top navigational menus as per the logged in user role(s).

The footer shall display, the copyright and other static information in the given format.

R14: The Menu.

Prerequisite: The user must be logged in.

Upon successful log in, the system shall display the consistent menu for all the pages of the web application. The following menus must be displayed with the respective menu items as per the table below.

Menu ⇨	Home	Students	Admin	Reports	Help
Menu Items ⇨		Details	Add Student	Class	Legend
		Sem-I Results	Edit Student	Bus	FAQs
		Sem-II Results	Manage Results	Fees	Holiday Calendar
		Sem-I Attendance	Manage Attendance		Escalation Matrix
		Sem-II Attendance	Manage Fees		Fees Structure
		Fees			

Home Students Admin Reports Help

Add Student

Edit Student

Manage Result

Manage Attendance

Manage Fees

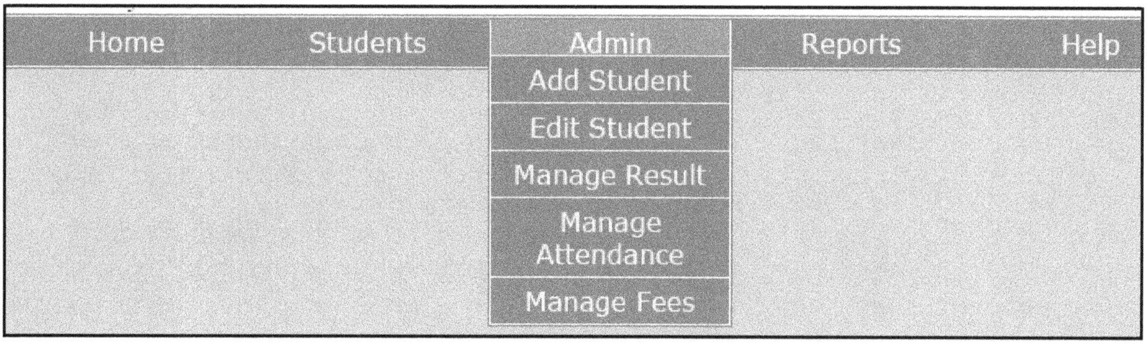

5

PROTOTYPING

The prototype models the UI of the web application to be build. The objective of the prototype is to ensure and verify what exactly the client is looking for. The prototype presents the actual UI. With these UI pages, the vendor should be able to explain the client what the UI looks like in detail and the vendor should also be able to explain the client the behavior of the application being built.

This is a set of html pages which exactly demonstrate how the application looks like. Typically, the graphics team understands the UI and UX requirements from the client and other stakeholders. Sometimes, the client shares the UI and UX requirements in the form of excel sheets or may be even image files. The graphics team comes up with the layout, headers, footers, color theme, page content area for the application to be built. This team provides a visualization of the looks of the actual application pages.

The prototype show cases how the applications looks and behaves. It is as near as possible mock up of the application interface and behavior.

In our case, we will build the mock up also known as prototype as HTML pages.

The purpose of prototype is to enable various stakeholders in the development of web application project to understand the system being built with utmost clarity. The prototype acts as supplementary practical, graphic version of requirements specification. The developers who build the UI generally don't read the requirements specifications word by word rather they build what they see in the prototype. In case of any ambiguity or doubt the requirements specifications must provide micro level clarity to the developers.

Page layout and template

The page layout in our case is simple, we have a header and a footer. The area in between the header and footer is used for the subjective page content. This is the dynamic region which holds the currently selected page by the user.

The Header

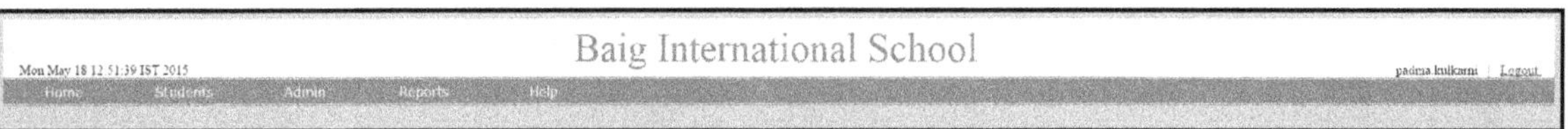

The header displays the school name in a banner mode. The header has the drop down menu which provides the universal navigation for the entire application. The header displays current date and time, the logged in user and the logout link.

The Footer

The footer generally displays the copyright information and disclaimers. In our case it shall display the copyright information and the book title.

The Dynamic Content Region

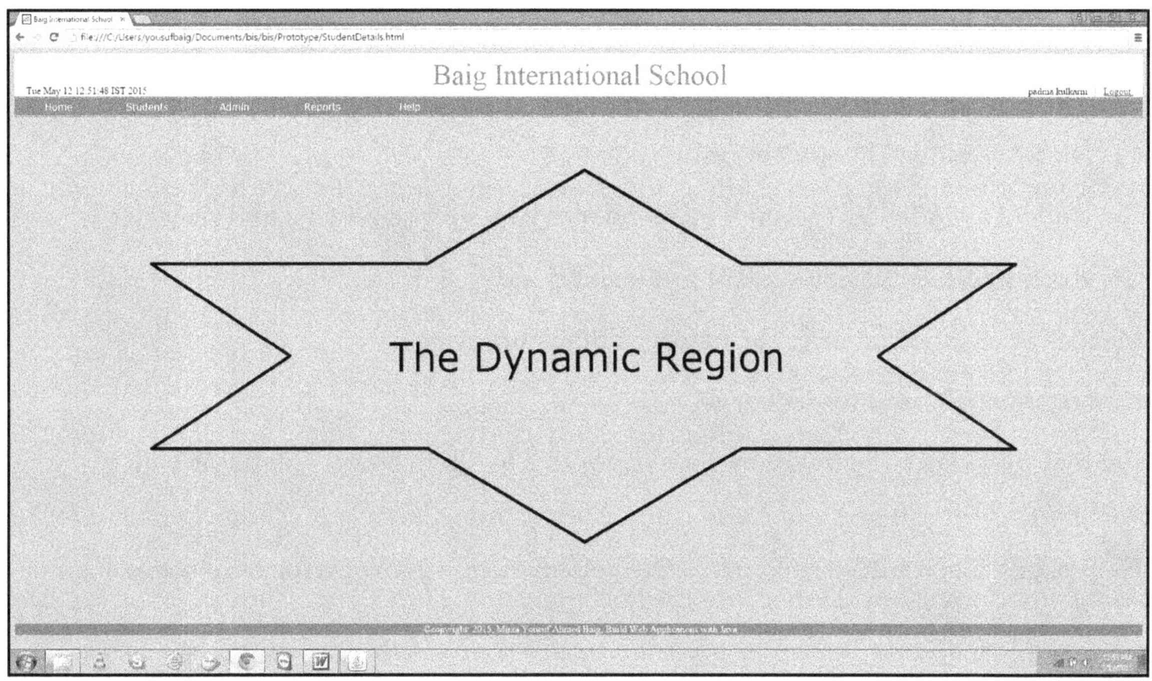

The header and footer are static and are always displayed for all the pages in the application. The dynamic region as shown in the figure displays the page the user is currently working on. Hence, in web applications we generally have a parent page called the home page template which has all the static contents like the header and footer. In some cases we have side navigation but in our case we don't have side navigation rather navigation is provided via top side menus. Based on the user interaction, the dynamic region is loaded with relevant pages. This saves the reloading of the same data and hence increases the application performance. It also saves network bandwidth by reducing the amount of data to be loaded. The developers focus on the functionalities of the individual pages and reuse the page template which is developed as a shared component.

Lets now build the prototype for all the pages of our sample application. Below is the list of use cases and their respective pages.

Authenticate user: The login page.

Authorize user and render dashboard based on role: The dashboard page.

Load student: The load student ajax region within the dashboard/home page.

Get student details: The student details page.

Get student results: The student results page.

Get student attendance: The student attendance pages for semester 1 and semester 2.

Get student fees status: the student fees status page.

Manage student attendance: The manage attendance page.

Add student: The add student page.

Get report by class: The report by class page. This has both report criteria as well as result/report display.

Help pages: The results legend page. The help pages are a set of static html pages.

Prototype 1: Login Page.

Specification Reference: R1

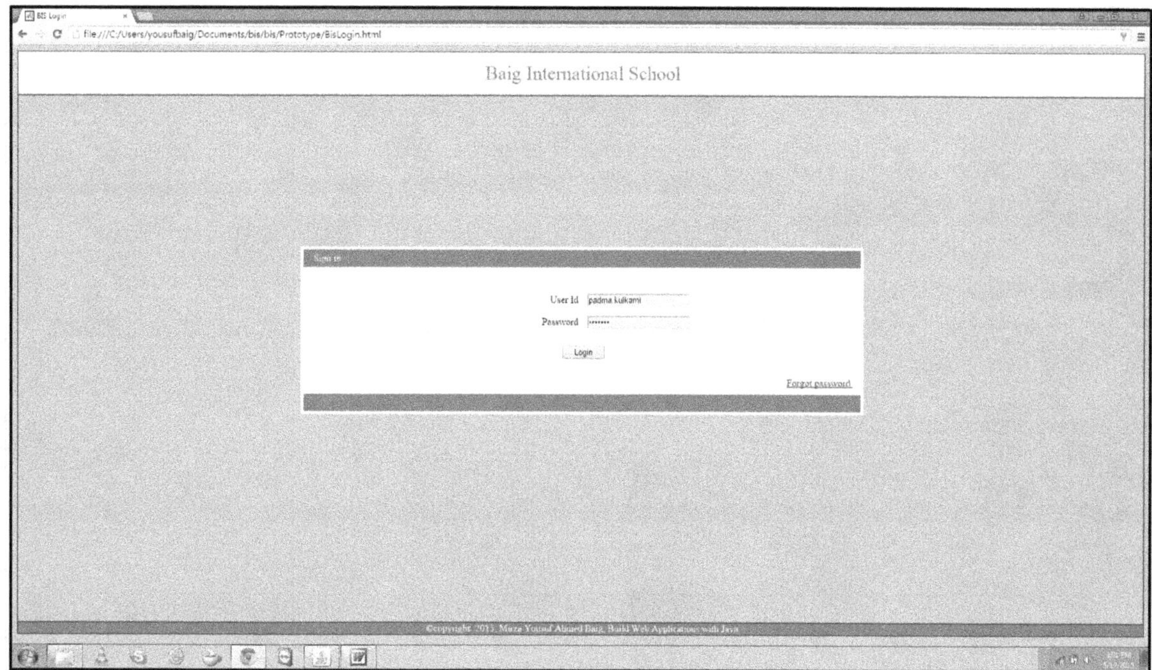

The BisLogin.jsp page is built using this html page. The source code for this page is available in chapter 15 under the authentication use case section.

Prototype 2: Dashboard/Home Page.

Specification Reference: R2

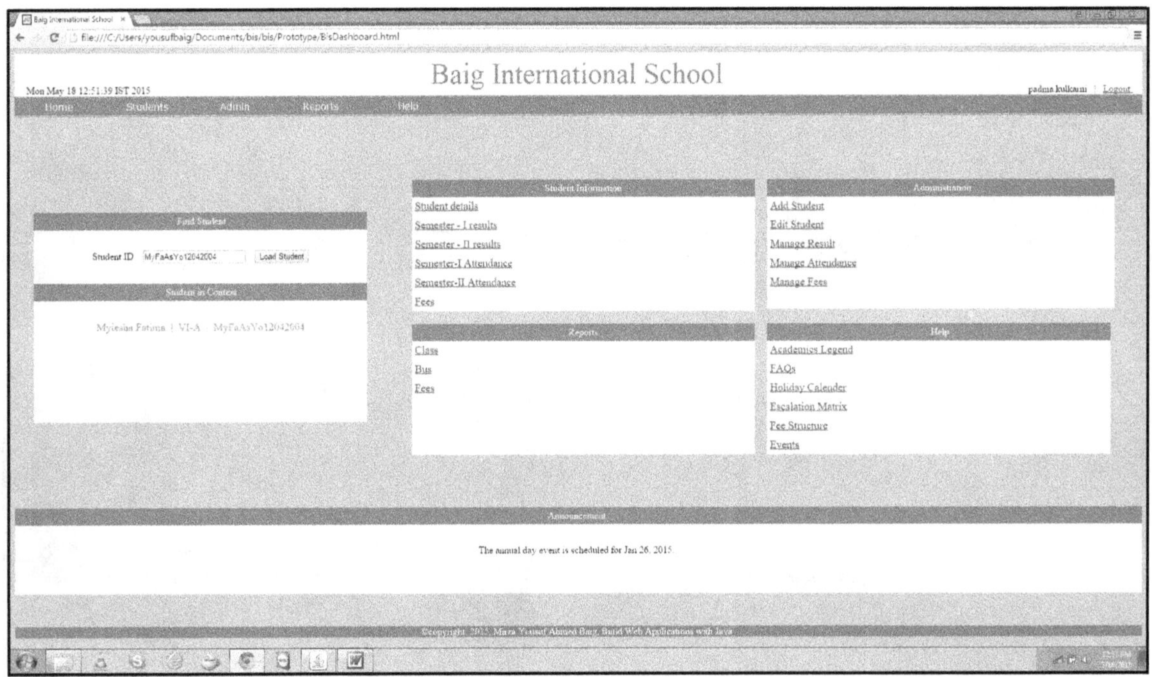

The BisDashboard.jsp page is built using this html page. The source code for this page is available in chapter 15 under the authorization use case section.

Prototype 3: Load Student.

Specification Reference: R3

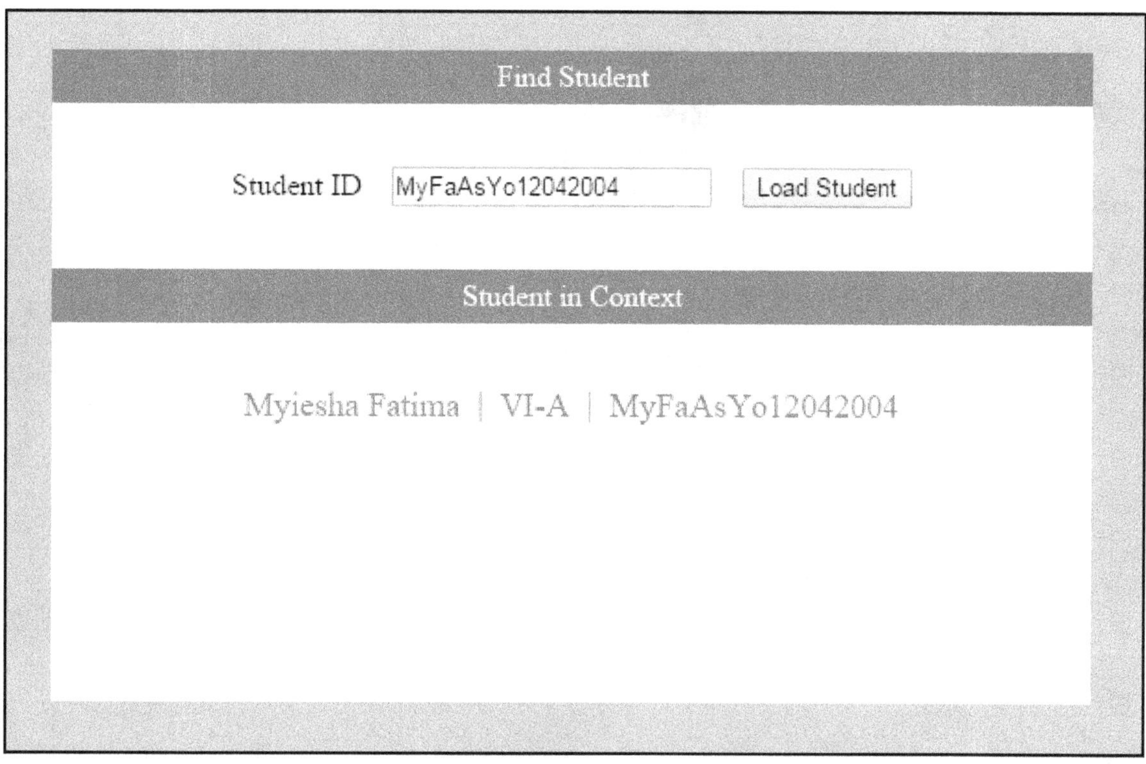

This region is within the BisDashboard.html page.

Prototype 4: Student Details Page.

Specification Reference: R4

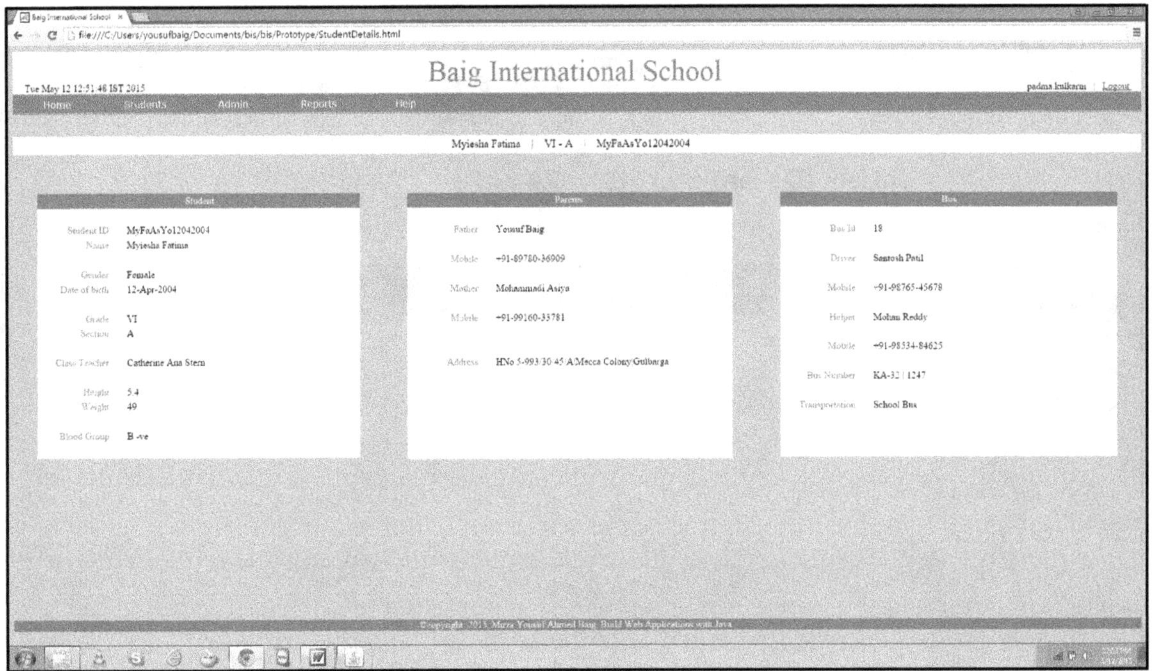

The StudentDetails.jsp page is built using this html page. The source code for this page is available in chapter 15 under the get student details use case section.

Prototype 5: Student Results Page for Semester 1.

Specification Reference: R6

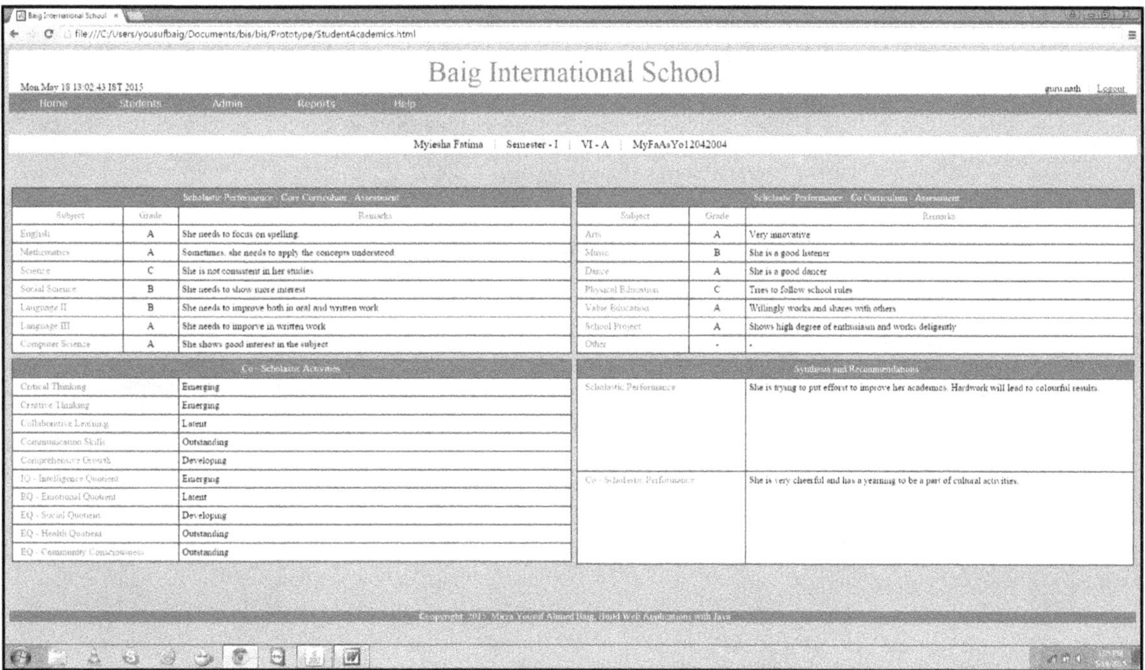

The StudentAcademics.jsp page is built using this html page. The source code for this page is available in chapter 15 under the get student results use case section.

Prototype 5: Student Results Page for Semester 2.

Specification Reference: R6

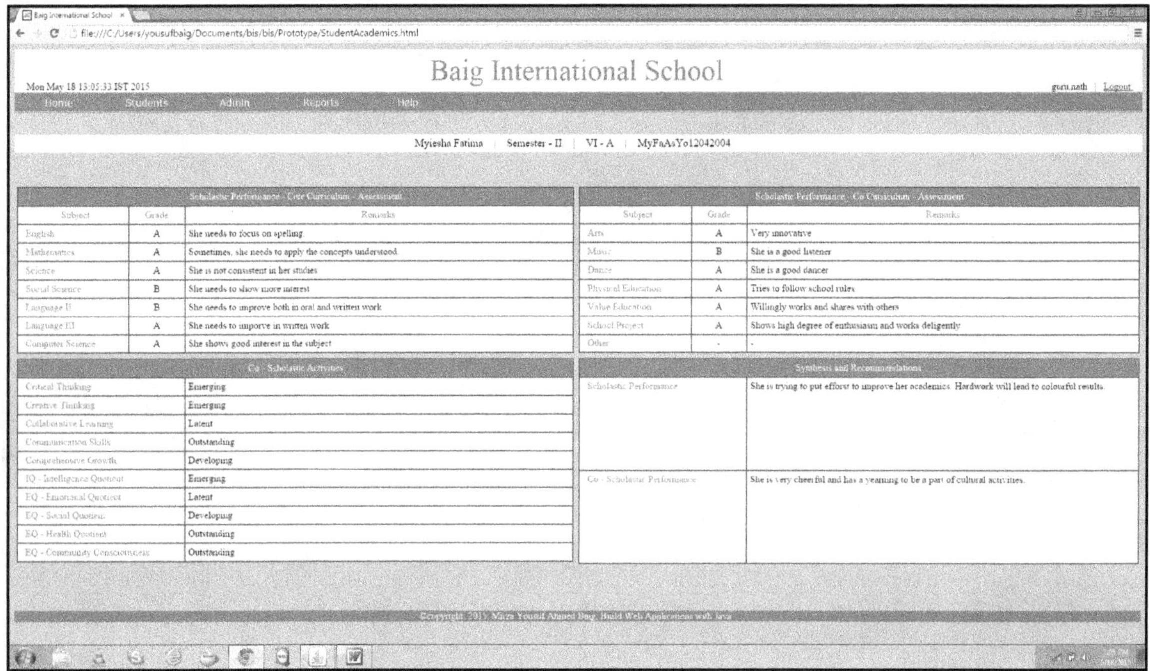

The StudentAcademics.jsp page is built using this html page. The source code for this page is available in chapter 15 under the get student results use case section.

Prototype 6: Student Attendance Page for Semester 1.

Specification Reference: R6

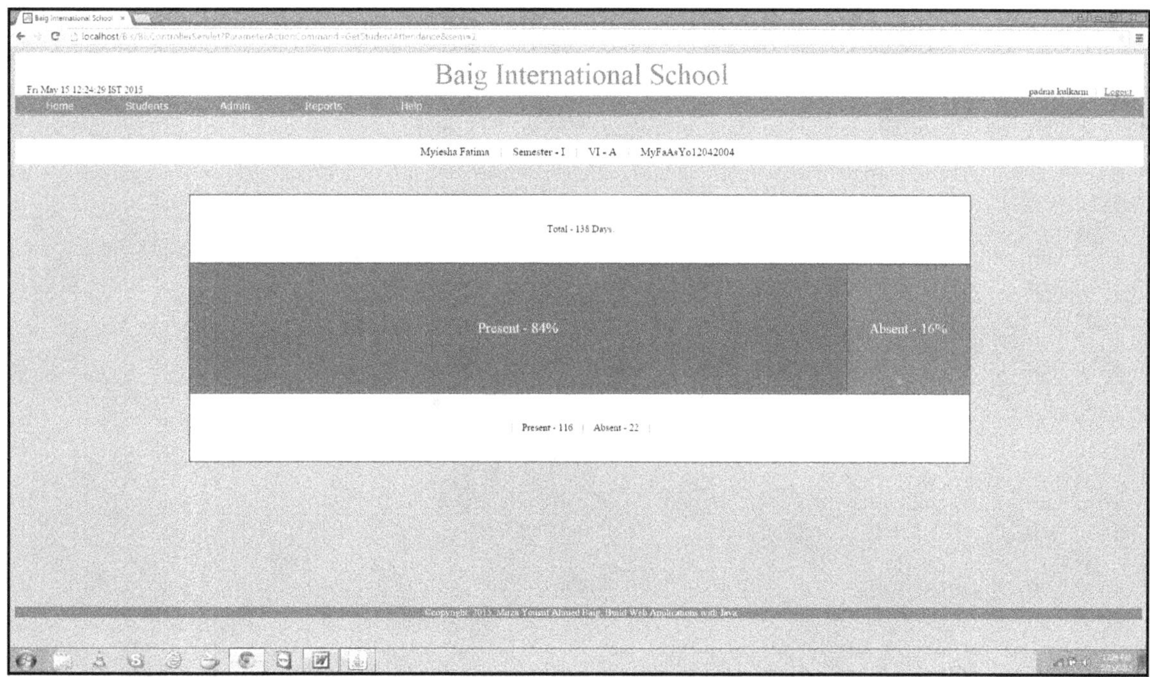

The StudentAttendance.jsp page is built using this html page. The source code for this page is available in chapter 15 under the get student attendance use case section.

Prototype 6: Student Attendance Page for Semester 2.

Specification Reference: R6

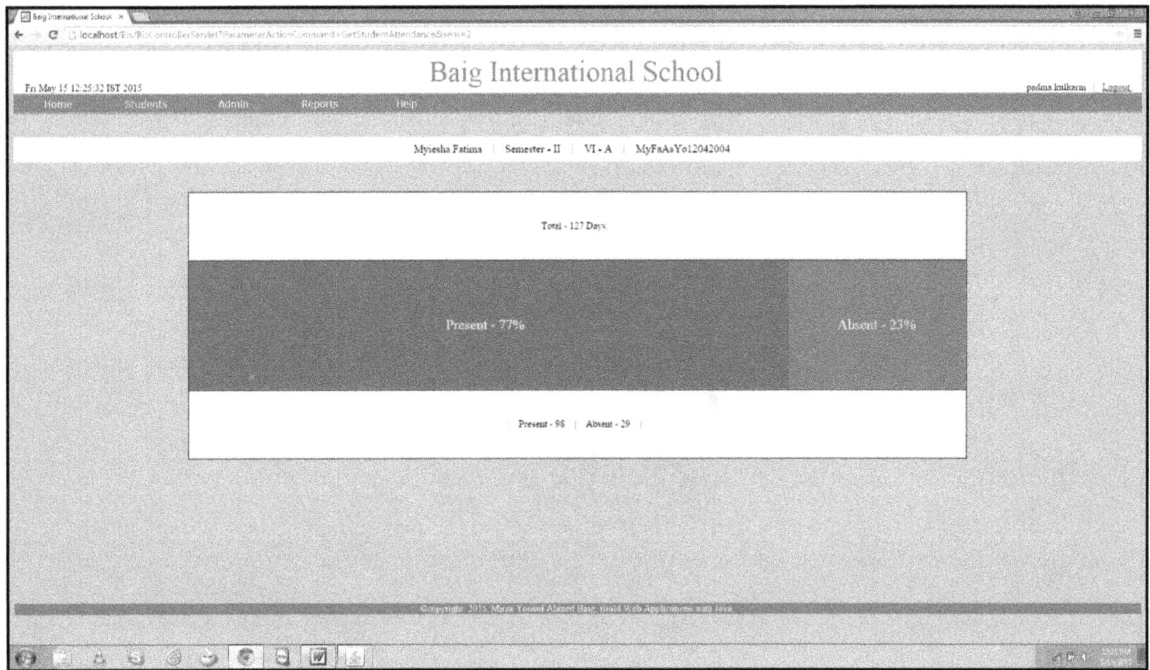

The StudentAttendance.jsp page is built using this html page. The source code for this page is available in chapter 15 under the get student attendance use case section.

Prototype 7: Fees Status Page.

Specification Reference: R8

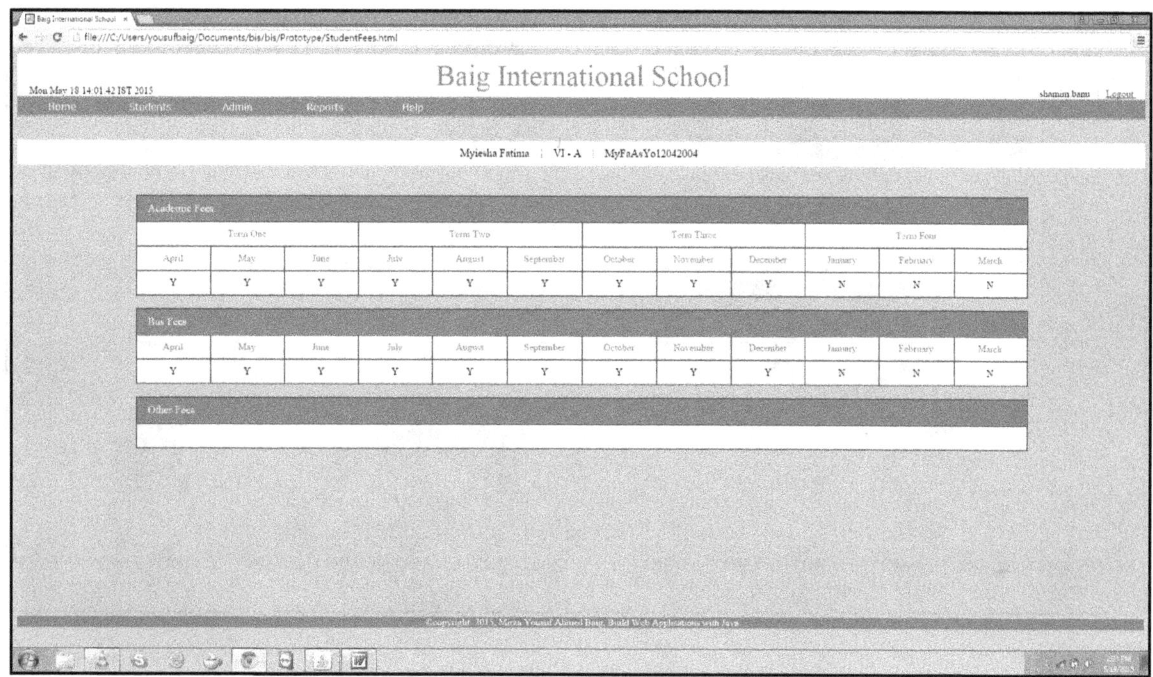

The StudentFees.jsp page is built using this html page. The source code for this page is available in chapter 15 under the get student fees use case section.

Prototype 8: Manage Attendance Page.

Specification Reference: R8

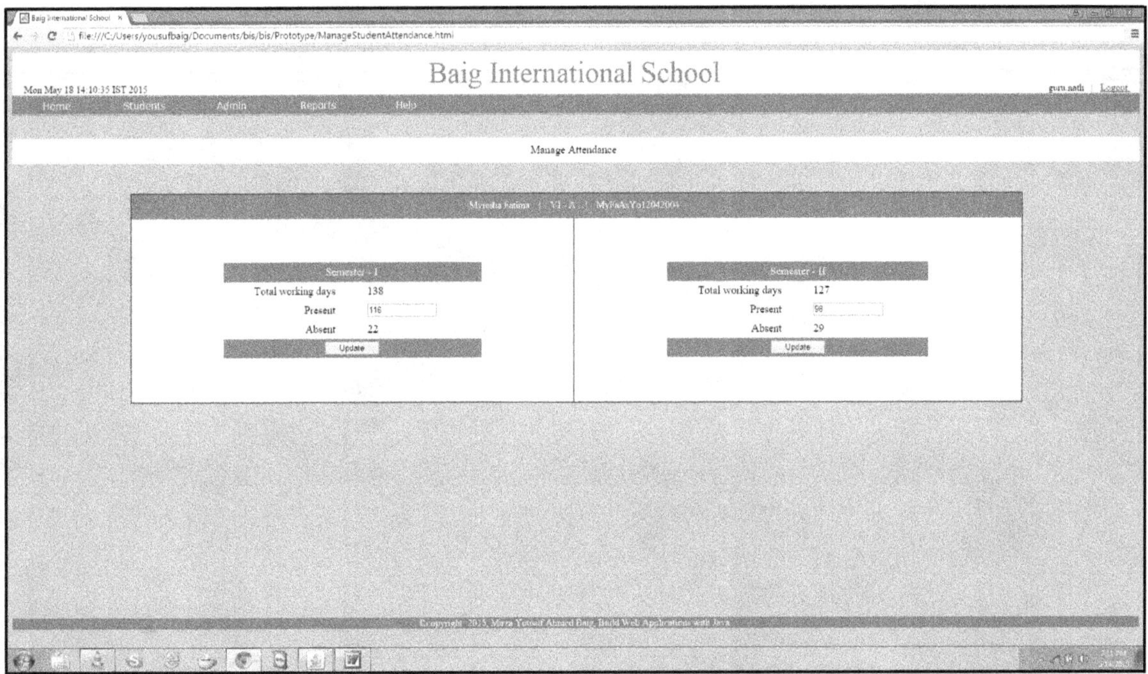

The ManageAttendance.jsp page is built using this html page. The source code for this page is available in chapter 15 under the manage student attendance use case section.

Prototype 9: Add Student Page.

Specification Reference: R9

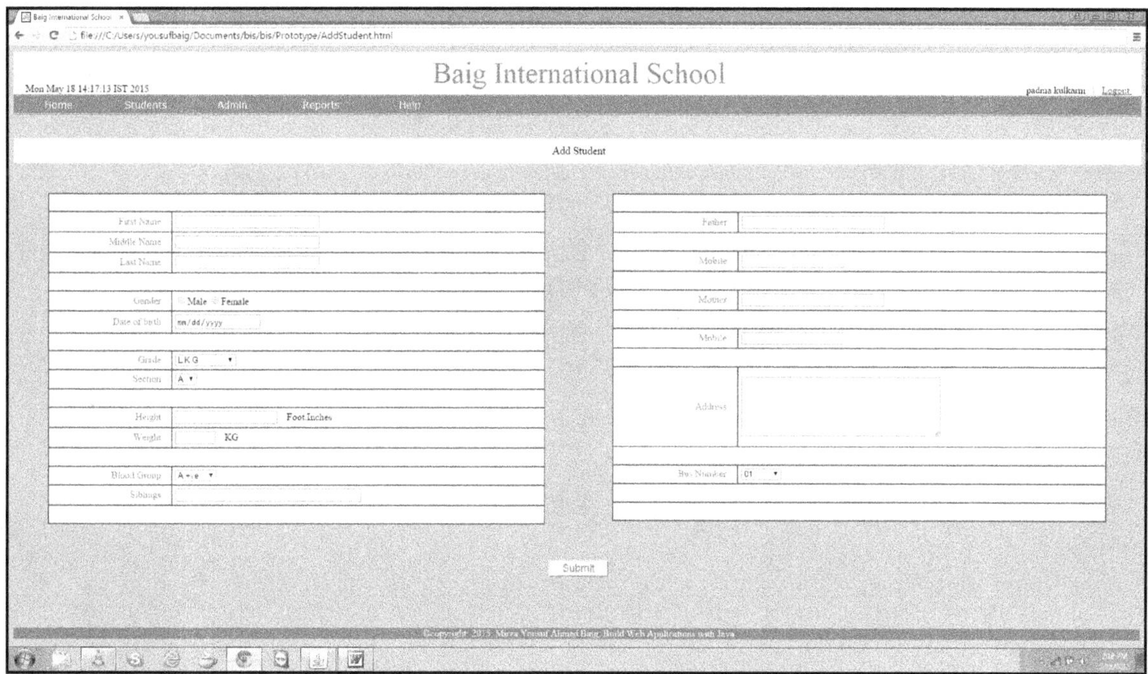

The AddStudent.jsp page is built using this html page. The source code for this page is available in chapter 15 under the add student use case section.

Prototype 10: Report by class page with report criteria options.

Specification Reference: R10

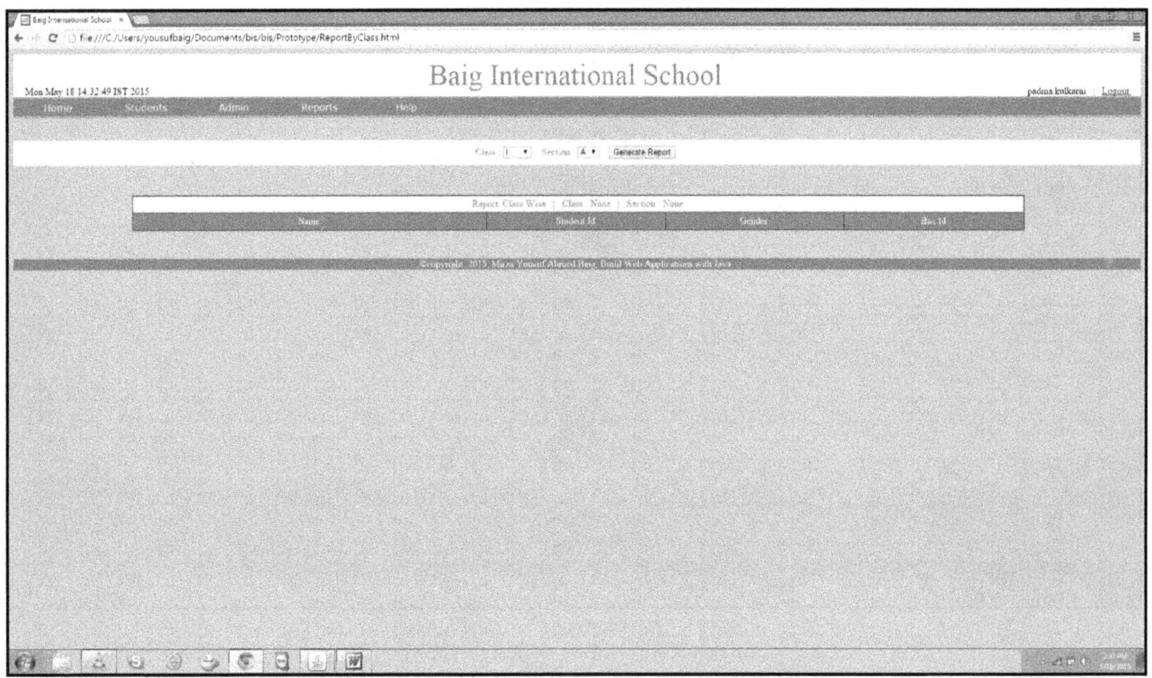

The ReportByClass.jsp page is built using this html page. The source code for this page is available in chapter 15 under the report by class use case section.

Prototype 10: Report by class page with report data.

Specification Reference: R10

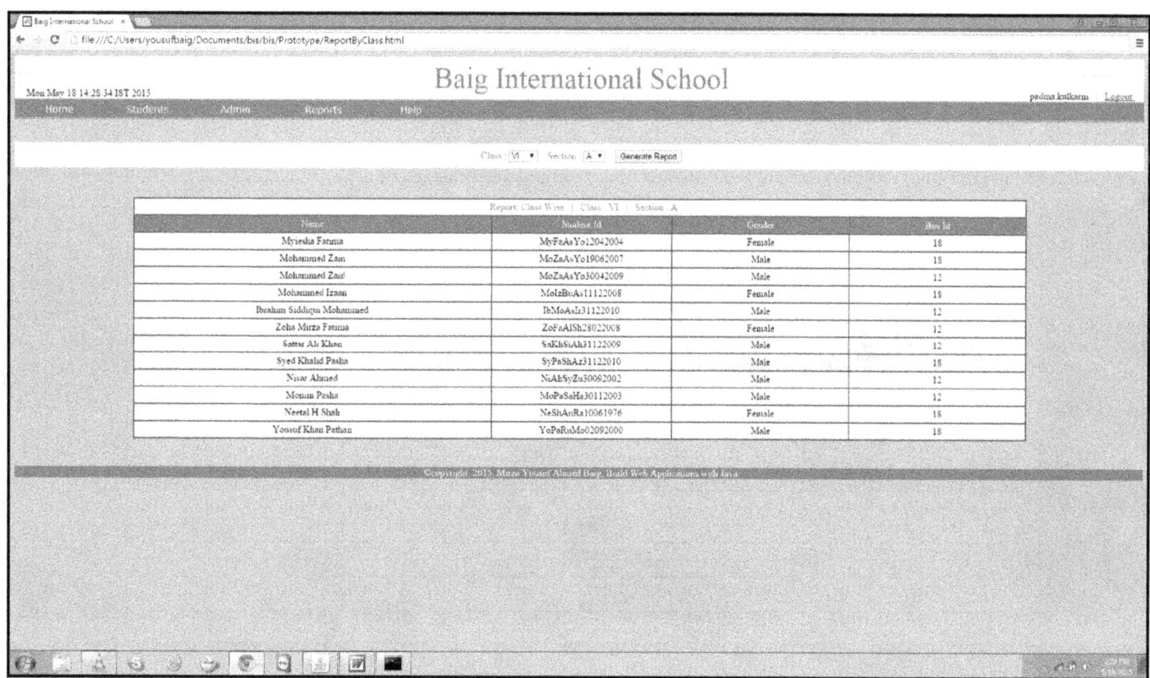

The ReportByClass.jsp page is built using this html page. The source code for this page is available in chapter 15 under the report by class use case section.

Prototype 11: Help pages, results legend page.

Specification Reference: R11

Type: Static html page.

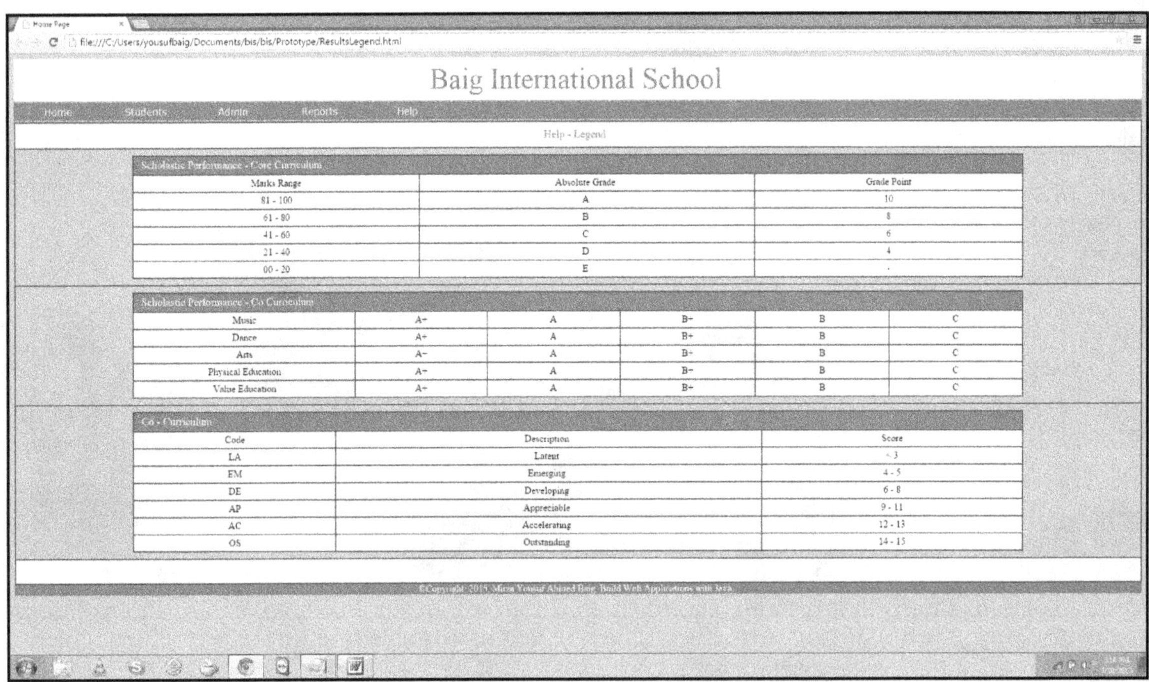

Baig International School

Home Students Admin Reports Help

Help - Legend

Scholastic Performance - Core Curriculum		
Marks Range	Absolute Grade	Grade Point
81 - 100	A	10
61 - 80	B	8
41 - 60	C	6
21 - 40	D	4
00 - 20	E	-

Scholastic Performance - Co Curriculum					
Music	A+	A	B+	B	C
Dance	A+	A	B+	B	C
Arts	A+	A	B+	B	C
Physical Education	A+	A	B+	B	C
Value Education	A+	A	B+	B	C

Co - Curriculum		
Code	Description	Score
LA	Latent	< 3
EM	Emerging	4 - 5
DE	Developing	6 - 8
AP	Appreciable	9 - 11
AC	Accelerating	12 - 13
OS	Outstanding	14 - 15

The source code for ResultsLegend.html page is available in chapter 15 under the help page use case section.

6

THE CLIENT SIDE

The face of a web application is a browser. The browser is a smart client and it has computational capabilities. The browser is not just for displaying the content it also provides computational functionalities and platform for other web 2.0 features. The most commonly used technologies used in almost all the browser based applications are JavaScript and Cascaded Style Sheets. In our sample application we are using one .js (javascript) file and one .css (cascaded style sheet) file. In this chapter we will go through these two files in detail.

JavaScript

This is the most popular scripting language used on the client side. There are even many frameworks built with JavaScript and they are pretty popular too. JavaScript is a object based programming language and is used for various computations at client side. The most common usage is form validation and executing other client side logic.

The javascript code can directly be embedded in a jsp or a html page. But the preferred way is to have separate .js file and include that file in the jsp or html page wherever required. In our sample application, we are using BisScript.js file and this is included in the home page template. The home page template in turn includes all the other jsp pages. Thereby, we don't have to include this file in all individual jsp pages. It is available to us in all the pages as we have included this in the home page template.

BisScript.js

```
function submitAddStdForm()    {
      document.getElementById("paramAddStdFrmSubmitted").value = "Yes";
      document.getElementById("frmAddStudent").submit();
}

function generateRptByCls()    {
      document.getElementById("frmReportByCls").submit();
}

function updateAttendance(sem)       {
      if (sem == '1')    {
            document.getElementById("ParameterUpdateSemAttendance").value
            = "1";
      }
      else if (sem == '2')     {
            document.getElementById("ParameterUpdateSemAttendance").value
            = "2";
      }
      document.getElementById("paramUpdateAttFrmSubmitted").value= "Yes";
      document.getElementById("frmManageAttendance").submit();
}

var xmlHttpReq=false;

function getStudentAJAX()      {

      var stdId = document.getElementById("txtStdId").value;
      var   url =
      "BisAjaxControllerServlet?ParameterActionCommand=LoadStudent&txtStd
      Id=";
      url = url + stdId;

      xmlHttpReq = new XMLHttpRequest();
      xmlHttpReq.open("GET",url, true);
      xmlHttpReq.send();
      xmlHttpReq.onreadystatechange=getStudentAjaxCallBack;

}

function getStudentAjaxCallBack()   {

      if (xmlHttpReq.readyState == 4 && xmlHttpReq.status == 200)    {

            document.getElementById("dvStdSmry").innerHTML
            = xmlHttpReq.responseText;
      }
```

}

The javascript function submitAddStdForm performs the following tasks:

⇒ Sets the value Yes to paramAddStdFrmSubmitted flag and submits the form. On the server side this flag is used to identify whether the user has submitted the filled form or is requesting the add student form page to be filled and submitted.

The javascript function generateRptByCls performs the following tasks:

⇒ Submits the form.

The javascript function updateAttendance performs the following tasks:

⇒ Sets the semester in context.

⇒ Marks the update flag to Yes.

⇒ Submits the form.

The javascript variable xmlHttpReq is used by the two Ajax javascript functions.

The load student use case details the other two Ajax functions getStudentAJAX and getStudentAjaxCallBack.

Cascaded Style Sheet

The css is the most common way of presenting the content to the browser. In css we define the styles for elements and these can be referenced from the html or Jsp documents. Each html style can be defined inline or at a document level or in a separate .css file. This file can be included in the jsp or html page and the style definitions in it can be tied to the html elements in the page. In our sample application, we are using only one css file. The styles for all the pages in our application are defined in this file. Also, the style for the menus and menu items are all defined in this file. Lets have a closer look at this file.

BISStyle.css

```
body {
      background-color: #BBBBBB;
}

#dashboardlink {
      color: Blue;
      font-size: large;
}

#trbgred {
      color: white;
      background-color: red;
}

#bigwhtxt {
      color: White;
      font-size: x-large;
}

#regfont {
      color: white;
}

#headingfont {
      color: Red;
      size: 7;
      style: bold;
}

#headingtxt {
      color: Red;
      font-size: large;
}

#redFontWhiteBg {
      color: red;
      background-color: White;
}

#whiteBg    {
      background-color: White;
      font-size: large;
}

#submitButton    {
      color: red;
```

```
        background-color: White;
        font-size: large;
}

#clred {
        color: red;
}

#cssmenu {
        width: auto;
        border: 1px solid #ff0000;
        background: #ff0000;
}

#cssmenu > ul {
        padding: 1px 0;
        margin: 0px;
        list-style: none;
        width: 100%;
        height: 27px;
        border-top: 1px solid #FFFFFF;
        border-bottom: 1px solid #FFFFFF;
        font: normal 12pt verdana, arial, helvetica;
}

#cssmenu > ul li {
margin: 0;
padding: 0;
display: block;
float: left;
position: relative;
width: 148px;
}

#cssmenu > ul li a:link, #cssmenu > ul li a:visited {
padding: 4px 0;
display: block;
text-align: center;
text-decoration: none;
background: #ff0000;
color: #ffffff;
width: 148px;
}

#cssmenu > ul li:hover a, #cssmenu > ul li a:hover, #cssmenu > ul
li a:active {
padding: 4px 0;
display: block;
text-align: center;
```

```
text-decoration: none;
background: #ff4d4d;
color: #ffffff;
width: 146px;
border-left: 1px solid #ffffff;
border-right: 1px solid #ffffff;
}

#cssmenu > ul li ul {
margin: 0;
padding: 1px 1px 0;
list-style: none;
display: none;
background: #ffffff;
width: 146px;
position: absolute;
top: 21px;
left: -1px;
border: 1px solid #ff0000;
border-top: none;
}

#cssmenu > ul li:hover ul {
      display: block;
}

#cssmenu > ul li ul li {
      clear: left;
      width: 146px;
}

#cssmenu > ul li ul li a:link, #cssmenu > ul li ul li a:visited {
clear: left;
background: #ff0000;
padding: 4px 0;
width: 146px;
border: none;
border-bottom: 1px solid #ffffff;
position: relative;
z-index: 1000;
}

#cssmenu > ul li ul li:hover a, #cssmenu > ul li ul li a:active,
#cssmenu > ul li ul li a:hover {
clear: left;
background: #ff4d4d;
padding: 4px 0;
width: 146px;
border: none;
```

```
border-bottom: 1px solid #ffffff;
position: relative;
z-index: 1000;
}

#cssmenu > ul li ul li ul.navigation-3 {
display: none;
margin: 0;
padding: 0;
list-style: none;
position: absolute;
left: 145px;
top: -2px;
padding: 1px 1px 0 1px;
border: 1px solid #ff0000;
border-left: 1px solid #ff0000;
background: #ffffff;
z-index: 900;
}

#cssmenu > ul li ul li:hover ul.navigation-3 {
      display: block;
}

#cssmenu > ul li ul li ul.navigation-3 li a:link, #cssmenu > ul li
ul li ul.navigation-3 li a:visited {
      background: #ff0000;
}
```

The BISStyle.css and BISScript.js files are included in the BisHome.jsp page. This page in turn includes all other jsp pages based on the use case. In order to use these files, the following code is added in BisHome.jsp page. Accordingly, the BISStyle.css files is placed under resources/css folder and the BISScript.js file is placed under resources/js folder.

```
<head>
      <link rel="stylesheet" type="text/css"
      href="resources/css/BISStyle.css">
      </link>
      <script src="resources/js/BISScript.js">
      </script>
</head>
```

Menus

For the implementation of the menus, please refer the BISStyle.css source code in this chapter and BisHome.jsp source code in chapter 14.

7
THE PATTERNS

A pattern is a proven way of approaching the solution for a know type of problem. A given problem can be solved in many ways. The approach which provides the best solution and which is already tried and tested by others constitute a pattern. Patterns provide ready made solutions for a known type of problem. Patterns basically reuse human efforts and intelligence which is already invested by others.

Let us understand pattern with an example from our day today life. A school bus driver picks and drops 20 students from various locations in a city. The driver has a pattern for the pick up based on the no entries, traffic conditions, weather etc during morning hours. The driver also has a pattern for dropping the students based on the said conditions in the evening. The driver will pick and drop students in a particular order. This order evolves after few weeks from the beginning of the academic year. The driver may pick the student nearest to the school in the last and the driver may drop the same student first in the evening. The driver of this school bus thus eventually has the best way after few weeks to save time, fuel and efforts for this task. The driver sticks to this pattern to achieve the said goals.

Now, lets take a scenario where the driver quits the job. In this case, the new driver will not reinvent the wheel. The new driver will learn the path and the order etc from the old driver who is quitting. We can now say that, the old driver has put intelligence, efforts, time, money etc to come up with the best pattern for picking up and dropping the students. The new driver has to just reuse this human effort and intelligence which is tried, tested and proven . This is nothing but establishing a pattern and reusing it.

Architectural Patterns

These are patterns at architectural level. These patterns focus at a bigger picture at the system level structure of modules, components and even applications within and outside an enterprise. Service Oriented Architecture (SOA), Model View Controller (MVC) and dependency injection are the most commonly used architectural patterns.

MVC

Please refer chapter 10 for detailed explanation and implementation of a MVC based architectural pattern.

Design Patterns

These are the patterns at design level. The design patterns provide solutions to the commonly encountered design problems. The most commonly used design patterns are Singleton, Factory, Command, Iterator, Bridge and Adapter etc.

Lets have a closer look at the patterns used in our sample application.

Command Pattern

This is basically a design pattern and is further categorized under behavioral patterns. In command pattern, the client sends a command and based on the command the server executes a functionality and returns the result to the client.

In our sample application and MVC based framework we exploit command pattern. Lets see this with an example of a use case. If you look at the get student details use case, The user click get student details, this sends the "getStudentDetails" command to the server. The server invokes the controller servlet, within the controller servlet we use a command processor class for each command. In this case, the controller servlet instantiates

GetStudentDetailsCP class and invokes the execute method. This class holds the business logic for get student details command. This class leverages other service classes and utility classes to get the student details from the database. And finally returns the view with the student details.

Hence, in command pattern we see that the client sends a request or a command to the server. The server delegates this command to the framework which in turn invokes the specific command handler. The command handler executes the business logic pertaining to the command and navigates the user to an appropriate view. For more details on command pattern please go through the Bis MVC framework flow description in chapter 10 and also please go through the individual use cases implementation to get further understanding and clarity.

Front Controller Design Patten

In this design pattern, we have a centralized entry point for particular type of client requests. This pattern is commonly used in frameworks which are used for building web applications.

In our framework, we use BisControllerServlet as an entry point for all the client requests. We have another controller servlet which is the entry point for all Ajax requests from the client. The BisAjaxControlerServlet handles only ajax requests in our framework and it acts as front controller for all the Ajax calls from the client.

This pattern helps a lot in debugging. By setting a break point at the controller servlet we can trace all the execution flows.

Value Object Design Pattern

In this pattern we use simple java beans with private fields and public getters and setters methods for those fields. In our sample application we use this pattern heavily. For example in the get student details use case, we add all the data related to student to a StudentDetailsBean. This data is fetched from one or more tables from the database. This gives us a handy object to process the student related data at the java tier. We add this object to the session and consume it for the view purpose at the jsp page level. This pattern helps in creating a view based on the use case requirements. This also helps in putting relevant or related data in a single object which is very handy for the developers.

There are other design patterns which are used in our sample applications. There are many other design patterns which can be used in our sample application. Based on the requirements, architecture, performance criteria, user base, support requirements, type of application and many other factors the design patterns have to be chosen and implemented.

8

THE ARCHITECTURE

Architecture is the blueprint of the application. This gives the ariel view of the system to be built. The architecture provides the bigger picture in a single view comprising of all the significant building blocks of the system.

The architecture is a very broad and old term used in almost all branches of engineering. Lets take an example of a civil engineering project to understand what an architecture is. Lets take the example of "Baig Apartments", this apartment needs to have 7 floors and each floor must have 3 flats. The plot size to build this apartment is 10,000 square feet. The requirement is very basic and quantified at a very high level in this case. The architecture needs to be built first, than comes the structural design and then the actual building will be built based on the design.

The architecture in this case provides the ariel view or the bigger picture of the apartment to be built. The architecture details the placement of each flat on a floor with the dimensions of each room, hall, kitchen etc. The architecture details the space for utilities, parking and other significant entities of a building of this size like the lift, staircase etc. The color of the walls, the material used for flooring, the interior of the kitchen etc are outside the scope of the architectural details. A good architecture is essential to build a system. It provides us the flexibility to visualize, model, design and modify a system before it is built.

The BIS-SMS Application Architecture

In software engineering, the architecture details all the building block of the application. It also details the interaction and the type between various components of a software system to be built. Lets now draw the architecture of BIS-SMS application. This architecture must show case us from browser to browser trace in a bigger picture. That is, it must show us what happens when a request is sent from a browser till we receive back the response to the browser. This must be depicted in a diagram at a component or modular level.

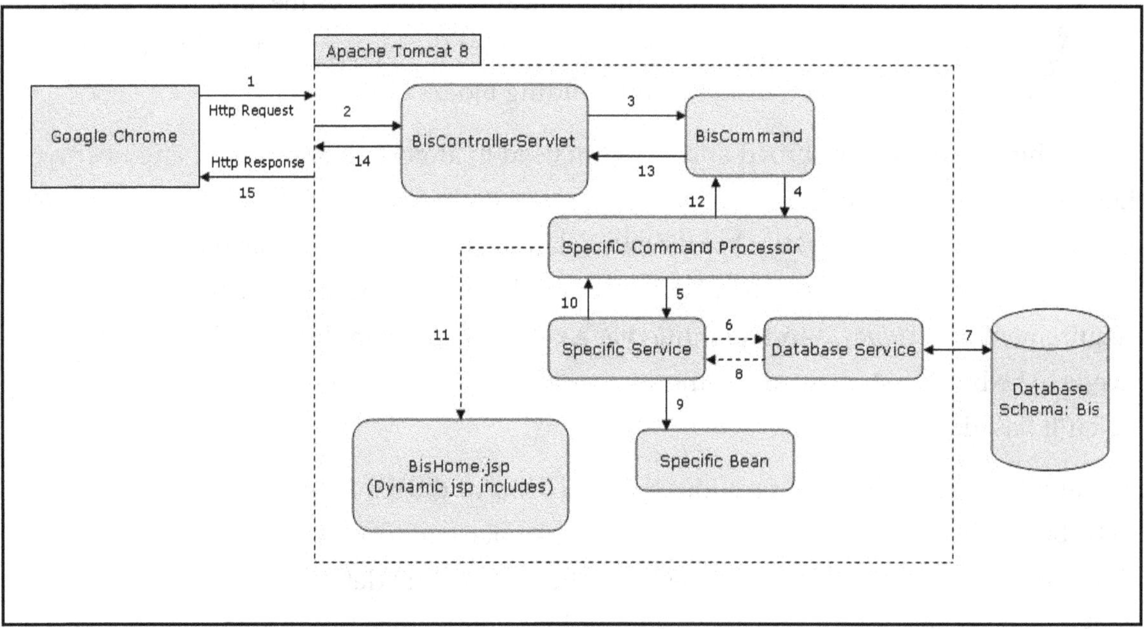

The browser sends a http request to the server. The server identifies the request and invokes the controller servlet. The controller servlet identifies the command and invokes the appropriate command processor. The command processor based on the use case leverages one of more service classes. The service classes hold the business logic and may interact with the database using database service class. The service classes provide the services for specific use cases. Based on the request type, the service classes cook up the beans and populate the data in one or more beans to provide it back with the response. In case of insert or update operations, the service classes will provide only a flag conveying success or failure. In case of a view request, the service classes, query the database add these values to beans and return the control to the command processor for rendering a specific view.

Note that in the above architectural diagram and description we have looked at the things in a bigger picture and not dwelled into the micro details of any specific interaction or component.

We build this architecture after having a clarity with requirements and after technology selection. The next thing is to list and detail all the use cases and then create detailed design for each use case. The detailed design must be provided with various UML diagrams. The objective of the architecture is served if it helps in coming up with detailed design. Once the detailed design is ready, the system can be implemented (Generally via coding). It is important that the implemented system must be in compliance with the architecture.

9

DATABASE DESIGN

Once we have complete clarity with the requirements i.e. once we have the frozen and signed requirements specifications, we come up with the database design.

For BIS SMS web application, we need following two schemas:

BisSecurityRealm Schema

This schema is exclusively used for users, roles and permissions. In this schema we have two tables one for users and other for the roles. The ER-diagram below details these tables.

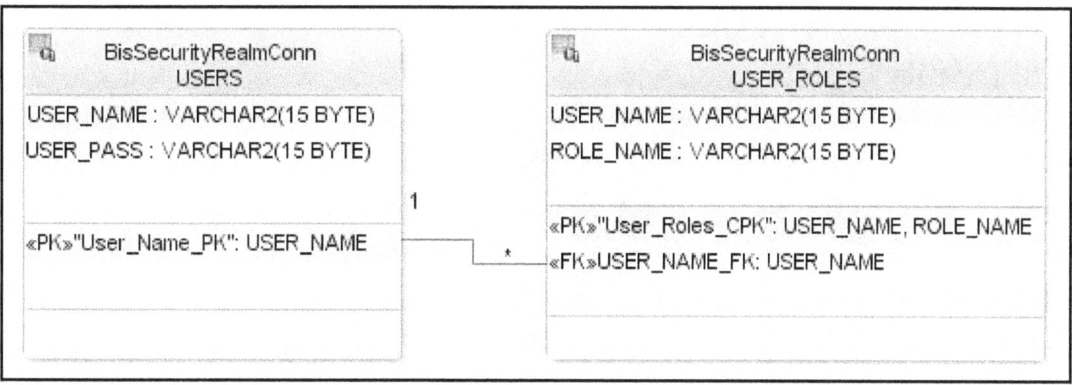

Users Table

The users table has two columns. The user name column stores the user name and is a primary key for this table. The user password column stores the password.

User Roles Table

The user roles table also has two columns. The user name column stores the user name and is a foreign key to the user name column in users table. The role name column stores the role.

Bis Schema

This is the application schema and is used for application specific data. The ER-diagram below details the tables. For the sample application we are only using database tables and not other database entities like view, triggers etc. The database is designed for a particular academic year and hence, the data has to be purged at the end of each academic year. However, this design can be enhanced for multiple academic years.

Lets take a closer look at each of these tables and their relationships.

Student Details Table

The student details table holds one record for each student and is uniquely identified by student id. This is the core table for all the information related to students.

Parent Details Table

This table holds the details of the student's parent's/guardian's. The student id here is a foreign key to the student details table.

Employee Details Table

This table provides us all the relevant information about the employees of the school. The employees include, the teaching staff and the non teaching staff. For example, this table provides us the information of the class teacher as well as the bus driver.

Transportation Details Table

The student's commute information is fetched from this table.

Class Teacher Mapping Table

This is a look up table which provides us identifying class teacher for a given class and section.

Student Attendance Table

For a given semester and for a given student, this table provides the attendance details. This table is designed to provide the attendance only for the current academic year.

Student Fees Table

For a given student, this table provides all the information about Tuition as well as transportation fees.

Scholastic Results/Co Scholastic Results Tables

These two table hold all the details about the student's results. These are example tables for learning purpose only and are not designed for any particular board or a body. These tables have to be designed accordingly for a specific board or a body (based on the country and education system).

BIS Constants Table

This table is used only for stories properties with a value. For e.g. the school telephone number can be stored in this table. If the telephone number changes, we have to update it in this table for a given property.

The applications consuming this table must be designed accordingly. Hence, we get smart applications where we neither have to modify the code nor have to redeploy the application.

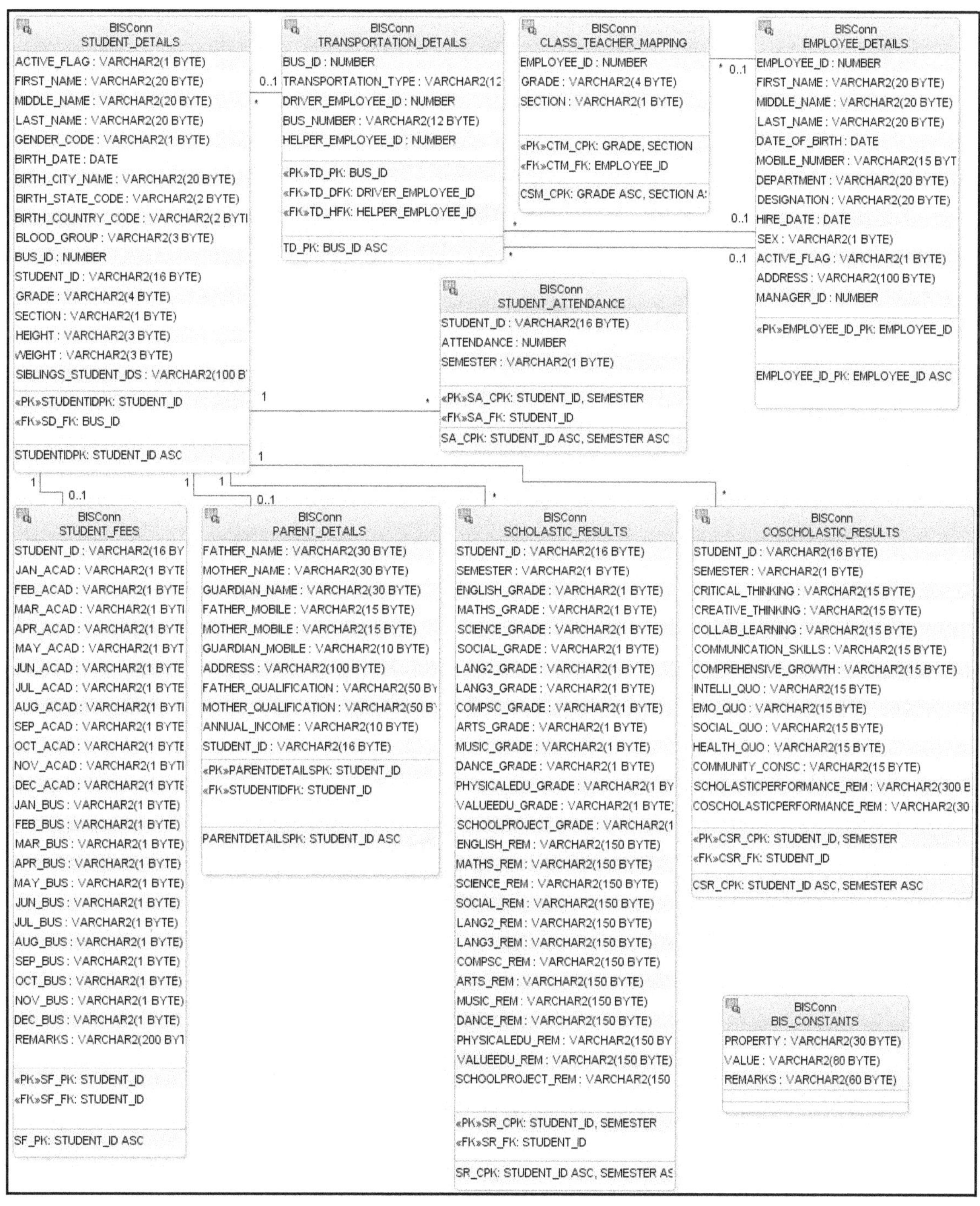
BISConn
STUDENT_DETAILS
ACTIVE_FLAG : VARCHAR2(1 BYTE)
FIRST_NAME : VARCHAR2(20 BYTE)
MIDDLE_NAME : VARCHAR2(20 BYTE)
LAST_NAME : VARCHAR2(20 BYTE)
GENDER_CODE : VARCHAR2(1 BYTE)
BIRTH_DATE : DATE
BIRTH_CITY_NAME : VARCHAR2(20 BYTE)
BIRTH_STATE_CODE : VARCHAR2(2 BYTE)
BIRTH_COUNTRY_CODE : VARCHAR2(2 BYTI
BLOOD_GROUP : VARCHAR2(3 BYTE)
BUS_ID : NUMBER
STUDENT_ID : VARCHAR2(16 BYTE)
GRADE : VARCHAR2(4 BYTE)
SECTION : VARCHAR2(1 BYTE)
HEIGHT : VARCHAR2(3 BYTE)
WEIGHT : VARCHAR2(3 BYTE)
SIBLINGS_STUDENT_IDS : VARCHAR2(100 B
«PK»STUDENTIDPK: STUDENT_ID
«FK»SD_FK: BUS_ID
STUDENTIDPK: STUDENT_ID ASC
BISConn
TRANSPORTATION_DETAILS
BUS_ID : NUMBER
TRANSPORTATION_TYPE : VARCHAR2(12
DRIVER_EMPLOYEE_ID : NUMBER
BUS_NUMBER : VARCHAR2(12 BYTE)
HELPER_EMPLOYEE_ID : NUMBER
«PK»TD_PK: BUS_ID
«FK»TD_DFK: DRIVER_EMPLOYEE_ID
«FK»TD_HFK: HELPER_EMPLOYEE_ID
TD_PK: BUS_ID ASC
BISConn
CLASS_TEACHER_MAPPING
EMPLOYEE_ID : NUMBER
GRADE : VARCHAR2(4 BYTE)
SECTION : VARCHAR2(1 BYTE)
«PK»CTM_CPK: GRADE, SECTION
«FK»CTM_FK: EMPLOYEE_ID
CSM_CPK: GRADE ASC, SECTION A:
BISConn
EMPLOYEE_DETAILS
EMPLOYEE_ID : NUMBER
FIRST_NAME : VARCHAR2(20 BYTE)
MIDDLE_NAME : VARCHAR2(20 BYTE)
LAST_NAME : VARCHAR2(20 BYTE)
DATE_OF_BIRTH : DATE
MOBILE_NUMBER : VARCHAR2(15 BYT
DEPARTMENT : VARCHAR2(20 BYTE)
DESIGNATION : VARCHAR2(20 BYTE)
HIRE_DATE : DATE
SEX : VARCHAR2(1 BYTE)
ACTIVE_FLAG : VARCHAR2(1 BYTE)
ADDRESS : VARCHAR2(100 BYTE)
MANAGER_ID : NUMBER
«PK»EMPLOYEE_ID_PK: EMPLOYEE_ID
EMPLOYEE_ID_PK: EMPLOYEE_ID ASC
BISConn
STUDENT_ATTENDANCE
STUDENT_ID : VARCHAR2(16 BYTE)
ATTENDANCE : NUMBER
SEMESTER : VARCHAR2(1 BYTE)
«PK»SA_CPK: STUDENT_ID, SEMESTER
«FK»SA_FK: STUDENT_ID
SA_CPK: STUDENT_ID ASC, SEMESTER ASC
0..1
*
0..1
0..1
0..1
1
1
1
1
1
0..1
0..1
BISConn
STUDENT_FEES
STUDENT_ID : VARCHAR2(16 BY
JAN_ACAD : VARCHAR2(1 BYTE
FEB_ACAD : VARCHAR2(1 BYTE
MAR_ACAD : VARCHAR2(1 BYTI
APR_ACAD : VARCHAR2(1 BYTE
MAY_ACAD : VARCHAR2(1 BYT
JUN_ACAD : VARCHAR2(1 BYTE
JUL_ACAD : VARCHAR2(1 BYTE
AUG_ACAD : VARCHAR2(1 BYTI
SEP_ACAD : VARCHAR2(1 BYTE
OCT_ACAD : VARCHAR2(1 BYTE
NOV_ACAD : VARCHAR2(1 BYTI
DEC_ACAD : VARCHAR2(1 BYTE
JAN_BUS : VARCHAR2(1 BYTE)
FEB_BUS : VARCHAR2(1 BYTE)
MAR_BUS : VARCHAR2(1 BYTE)
APR_BUS : VARCHAR2(1 BYTE)
MAY_BUS : VARCHAR2(1 BYTE)
JUN_BUS : VARCHAR2(1 BYTE)
JUL_BUS : VARCHAR2(1 BYTE)
AUG_BUS : VARCHAR2(1 BYTE)
SEP_BUS : VARCHAR2(1 BYTE)
OCT_BUS : VARCHAR2(1 BYTE)
NOV_BUS : VARCHAR2(1 BYTE)
DEC_BUS : VARCHAR2(1 BYTE)
REMARKS : VARCHAR2(200 BYT
«PK»SF_PK: STUDENT_ID
«FK»SF_FK: STUDENT_ID
SF_PK: STUDENT_ID ASC
BISConn
PARENT_DETAILS
FATHER_NAME : VARCHAR2(30 BYTE)
MOTHER_NAME : VARCHAR2(30 BYTE)
GUARDIAN_NAME : VARCHAR2(30 BYTE)
FATHER_MOBILE : VARCHAR2(15 BYTE)
MOTHER_MOBILE : VARCHAR2(15 BYTE)
GUARDIAN_MOBILE : VARCHAR2(10 BYTE)
ADDRESS : VARCHAR2(100 BYTE)
FATHER_QUALIFICATION : VARCHAR2(50 BY
MOTHER_QUALIFICATION : VARCHAR2(50 B
ANNUAL_INCOME : VARCHAR2(10 BYTE)
STUDENT_ID : VARCHAR2(16 BYTE)
«PK»PARENTDETAILSPK: STUDENT_ID
«FK»STUDENTIDFK: STUDENT_ID
PARENTDETAILSPK: STUDENT_ID ASC
BISConn
SCHOLASTIC_RESULTS
STUDENT_ID : VARCHAR2(16 BYTE)
SEMESTER : VARCHAR2(1 BYTE)
ENGLISH_GRADE : VARCHAR2(1 BYTE)
MATHS_GRADE : VARCHAR2(1 BYTE)
SCIENCE_GRADE : VARCHAR2(1 BYTE)
SOCIAL_GRADE : VARCHAR2(1 BYTE)
LANG2_GRADE : VARCHAR2(1 BYTE)
LANG3_GRADE : VARCHAR2(1 BYTE)
COMPSC_GRADE : VARCHAR2(1 BYTE)
ARTS_GRADE : VARCHAR2(1 BYTE)
MUSIC_GRADE : VARCHAR2(1 BYTE)
DANCE_GRADE : VARCHAR2(1 BYTE)
PHYSICALEDU_GRADE : VARCHAR2(1 BY
VALUEEDU_GRADE : VARCHAR2(1 BYTE)
SCHOOLPROJECT_GRADE : VARCHAR2(1
ENGLISH_REM : VARCHAR2(150 BYTE)
MATHS_REM : VARCHAR2(150 BYTE)
SCIENCE_REM : VARCHAR2(150 BYTE)
SOCIAL_REM : VARCHAR2(150 BYTE)
LANG2_REM : VARCHAR2(150 BYTE)
LANG3_REM : VARCHAR2(150 BYTE)
COMPSC_REM : VARCHAR2(150 BYTE)
ARTS_REM : VARCHAR2(150 BYTE)
MUSIC_REM : VARCHAR2(150 BYTE)
DANCE_REM : VARCHAR2(150 BYTE)
PHYSICALEDU_REM : VARCHAR2(150 BY
VALUEEDU_REM : VARCHAR2(150 BYTE)
SCHOOLPROJECT_REM : VARCHAR2(150
«PK»SR_CPK: STUDENT_ID, SEMESTER
«FK»SR_FK: STUDENT_ID
SR_CPK: STUDENT_ID ASC, SEMESTER AS
BISConn
COSCHOLASTIC_RESULTS
STUDENT_ID : VARCHAR2(16 BYTE)
SEMESTER : VARCHAR2(1 BYTE)
CRITICAL_THINKING : VARCHAR2(15 BYTE)
CREATIVE_THINKING : VARCHAR2(15 BYTE)
COLLAB_LEARNING : VARCHAR2(15 BYTE)
COMMUNICATION_SKILLS : VARCHAR2(15 BYTE)
COMPREHENSIVE_GROWTH : VARCHAR2(15 BYTE)
INTELLI_QUO : VARCHAR2(15 BYTE)
EMO_QUO : VARCHAR2(15 BYTE)
SOCIAL_QUO : VARCHAR2(15 BYTE)
HEALTH_QUO : VARCHAR2(15 BYTE)
COMMUNITY_CONSC : VARCHAR2(15 BYTE)
SCHOLASTICPERFORMANCE_REM : VARCHAR2(300 E
COSCHOLASTICPERFORMANCE_REM : VARCHAR2(30
«PK»CSR_CPK: STUDENT_ID, SEMESTER
«FK»CSR_FK: STUDENT_ID
CSR_CPK: STUDENT_ID ASC, SEMESTER ASC
BISConn
BIS_CONSTANTS
PROPERTY : VARCHAR2(30 BYTE)
VALUE : VARCHAR2(80 BYTE)
REMARKS : VARCHAR2(60 BYTE)

10

THE FRAMEWORK

A framework provides the platform to quickly build applications using it. The framework holds all the common functionalities. A framework is a reusable entity and it helps in quickly building applications by focusing only on the application specifics. Reusability, productivity, best practices, proven patterns, fine tuned performance, scalability, compliance to standards, plug and play are the main advantages of using frameworks.

There are many open source and paid frameworks available in the market which are based on many proven architectural and design patterns.

The MVC Based Java Framework

In this chapter we will build our own light weight MVC based Java Framework for web applications. This will give us a complete insight and know how of a framework. This framework will than be used for building our applications on top of it. We will follow the industry recognized and proven MVC pattern. In this architectural pattern, there are three entities: the model, the view and the controller. Each entity has its own specific functionality.

View Layer

This is the user interface (UI) layer which the end user sees and interacts with it. On a desktop browser view is rendered as html document which has content and the presentation. In our framework, the html and jsp pages constitute the view.

Model Layer

Model represents the state of data during runtime on the server side. In Java, we use beans for model. These beans hold the data in a particular state.

Controller Layer

As the name suggests, the controller layer takes charge of the control and flow. The controller decides what functionality needs to be invoked on a particular interaction from the user. The controller also decides navigation flow and the view to be rendered to the user. Typically, a Servlet is used as a controller.

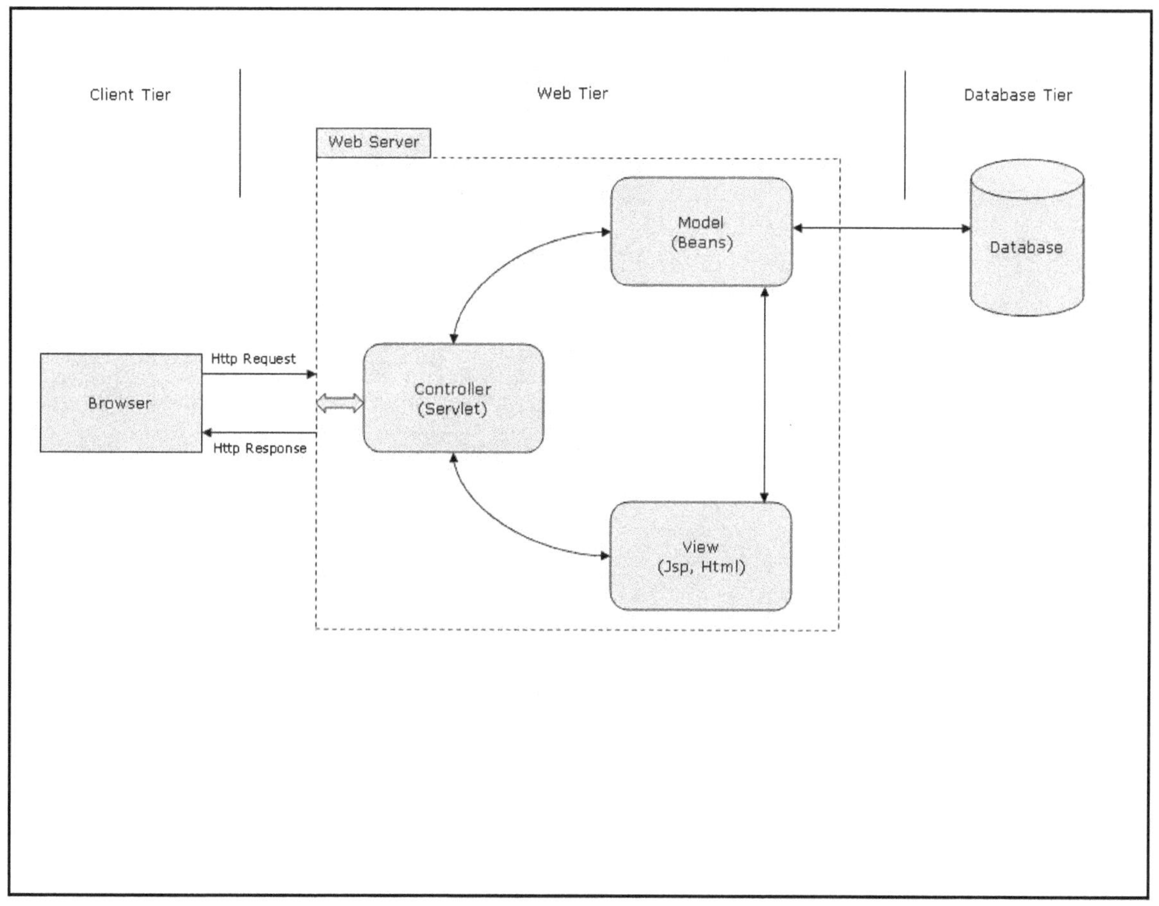

All the http requests from the client and all the http responses to the client (typically, a web browser) goes via the controller. Based on the client request, the controller invokes particular service. The service in turn prepares model and finally the view is rendered back to the client.

BisFramework

We will now build our own light weight MVC based Java framework. Lets call it BisFramework.

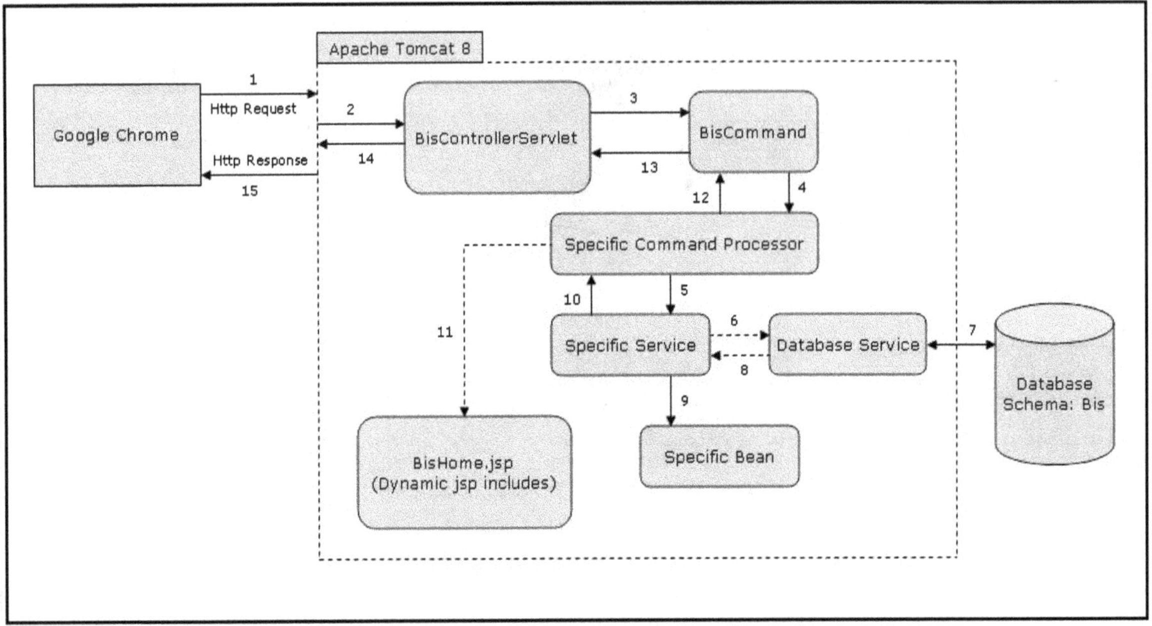

The BisFramework Architecture

In the above figure, we have 3 tiers. The client tier, the web server tier and the database tier.

Client Tier

The client tier typically consists of a web browser. The figure shows Google chrome as the client.

Database Tier

The database tier consists of a database. In our case we are using Oracle XE with two schemas one for authentication and authorization and other for the application.

Web Server Tier

The web server tier is comprised of Apache Tomcat. This provides us the capability of a web server and a Servlet container. The web server deals with the http protocol requests and responses and the Servlet container provides the runtime environment for the Servlets and JSP (JSPS are compiled to Servlets at runtime).

View Layer

The view layer takes care of managing the UI. It captures the user interactions and displays the output. The constituents of view are Jsp and html pages. The JavaScript .js and the cascaded style sheet .css files belong to the view. BisHome.jsp is an example view shown in the figure.

Controller Layer

The controller typically consists of one or more Servlets (generally one controller Servlet) In our case the controller Servlet is BisControllerServlet. All the requests and responses to the client flow through this Servlet. This controller primarily takes charge of invocation of services based on request and navigation flow.

Model Layer

The model comprises of the service classes and the beans classes. The beans represent the state of data in during the runtime. The service classes implement the business logic. The API that interacts with the database are leveraged from the Model layer.

Command Processor

The command processor takes charge form the controller Servlet. For a given request command, the subjective command processor is dynamically executed by the controller Servlet. Each command object than orchestrates the execution on the Model for the specific use case. To put it simple, the controller reads the client request and hand overs the task to a particular command object. The command object in turn invokes the model to achieve the specific task.

To achieve this, the controller just calls the execute method of the command.

BisCommand is an interface which holds only one method called execute. All the command processors implement the interface BisCommand to qualify as command processor. The command processor classes are suffixed with "CP", e.g. AddStudentCP. Each CP is subjective for its action. The CPs call the subjective services for a given task. Upon execution of the complete flow, either a bean is populated or a change is made in the database. If it is a view, the bean is populated and added to session. The view than consumes the bean and displays the output.

The Control Flow

In order to understand the control flow, lets trace the flow from the browser request till response. In the figure above lets have a closer look at each flow numbered from 1 to 15.

1. In this flow, the browser sends a http request to the server.

2. The server invokes the requested Servlet, in this case the BisControllerServlet.

3. All command processors implement the BisCommand interface in order to qualify as a command processor. This helps the controller servlet to leverage Java's polymorphic feature to dynamically execute a specific command processor. Please refer the service method of the controller servlet's code to get more clarity on this.

4. The controller servlet instantiates a specific command processor based on the request command passed by the view. This command is typically passed as a html hidden type

from the view. The command is generally a verb which conveys the user interaction with the UI. The controller servlet invokes the execute method of the command processor.

5. The command processor instantiates and invokes the required service classes.

6,7,8. The control flow takes this route if the service class needs an interaction with the database. DatabaseService is a java class which provides all the methods to interact with a particular database.

9. The service class populates one or more java beans via setters if the use is a get request for data.

In case of insert or update action to the database, the control flow varies. The beans are first populated from the request and than the values are passed to the database.

10, 11, 12, 13 Upon success or failure, the service class returns back the control to the command processor. Based on the result, the command processor assigns the next view name and returns back the control to BisControllerServlet.

14. The controller servlet uses the returned view name and based on that redirects the http response to a particular view (Jsp page).

15. The server sends back the http response of the view (Jsp page) to the browser. The user sees the next page which he/she had requested.

11

THE LOGGING

What is logging and why it is needed?

Logging is a mechanism to record the activities performed by a software program during execution. When a software program is executed line by line it accomplishes certain intended task. During the execution, the program logs the success, failures, important action or any other significant information into a file. This file is known as a log file and is used to monitor the health as well as the job of the software. The most common usage of logging is to identify system and business errors and it helps in fixing them. Logging helps in smoothly running the software system by providing the required information to the support team. In a broader sense, logging helps a lot in software system governance.

In our sample application we are using Log4j. Apache log4j is a logging utility and it provides ready made mechanism to enable logging in java applications with little configurations.

Logging Levels

In some applications or use cases we need extensive logging whereas in some other applications or use cases we may need logging only in case of an error or if something goes really fatal. Logging levels provide us an option to configure what level of logging is needed. For example, if the support team is analysis a bug they may set the logging at highest level as log at ALL levels provides more information. With log4j the following log levels are available.

ALL - Logs everything.

DEBUG - While debugging an issue.

ERROR - Logs errors and exceptions.

FATAL - Logs critical errors that could potentially terminate the application.

INFO - Provides information about the progress of the application for e.g. a new student is successfully added.

OFF - For turning off the logging.

WARN - For warnings. For e.g. a sql injection is attempted.

TRACE, TRACE_INT and are the other finer grained levels of logging.

Using Log4j in jdeveloper

In order to use Log4j download the latest version of Log4j.jar file and add it to the library. In order to add a jar file to a project library in jdeveloper, please follow the steps below:

Step 1: Right click the BISViewController project and select project properties as shown in the figure below.

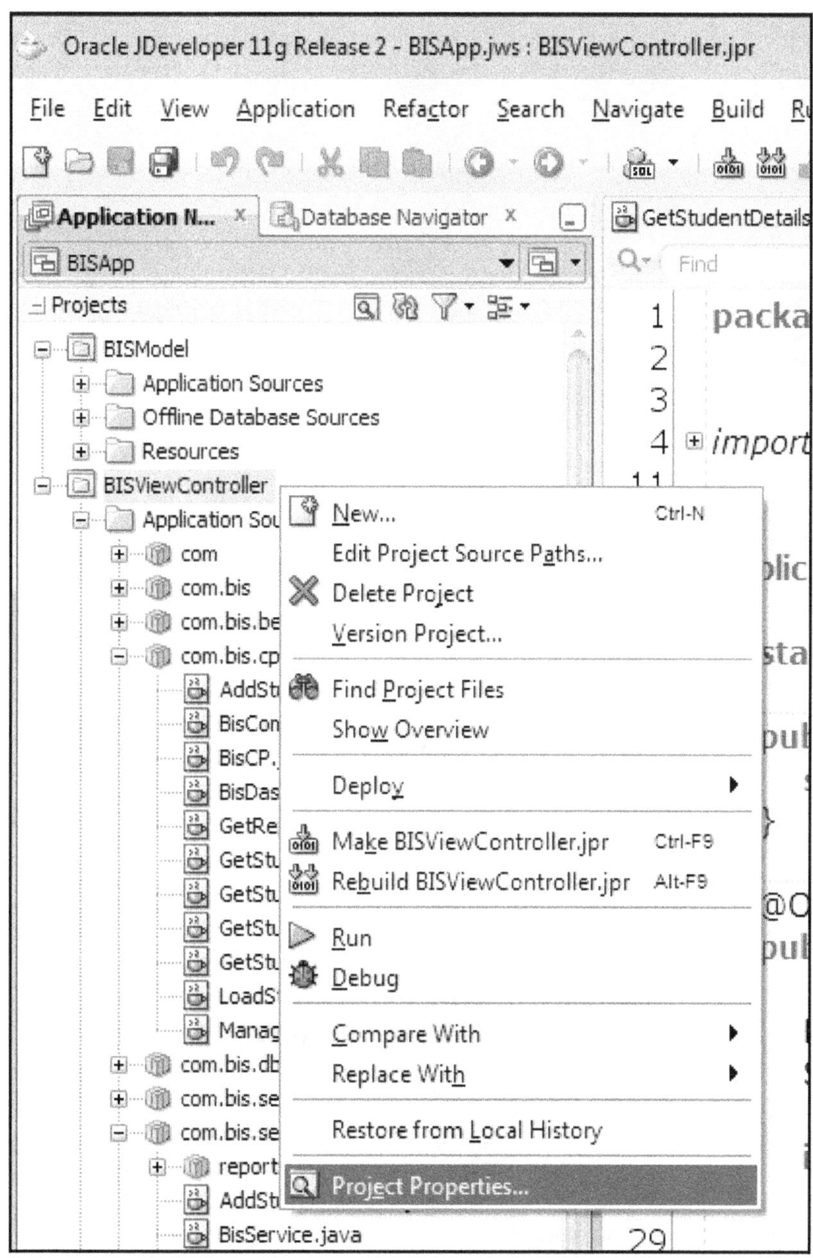

Step 2: The project properties window opens up. In this window, select libraries and classpath as shown in the figure.

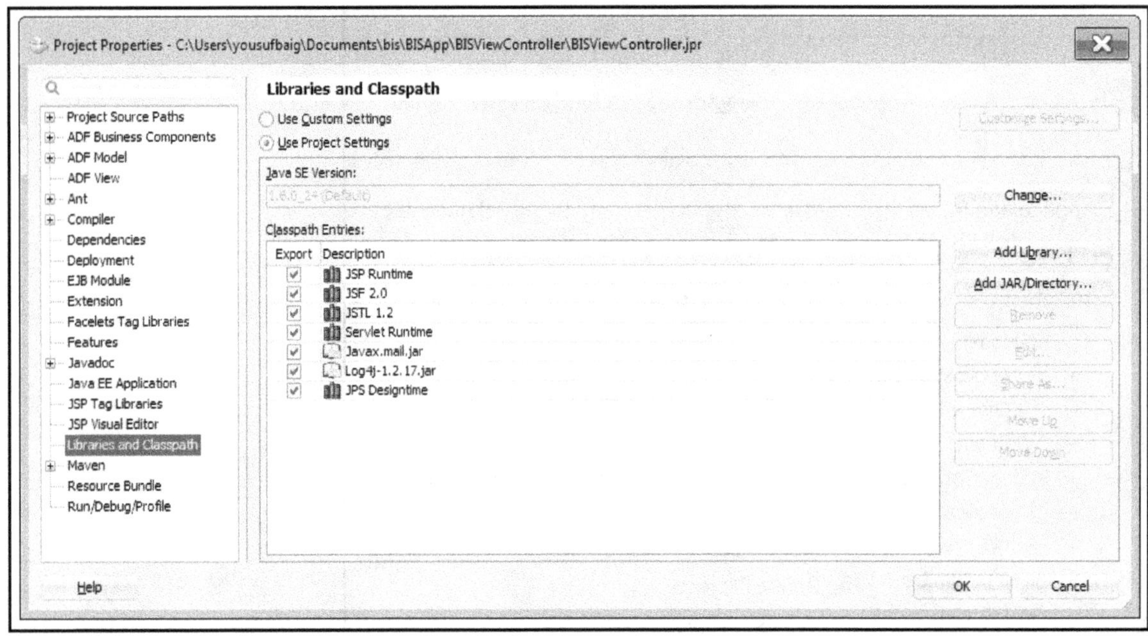

Step 3: Click add JAR/Directory button and then browse and select the Log4j.jar file. Click OK to close the window.

The Log4j.jar file is now added to the project library.

Using logger in java classes:

In order to use the logger within the java classes, declare a static class variable for the logger as shown below.

```
public class LoadStudentCP extends BisCP implements BisCommand {
      static Logger logger = Logger.getLogger(LoadStudentCP.class);
```

Note that the specific class name must be passed as an argument to the getLogger method. In the above code snippet, the class name is passed as LoadStudentCP.class as this logger is used within the class LoadStudentCP.

The logger handle can now be used within the scope of this java class to perform various loggings. We can now use various methods available in the logger for logging errors or information or any other details we want to log at various points in our code.

For example we will use the following code in order to log the exception message at error level.

```
catch (Exception e) {
      logger.error(e.getMessage());
}
```

Similarly, to log something as fatal, info and debug we use the respective methods. Please refer the application java code to see how logging is used at various levels.

The log4j.properties file

The log4j.properties file is used to perform various configurations for the logger. This properties file is most commonly modified for changing the logging levels. The sample web application is deployed in Apache Tomcat server hence the log4j.properties file must be added to the $CATALINA_BASE/webapps/Bis/WEB-INF/classes folder. The logger configurations we used for sample application is as shown below.

```
log4j.debug=true
log4j.rootLogger=INFO, CATALINA
log4j.appender.CATALINA=org.apache.log4j.FileAppender
log4j.appender.CATALINA.file=${catalina.base}/logs/bis.log
log4j.appender.CATALINA.encoding=UTF-8
log4j.appender.CATALINA.layout=org.apache.log4j.PatternLayout
log4j.appender.CATALINA.layout.conversionPattern
= %d [%t] %-5p %c - %m%n
log4j.appender.CATALINA.append=true
```

These configuration properties have self explanatory names, for example log4j.appender.CATALINA.file is the name of the log file to be created or used. The value for this is ${catalina.base}/logs/bis.log this means that the log file named bis.log within the folder logs will be created or used.

Below are the sample error messages from the bis.log file.

```
2015-04-23 10:51:07,384 [http-nio-80-exec-4] ERROR
com.bis.cp.BisDashboardCP - Student id is null
2015-04-23 10:51:10,034 [http-nio-80-exec-7] ERROR
com.bis.session.reports.ReportByClassService - Section/Class is
null
```

```
2015-04-23 10:51:18,038 [http-nio-80-exec-2] ERROR
com.bis.cp.BisDashboardCP - Student id is null
2015-04-23 10:51:28,966 [http-nio-80-exec-6] ERROR
com.bis.session.StudentDetailsService - Invalid column name
```

12

SESSION MANAGEMENT

Understanding Session

An interaction between a user and the application where an objective of the user is served is called the session. For this interaction to take place, the user starts with the log in activity and then the user performs one of more other activities with the application to achieve his/her objective of that particular interaction. Then the user logs out. This interaction between the user and the system where in which the user logs in, performs one or more interactions and then logs out is called session. The period between a user's log in and log out is called the session period. During the session the logged in user accesses the various functionalities of the web application.

For example, we use email services like yahoo mail and gmail. In order to use these email services we log in first, then we perform one or more of the following activities: check email, read one or more emails, delete one or more emails, send one or more emails etc. Once our tasks is done we log out of the email service. This is known as a session between the user and the email service.

Once a user log in to our BIS-SMS application we need to track the state of the user's interaction. That is, we need to remember attributes of the user's interaction with the system. Like, the student currently in context. There are various ways to remember and use such values.

The other significant requirement for session management is the identification of users. Suppose ten different users have logged into the system with different user ids and roles. There should be a mechanism to uniquely identify each user at the server side. This is achieved using session ids. Each logged in user at the server side is uniquely identified with a session id.

Leveraging Http Session

In our application we use HttpSession for session management. HttpSession is an interface in javax.servlet.http package. This interface enables us to identify a user across more than one page request to a web application. This interface also provides us an option to store information about that user. For e.g. The logged in user padma.kulkarni might be browsing the student Zain Baig and the other logged in user shamim.banu might be browsing the student Neetal Shah. All these information are stored in user specific Http Session object for each logged in user. The servlet container uses HttpSession interface to create a session between a http client and a http server.

Below is the code snippet to add student id to the http session within the command processor.

```
HttpSession session = null;
strStudentId = request.getParameter("txtStdId");
session = request.getSession();
session.setAttribute("StudentId", strStudentId);
```

This code is from the load student command processor. Here we get the student id entered by the user via request.getParameter("txtStdId").

For the logged in user this student id remains in the session. When this user clicks get student details. The student id is fetched from the session. Below is the code snippet for that.

```
HttpSession session = request.getSession();
strStudentId = (String) session.getAttribute("StudentId");
```

The student id is tied to a http session and this http session belongs to a particular http client. When the same client (browser or the user) sends a request for student details page. The student id is read from the http session belonging to this http client.

The session for a user is either invalidated automatically with time out or explicitly invalidated when the user logs out.

There are many ways to manage session in a web application. In our sample application we did not use cookies for session management. Primarily, we have used HttpSession from the servlet API for the session management in our sample web application. Besides this, we have we also used hidden variables for some use cases implementation. Please refer the individual use cases in the implementing use cases chapter to get more clarity.

13
INTERACTING WITH THE DATABASE

In our sample application we have 3 tier architecture: the client tier, the web server tier and the database tier. The client interacts with the web server and for most of the use cases the server interacts with the database tier. In our database tier we have two schemas one used by the server for authentication and authorization and the other used by the application.

We need lots of interaction between our application and the database. All our application tables are in the Bis schema. In this chapter we will take a closer look at all the type of interactions that happen between our application/server and the database server.

The approaches for database connectivity

Java Database Connectivity (JDBC) is the technology used in Java for interacting with the databases. We can get a database connection by directly using the oracle's drivers for JDBC connectivity. The other way is to get the database connection from the server via a JNDI look up for the data source. Using data source is a better approach as we get lot of out of the box advantages with it. Also using data sources is the right approach in the distributed computing paradigm. Hence, in our application we have taken this approach.

Using Data Source

Working with data sources has two parts. One, creating a data source with connection pool on the server. Two, looking up this data source from the application code.

In the popular application servers, we get GUI for creating connection pool and data sources. In case of Apache Tomcat server we need to add an entry to context.xml file to create a data source. Chapter 21 details how to create data source in Apache Tomcat 8. In components chapter under the DatabaseService.java section we see how to look up the data source via JNDI and we also see how to get connection and release database resources. The various use cases in the chapter implementing use cases detail how to perform create, update, delete and read operations. This is explained in detail with the source code for each type of operation.

14

THE BIS-SMS PROJECT COMPONENTS

The sample project Baig International School - Student Management System is built using the following software components:

- Java Servlets
- Command Processors
- Service Classes
- Java Beans
- Utility Classes
- Java Server Pages (jsp)
- Log4j

Java Servlets

A java program that runs on the server side. A java class gets qualified as a servlet by implementing the Servlet interface. The life cycle of a servlet is managed by the servlet container. In BIS-SMS application we use two servlets, the ControllerServlet and AjaxControllerServlet.

The ControllerServlet is the centralized point for all the client http requests except for the Ajax calls. The controller servlet returns a view as a jsp. The AjaxControllerServlet is a dedicated centralized point for all the client Ajax calls. The ajax controller servlet returns a response text.

Both the controller servlet and the ajax controller servlet extend HttpServlet and override the service method. The HttpServlet extends the GenericServlet which in turn implements the Servlet and ServletConfig interfaces.

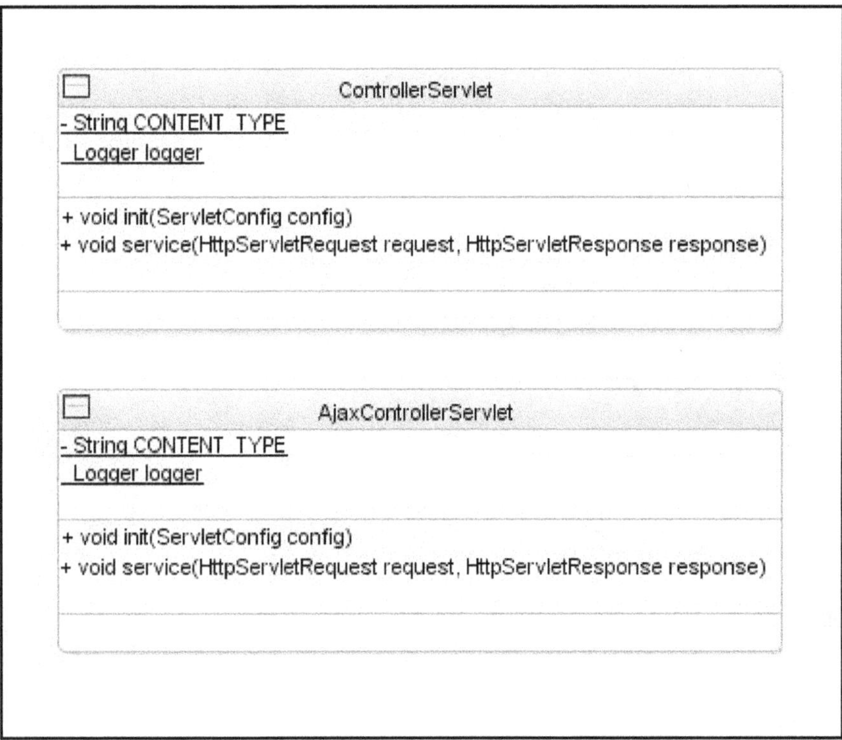

ControllerServlet.java

```
/*
 * @Author Mirza Yousuf Ahmed Baig
 * @ControllerServlet.java
 * @Copyright: Build web applications with Java.
 */

package com.bis.servlet;

import com.bis.cp.BisCommand;
import java.io.IOException;
import javax.servlet.RequestDispatcher;
import javax.servlet.ServletConfig;
import javax.servlet.ServletException;
import javax.servlet.http.HttpServlet;
import javax.servlet.http.HttpServletRequest;
import javax.servlet.http.HttpServletResponse;
import org.apache.log4j.Logger;

public class ControllerServlet extends HttpServlet {

      private static final String CONTENT_TYPE = "text/html;
      charset=windows-1252";
      static Logger logger = Logger.getLogger(ControllerServlet.class);

      public void init(ServletConfig config) throws ServletException {
            super.init(config);
      }

      public void service(HttpServletRequest request, HttpServletResponse
                  response) throws ServletException, IOException {

        String commandCP = null;
        String view = null;
        commandCP = request.getParameter("ParameterActionCommand");

        if (commandCP != null)    {

            // Added security to avoid mal invocation of the commands.
            String StrCommandClass = "com.bis.cp."+commandCP+"CP";
            try {
                Class myClass   = Class.forName(StrCommandClass);
                BisCommand bisCommand = (BisCommand)
                myClass.newInstance();
                view = bisCommand.execute(request, response);
```

```
                if (view == null || view.trim().equalsIgnoreCase("") ) {
                  view = "BisError";
                  // Add error message in session and display that in the
                  jsp.
                  logger.debug("A null value returned for view");
                  }

                  RequestDispatcher requestDispatcher =
                  request.getRequestDispatcher
                  ("/BisHome.jsp?prmDynInclPage="+view);
                  requestDispatcher.forward(request, response);
            } catch (ClassNotFoundException cnfe) {
                logger.error(cnfe.getMessage());
            } catch (InstantiationException inse) {
                logger.error(inse.getMessage());
            } catch (Exception excep) {
                logger.error(excep.getMessage());
            }
            }
        else {
            logger.fatal("Action command is null");
        }
    }
}
```

The service method performs the following tasks:

⇒ Gets the request command from the request parameter.

⇒ Loads the command processor class pertaining to the command.

⇒ Creates an instance of the command processor and invokes the execute method.

⇒ Forwards the view returned to the browser.

It is mandatory for the command processor to implement BisCommand interface to be qualified as a command processor. The execute method is invoked using the reference of the interface (BisCommand) and not specific command processor class. It is the polymorphic feature of java which invokes the execute method of the specific command processor object in question. This is the reason why each command processor must have to implement the BisCommand interface. This is one of the best example for late binding and polymorphic features in java language.

If the command is AddStudent, AddStudentCP is loaded and execute method is invoked. The AddStudentCP implements BisCommand interface which has the execute method. Since AddStudentCP implements BisCommand it has to provide implementation for execute method pertaining to adding a student. The object of AddStudentCP which implements BisCommand is referenced via the BisCommand interface reference. Similarly, if it is other command, the respective class is loaded and execute method of the command processor class is invoked. This is one of the best example of usage of interface reference to exploit runtime dynamic polymorphic feature of the java programming language.

AjaxControllerServlet.java

```
package com.bis.servlet;

import com.bis.cp.BisCommand;
import java.io.IOException;
import java.io.PrintWriter;
import javax.servlet.ServletConfig;
import javax.servlet.ServletException;
import javax.servlet.http.HttpServlet;
import javax.servlet.http.HttpServletRequest;
import javax.servlet.http.HttpServletResponse;
import org.apache.log4j.Logger;

public class AjaxControllerServlet extends HttpServlet {

      private static final String CONTENT_TYPE =
      "text/html;charset=windows-1252";
      static Logger logger =
      Logger.getLogger(AjaxControllerServlet.class);

      public void init(ServletConfig config) throws ServletException {
            super.init(config);
      }

      public void service(HttpServletRequest request, HttpServletResponse
                  response) throws ServletException, IOException {

        response.setContentType(CONTENT_TYPE);
        PrintWriter out = response.getWriter();
        String strAjaxResponseText = "";
        String commandCP = null;
```

```
        commandCP = request.getParameter("ParameterActionCommand");

        if (commandCP != null)    {
            if ( !( commandCP.trim().equalsIgnoreCase("") ) )   {

            // Added security to avoid mal invocation of the
            commands.
            String StrCommandClass = "com.bis.cp."+commandCP+"CP";

            try {
                    Class myClass    = Class.forName(StrCommandClass);
                    BisCommand bisCommand = (BisCommand)
                    myClass.newInstance();
                    strAjaxResponseText = bisCommand.execute(request,
                    response);
            } catch (ClassNotFoundException cnfe) {
                logger.error(cnfe.getMessage());
            } catch (InstantiationException inse) {
                logger.error(inse.getMessage());
            } catch (Exception excep) {
                logger.error(excep.getMessage());
            }
            }
        else {
            logger.fatal("Action Command is missing.");
        }
        }
        else    {
            logger.fatal("Action Command is null.");
        }
        out.println(strAjaxResponseText);
        out.close();
    }
}
```

The service method performs the following tasks:

⇒ Gets the request command from the request parameter.

⇒ Loads the command processor class pertaining to the command.

⇒ Creates an instance of the command processor and invokes the execute method.

⇒ Returns the Ajax Response Text to the browser.

The difference between the AjaxControllerServlet and the ControllerServlet is that the controller servlet returns a view via a jsp page whereas the ajax controller servlet returns a response text only. Both of these servlets belong to the BIS MVC Framework one dedicated for the regular http requests and the other for ajax requests.

The Command Processors

For the sample application and for our framework, the command processors are java classes that extend BisCP class and implement BisCommand interface. The BisCP is a concrete class with a set of variables. The BisCommand interface has only one method and that is the execute method.

The following class diagram shows all the command processor classes used in our sample application. It also shows the relationship between these classes and the framework artifacts BisCP and BisCommand.

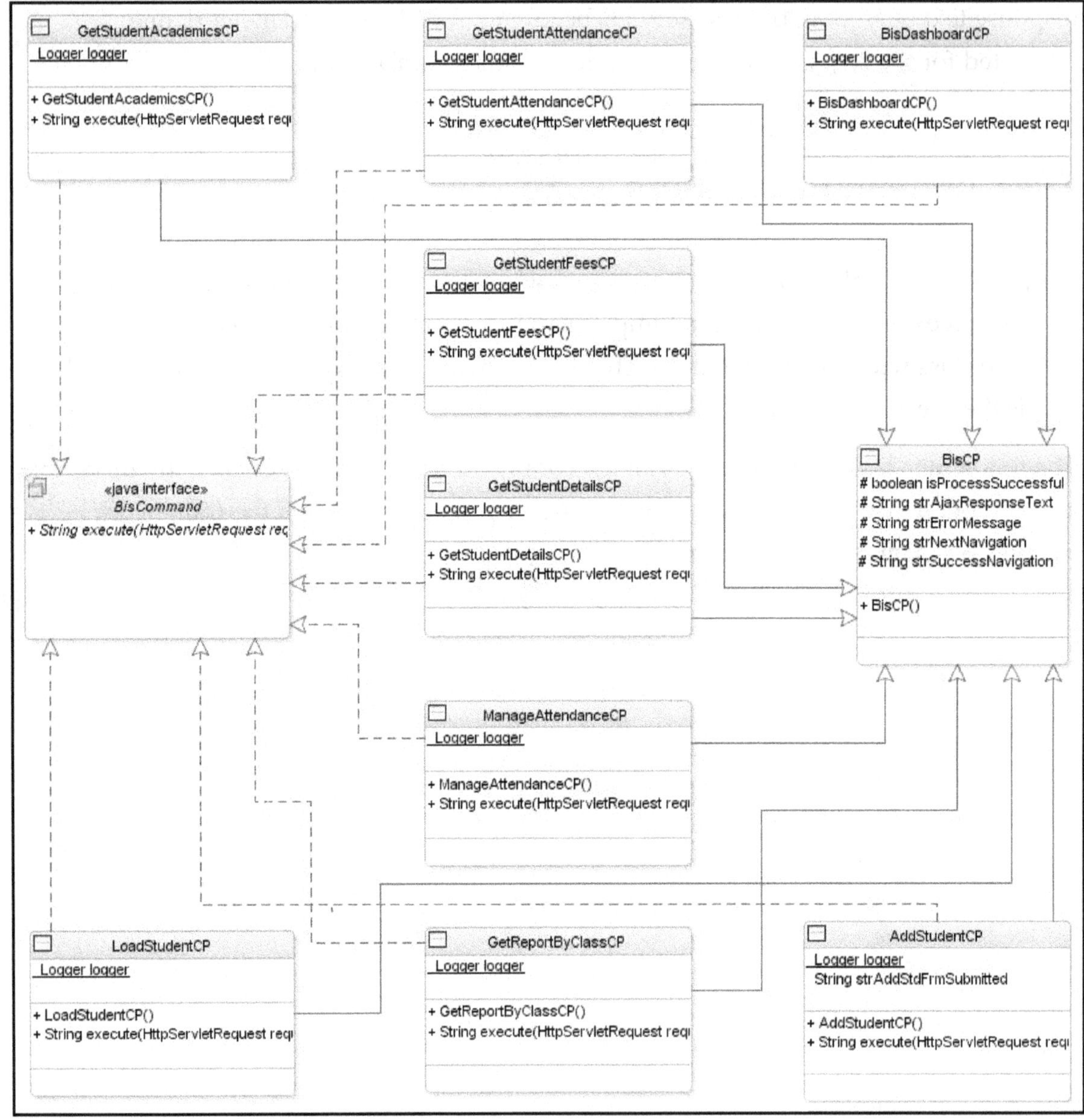
GetStudentAcademicsCP
Logger logger
+ GetStudentAcademicsCP()
+ String execute(HttpServletRequest requ
GetStudentAttendanceCP
Logger logger
+ GetStudentAttendanceCP()
+ String execute(HttpServletRequest requ
BisDashboardCP
Logger logger
+ BisDashboardCP()
+ String execute(HttpServletRequest requ
GetStudentFeesCP
Logger logger
+ GetStudentFeesCP()
+ String execute(HttpServletRequest requ
BisCP
boolean isProcessSuccessful
String strAjaxResponseText
String strErrorMessage
String strNextNavigation
String strSuccessNavigation
+ BisCP()
«java interface»
BisCommand
+ String execute(HttpServletRequest req
GetStudentDetailsCP
Logger logger
+ GetStudentDetailsCP()
+ String execute(HttpServletRequest requ
ManageAttendanceCP
Logger logger
+ ManageAttendanceCP()
+ String execute(HttpServletRequest requ
LoadStudentCP
Logger logger
+ LoadStudentCP()
+ String execute(HttpServletRequest requ
GetReportByClassCP
Logger logger
+ GetReportByClassCP()
+ String execute(HttpServletRequest requ
AddStudentCP
Logger logger
String strAddStdFrmSubmitted
+ AddStudentCP()
+ String execute(HttpServletRequest requ

BisCP.java

```
package com.bis.cp;

public class BisCP {

    public BisCP() {
        super();
    }

    protected boolean isProcessSuccessful;
    protected java.lang.String strSuccessNavigation;
    protected java.lang.String strNextNavigation;
    protected java.lang.String strErrorMessage;
    protected java.lang.String strAjaxResponseText;
}
```

The BisCP.java class has only variables which are used in the command processor classes that is the sub classes of BisCP class. The variable names used are self explanatory.

BisCommand.java

```
package com.bis.cp;

public interface BisCommand {

      public abstract String execute(
      javax.servlet.http.HttpServletRequest request,
      javax.servlet.http.HttpServletResponse response);

}
```

This interface has only one method and that is execute method. The implementing command processor class implements the business logic pertaining to the specific command processor for the execute method. Note that, it is mandatory to implement this interface in order to qualify a class as a command processor. This is one such example of compliances requirements when working with a particular framework. For Bis MVC Framework, a command processor must implement BisCommand interface. Otherwise, the execute method of the specific command processor will fail to be executed polymorphically with in the service method of the controller servlet.

The Service Classes

The job of the service classes is to implement the services i.e. the business logic. These classes orchestrate and implement the various actions required for a use case. For e.g. add student service class, inserts three records to three different tables in the database. The command processor only invokes the process add student method in the service class. This method in turn invokes multiple methods, takes care of transactional requirements, interacts with the database using database utility classes and gets the task done. The command processor is basically a client for these classes they request for services from the services classes. The services classes provide the services to their client. These are reusable components.

The services classes in our application and framework implements BisService interface. Note that, this is not a mandatory requirement. This is just to provide a scalability option in case we want to add common services functionality in future versions. The BisService interface as of now has only one method which provides the name of the class for the current service instance.

The following class diagrams shows all the services used in our application.

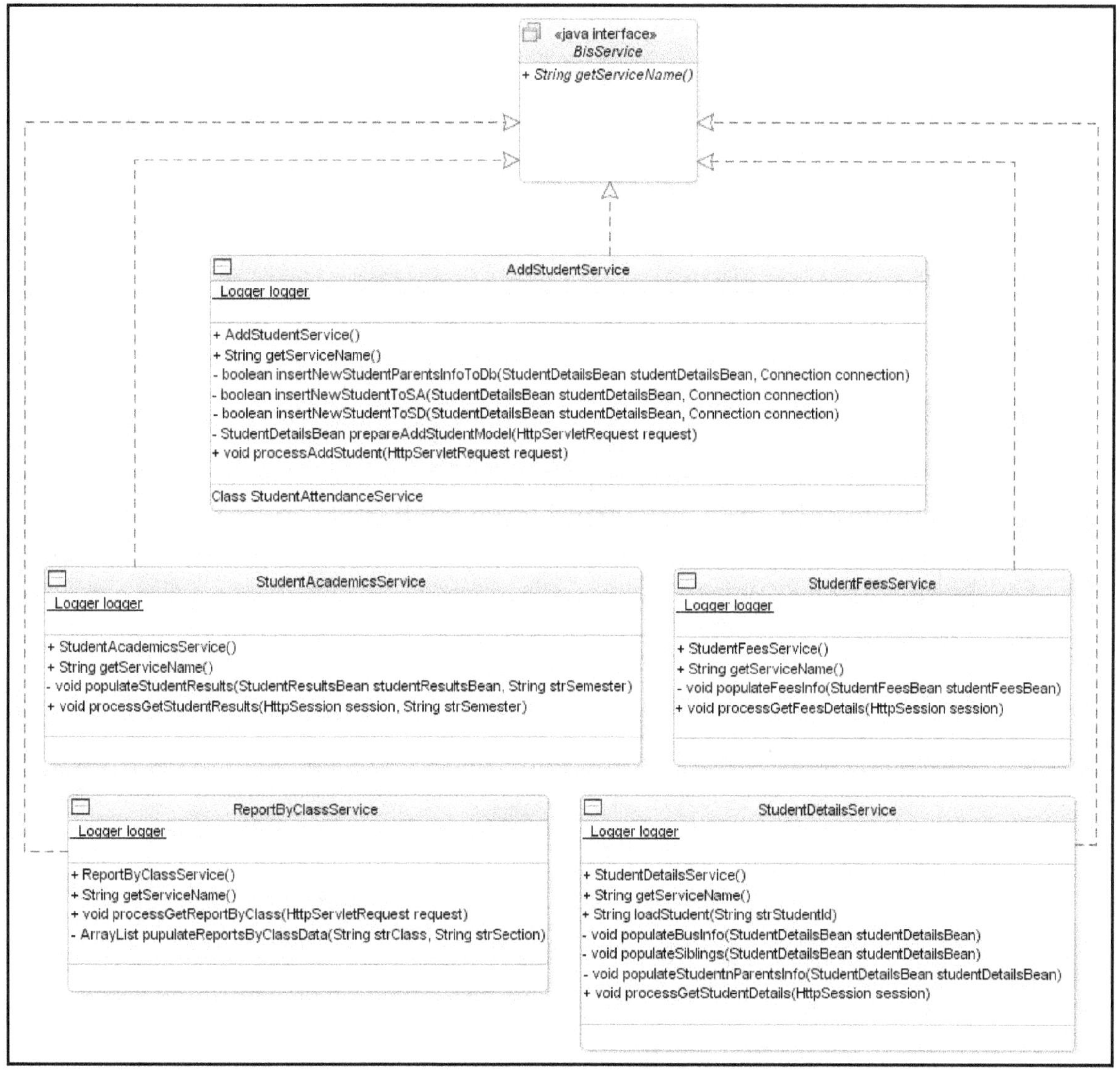
«java interface»
BisService
+ String getServiceName()
AddStudentService
Logger logger
+ AddStudentService()
+ String getServiceName()
- boolean insertNewStudentParentsInfoToDb(StudentDetailsBean studentDetailsBean, Connection connection)
- boolean insertNewStudentToSA(StudentDetailsBean studentDetailsBean, Connection connection)
- boolean insertNewStudentToSD(StudentDetailsBean studentDetailsBean, Connection connection)
- StudentDetailsBean prepareAddStudentModel(HttpServletRequest request)
+ void processAddStudent(HttpServletRequest request)
Class StudentAttendanceService
StudentAcademicsService
Logger logger
+ StudentAcademicsService()
+ String getServiceName()
- void populateStudentResults(StudentResultsBean studentResultsBean, String strSemester)
+ void processGetStudentResults(HttpSession session, String strSemester)
StudentFeesService
Logger logger
+ StudentFeesService()
+ String getServiceName()
- void populateFeesInfo(StudentFeesBean studentFeesBean)
+ void processGetFeesDetails(HttpSession session)
ReportByClassService
Logger logger
+ ReportByClassService()
+ String getServiceName()
+ void processGetReportByClass(HttpServletRequest request)
- ArrayList pupulateReportsByClassData(String strClass, String strSection)
StudentDetailsService
Logger logger
+ StudentDetailsService()
+ String getServiceName()
+ String loadStudent(String strStudentId)
- void populateBusInfo(StudentDetailsBean studentDetailsBean)
- void populateSiblings(StudentDetailsBean studentDetailsBean)
- void populateStudentnParentsInfo(StudentDetailsBean studentDetailsBean)
+ void processGetStudentDetails(HttpSession session)

BisService.java

```
package com.bis.session;

public interface BisService {
    public String getServiceName();
}
```

The implementing class provides it's name by implementing this method.

The Java Beans

These beans are plain java classes with private fields and their public getter and setter methods. All the beans implement serializable interface via the framework class hierarchy. All the beans used in the application eventually extend the class BisBean which implements Serializable interface.

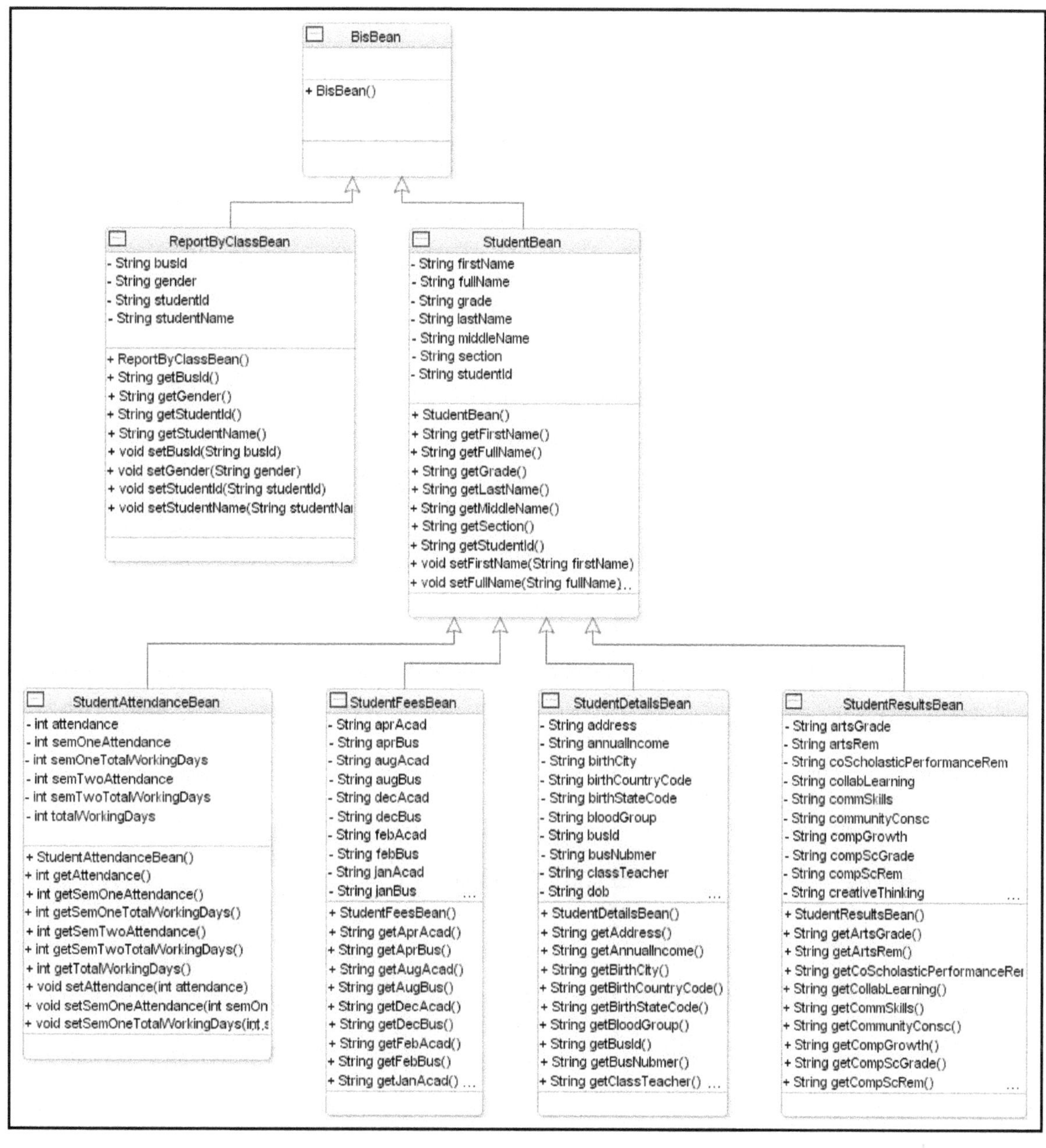
BisBean
+ BisBean()
ReportByClassBean
- String busId
- String gender
- String studentId
- String studentName
+ ReportByClassBean()
+ String getBusId()
+ String getGender()
+ String getStudentId()
+ String getStudentName()
+ void setBusId(String busId)
+ void setGender(String gender)
+ void setStudentId(String studentId)
+ void setStudentName(String studentNa
StudentBean
- String firstName
- String fullName
- String grade
- String lastName
- String middleName
- String section
- String studentId
+ StudentBean()
+ String getFirstName()
+ String getFullName()
+ String getGrade()
+ String getLastName()
+ String getMiddleName()
+ String getSection()
+ String getStudentId()
+ void setFirstName(String firstName)
+ void setFullName(String fullName)...
StudentAttendanceBean
- int attendance
- int semOneAttendance
- int semOneTotalWorkingDays
- int semTwoAttendance
- int semTwoTotalWorkingDays
- int totalWorkingDays
+ StudentAttendanceBean()
+ int getAttendance()
+ int getSemOneAttendance()
+ int getSemOneTotalWorkingDays()
+ int getSemTwoAttendance()
+ int getSemTwoTotalWorkingDays()
+ int getTotalWorkingDays()
+ void setAttendance(int attendance)
+ void setSemOneAttendance(int semOn
+ void setSemOneTotalWorkingDays(int s
StudentFeesBean
- String aprAcad
- String aprBus
- String augAcad
- String augBus
- String decAcad
- String decBus
- String febAcad
- String febBus
- String janAcad
- String janBus ...
+ StudentFeesBean()
+ String getAprAcad()
+ String getAprBus()
+ String getAugAcad()
+ String getAugBus()
+ String getDecAcad()
+ String getDecBus()
+ String getFebAcad()
+ String getFebBus()
+ String getJanAcad() ...
StudentDetailsBean
- String address
- String annualIncome
- String birthCity
- String birthCountryCode
- String birthStateCode
- String bloodGroup
- String busId
- String busNubmer
- String classTeacher
- String dob ...
+ StudentDetailsBean()
+ String getAddress()
+ String getAnnualIncome()
+ String getBirthCity()
+ String getBirthCountryCode()
+ String getBirthStateCode()
+ String getBloodGroup()
+ String getBusId()
+ String getBusNubmer()
+ String getClassTeacher() ...
StudentResultsBean
- String artsGrade
- String artsRem
- String coScholasticPerformanceRem
- String collabLearning
- String commSkills
- String communityConsc
- String compGrowth
- String compScGrade
- String compScRem
- String creativeThinking ...
+ StudentResultsBean()
+ String getArtsGrade()
+ String getArtsRem()
+ String getCoScholasticPerformanceRe
+ String getCollabLearning()
+ String getCommSkills()
+ String getCommunityConsc()
+ String getCompGrowth()
+ String getCompScGrade()
+ String getCompScRem() ...

StudentBean.java

This bean holds all the generics for the student related information. All the other beans that require these fields extend this bean. The student bean in turn extends BisBean.

```
package com.bis.beans;

public class StudentBean extends BisBean {

    public StudentBean() {
        super();
    }

    private java.lang.String studentId;
    private java.lang.String fullName;
    private java.lang.String grade;
    private java.lang.String section;
    private java.lang.String firstName;
    private java.lang.String middleName;
    private java.lang.String lastName;

    public void setStudentId(String studentId) {
        this.studentId = studentId;
    }

    public String getStudentId() {
        return studentId;
    }

    public void setFullName(String fullName) {
        this.fullName = fullName;
    }

    public String getFullName() {
        return fullName;
    }

    public void setGrade(String grade) {
        this.grade = grade;
    }

    public String getGrade() {
        return grade;
    }

    public void setSection(String section) {
```

```
        this.section = section;
    }

    public String getSection() {
        return section;
    }

    public void setFirstName(String firstName) {
        this.firstName = firstName;
    }

    public String getFirstName() {
        return firstName;
    }

    public void setMiddleName(String middleName) {
        this.middleName = middleName;
    }

    public String getMiddleName() {
        return middleName;
    }

    public void setLastName(String lastName) {
        this.lastName = lastName;
    }

    public String getLastName() {
        return lastName;
    }
}
```

BisBean.java

```
package com.bis.beans;

import java.io.Serializable;

public class BisBean implements Serializable {

    public BisBean() {
        super();
    }

}
```

All the beans in the application extends this bean. It is mandatory to extends this bean either directly or indirectly to be qualified as a bean. The application currently doesn't exchange bean instance by value but for the application to be scalable in the future versions this is mandated. Generally java beans are persistable and hence they have to implement serializable interface.

The Utility Classes

We have three utility classes used across the application for various common objectives. These classes are BisUtility, DatabaseService and BisConstants. In this, BisUtility and DatabaseService are concrete java classes and BisConstants is a java interface.

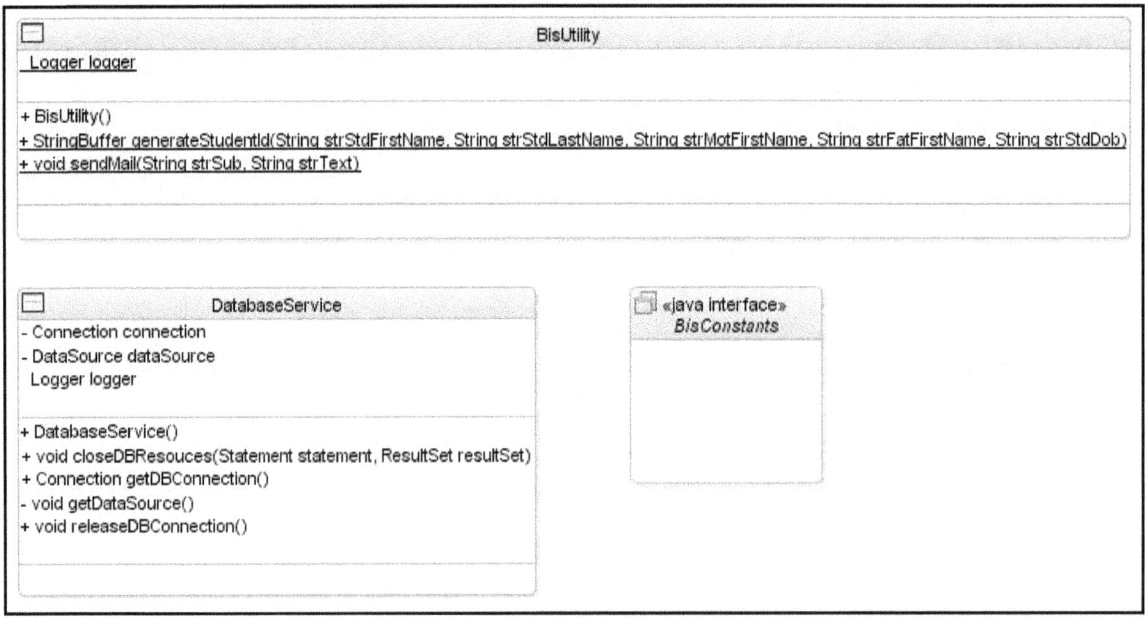

BisUtility
Logger logger
+ BisUtility()
+ StringBuffer generateStudentId(String strStdFirstName, String strStdLastName, String strMotFirstName, String strFatFirstName, String strStdDob)
+ void sendMail(String strSub, String strText)

DatabaseService
- Connection connection
- DataSource dataSource
Logger logger
+ DatabaseService()
+ void closeDBResouces(Statement statement, ResultSet resultSet)
+ Connection getDBConnection()
- void getDataSource()
+ void releaseDBConnection()

«java interface»
BisConstants

Bisutility.java

```
package com.bis.utility;
```

```
import java.util.Properties;
import java.util.StringTokenizer;
import javax.mail.Message;
import javax.mail.MessagingException;
import javax.mail.Session;
import javax.mail.Transport;
import javax.mail.internet.InternetAddress;
import javax.mail.internet.MimeMessage;
import org.apache.log4j.Logger;

public class BisUtility {

static Logger logger = Logger.getLogger(BisUtility.class);

      public BisUtility() {
        super();
      }

      public static StringBuffer generateStudentId(String
      strStdFirstName,String  strStdLastName, String
      strMotFirstName,String strFatFirstName, String  strStdDob) {

        StringBuffer sbStdId = new StringBuffer();
        StringBuffer sbDob = null;

        try {

            if (strStdFirstName != null &&
                  !(strStdFirstName.trim().equalsIgnoreCase(""))) {
                  sbStdId.append(strStdFirstName.substring(0, 2));
            } else {
                  logger.error("Failed to generate student id: Invalid
                  first name");
            }

            if (strStdLastName != null &&
                  !(strStdLastName.trim().equalsIgnoreCase(""))) {
                  sbStdId.append(strStdLastName.substring(0, 2));
            } else {
                  logger.error("Failed to generate student id: Invalid
                  last name");
            }

            if (strMotFirstName != null &&
                  !(strMotFirstName.trim().equalsIgnoreCase(""))) {
                  sbStdId.append(strMotFirstName.substring(0, 2));
            } else {
                logger.error("Failed to generate student id: Mother's
                first name is invalid");
```

```
        }

        if (strFatFirstName != null &&
              !(strFatFirstName.trim().equalsIgnoreCase(""))) {
              sbStdId.append(strFatFirstName.substring(0, 2));
        } else {
            logger.error("Failed to generate student id: Father's
            first name is invalid");
        }
        if (strStdDob != null &&
              !(strStdDob.trim().equalsIgnoreCase(""))) {

            StringTokenizer sTokenizer = new
            StringTokenizer(strStdDob,"-");
            String strYear = sTokenizer.nextToken();
            String strMonth = sTokenizer.nextToken();
            String strDay = sTokenizer.nextToken();
            sbDob = new StringBuffer();
            sbDob.append(strDay);
            sbDob.append(strMonth);
            sbDob.append(strYear);

            if (sbDob.length() == 8) {
                sbStdId.append(sbDob);
            } else {
              logger.error("Failed to generate student id: Invalid
              date of birth");
            }
        } else {
            logger.error("Failed to generate student id: Invalid date
              of birth");
        }
        if (sbStdId.length() != 16) {
            logger.error("Failed to generate student id:
              inappropriate size");
        }
    } catch (Exception e) {
        logger.error(e.getMessage());
        sbStdId = null;
    }

    return sbStdId;
}

public static void sendMail(String strSub, String strText) {

    String strTo = "yousuf.baig@gmail.com";
    String strFrom = "yousuf.baig@yahoo.com";
    String strHost = "localhost";
```

```
        int inPort=25;
        Properties properties = System.getProperties();
        properties.setProperty("mail.smtp.host", strHost);
        properties.put("mail.smtp.auth", "false");
        properties.put("mail.smtp.starttls.enable", "true");
        properties.put("mail.smtp.port", inPort);
        Session session = Session.getDefaultInstance(properties);

        try {
            MimeMessage message = new MimeMessage(session);
            message.setFrom(new InternetAddress(strFrom));
            message.addRecipient(Message.RecipientType.TO, new
            InternetAddress(strTo));
            message.setSubject(strSub);
            message.setText(strText);
            Transport.send(message);
        } catch (MessagingException mex) {
            logger.error(mex.getMessage());
        }
    }
}
```

The generateStudentId method performs the following tasks:

⇒ This method generates a unique student id for a given student from the student's first name, student's last name, student's mother's first name, student's father's first name and student's date of birth.

Lets split up an example student id: MyFaAsYo12042004

My - first two digits of student's first name Myiesha.

Fa - first two digits of student's last name Fatima.

As - first two digits of student's mother's first name Asiya.

Yo - first two digits of student's father's first name Yousuf.

12042004 - student's data of birth in DDMMYYYY

The generateStudentId method takes all these inputs and returns the generated student id as per the requirements above.

Though, a database sequence can be used to assign a unique student id for each student. This approach is taken to make sure that the id can be remembered with the known algorithm. This student id may have a rare conflict and in that case, the addition of birth time or any other such attribute will make it more unique and conflict free.

The sendMail method performs the following tasks:

⇒ This method is used for sending simple SMTP mail.

In production ready applications, these email properties are generally fetched from the application properties file. In case the host name changes, the support team will only update the host name or IP address in the properties file and redeploy the application to fetch the updated host. In our sample application, since we are working very closely with the code, this is directly added to the method itself for quick learning purpose. In serious applications, the recommend approach is to create application properties file and fetch these properties from that file.

DatabaseService.java

```
package com.bis.db;

import com.bis.utility.BisConstants;
import java.sql.Connection;
import java.sql.ResultSet;
import java.sql.SQLException;
import java.sql.Statement;
import javax.naming.Context;
import javax.naming.InitialContext;
import javax.naming.NamingException;
import javax.sql.DataSource;
import org.apache.log4j.Logger;

public class DatabaseService {

    private static DataSource dataSource = null;
    private static Connection connection = null;
    static Logger logger = Logger.getLogger(DatabaseService.class);

    private static void lookUpDataSource() {
        if (dataSource == null) {
            try {
                Context initialContext = new InitialContext();
                Context envContext =
                  (Context)initialContext.lookup("java:/comp/env");
```

```
        if (initialContext != null) {
              dataSource = (DataSource)envContext.lookup
              (BisConstants.BisDataSource);
            } else {
              // initial context is null, throw exception.
              logger.error("Initial context is null");
            }
        } catch (NamingException ne) {
            logger.error("Failed to look up data source." +
              ne.getMessage());
        }
    }
}

public DatabaseService() {
}

public static void releaseDBConnection() {
    if (connection != null) {
        try {
            connection.close();
        } catch (SQLException sqle) {
            logger.error(sqle.getMessage());
        }
    }
}

  public static void closeDBResouces(Statement statement,
                                      ResultSet resultSet) {
    try {
        if (resultSet != null) {
            resultSet.close();
        }
        if (statement != null) {
            statement.close();
        }
    } catch (SQLException sqle) {
        logger.error(sqle.getMessage());
    }
  }

  public static Connection getDBConnection() {
    if (dataSource == null) {
        lookUpDataSource();
    }
    try {
        if (connection == null || connection.isClosed()) {
            connection = dataSource.getConnection();
        }
```

```
        } catch (SQLException sqle) {
            logger.error(sqle.getMessage());
        }

        return connection;
    }
}
```

The lookUpDataSource method performs the following tasks:

⇒ Creates the initial context and performs JNDI look up for Bis data source.

Note that that data source name specified in the BisConstants interface must be created on the server prior to the deployment of the application war file. Otherwise the look up will fail and all operations related to database will not work.

The releaseDBConnection method performs the following tasks:

⇒ Closes the database connection.

The closeDBResouces method performs the following tasks:

⇒ Closes the result set and statement.

The getDBConnection method performs the following tasks:

⇒ Calls lookUpDataSource method if the data source is null.

⇒ Gets the database connection from the data source and returns it.

BisConstants.java

This is a simple java interface which is used for holding constant values.

```
package com.bis.utility;

public interface BisConstants {

      public static final String BisDataSource = "jdbc/bisDataSource";
}
```

Any change in value of the variables in this interface needs recompilation of this interface. Depending on the requirements either an interface can be used or application properties file can be used. The other approach is to fetch the constant values from a database table. The designer of the web application has to take multiple factors into account for a specific requirements or type of application to make a subjective design decision. In our sample application we are using an interface as well as a database table with property and values. This is purely with an intension to learn various pragmatic approaches to access variables that seldom change.

The Java Server Pages

JSP is a view technology which adds dynamism to static html or other mark up language. JSPs are generally used as a view with dynamic jsp capabilities along with static standard html tags. The content and presentation can be dynamically added to a web page at the server side based on the requirements. This makes jsp technology very powerful and useful for building web applications. The computational power of java clubbed with the presentation capability of html makes a jsp a perfect choice for the view layer of web applications.

In our sample BIS-SMS web application we use only jsps for the view layer. The header, footer and the menus remain constant part of the view between log in and log out session. The design for our view has one page template called BisHome.jsp. The user is always on this page during the session. The jsp page has all the common presentation part along with a dynamic region where the various pages are displayed as an include based on the user interaction. Please refer chapter 5 for more details on the dynamic and static view parts of the page.

The views (jsp pages) for all the use cases are dynamically included in the BisHome.jsp page. The individual jsp pages for the use cases does not hold any code or tags for the common part i.e. for the header, footer etc. The BisHome.jsp has all the static view part and given an area for the dynamic page. This area is called the dynamic region and in this region the various jsp pages based on the use case in question are displayed.

The BisHome.jsp page without any jsp included with dynamic region is shown in the below figure. Here, all the common view part like the header, footer, menus etc are displayed for all the pages. Only the dynamic part changes. For e.g. for the get student details use case the dynamic part will display StudentDetails.jsp page within the dynamic region.

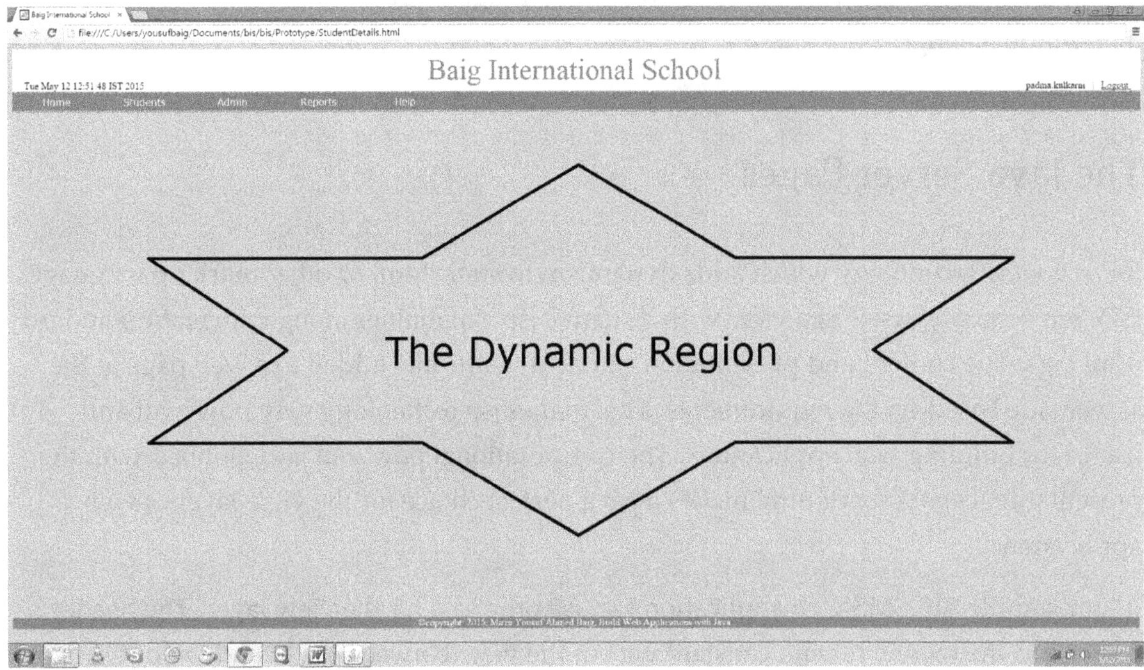

Plus (+)

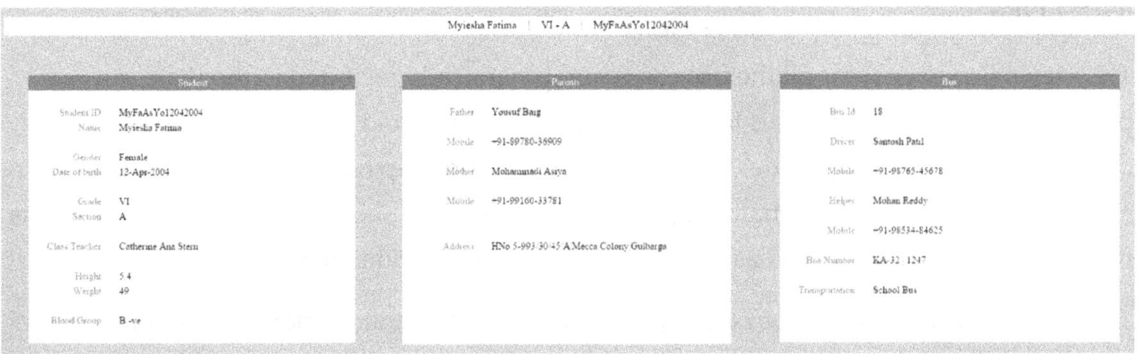

Is Equal To (=)

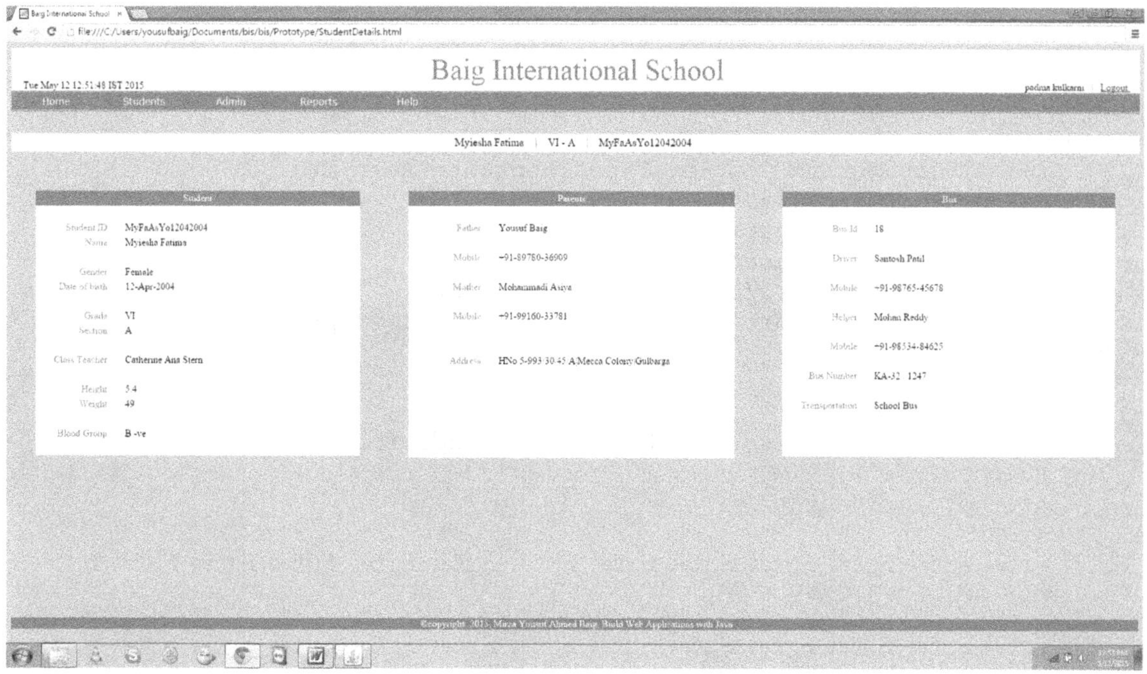

The view, only from the StudentDetails.jsp is as shown in the figure above. The BisHome.jsp page template plus the StudentDetails.jsp view will provide the final view for the complete page display as shown above.

Commons View + Dynamic View = Complete Page View.

BisHome.jsp

Here's the source code of the BisHome.jsp page. This has the header with the menus, the footer and the jsp:include tag for the dynamic jsp page to be included.

```
<!DOCTYPE HTML PUBLIC "-//W3C//DTD HTML 4.01 Transitional//EN"
"http://www.w3.org/TR/html4/loose.dtd">

<%@ page contentType="text/html;charset=windows-1252"%>
<%@ page import="java.util.Date"%>
```

```
<%
String strDynIncPage = "BisError.jsp";
strDynIncPage = request.getParameter("prmDynInclPage") + ".jsp";
%>

<html>

<head>
      <meta http-equiv="Content-Type" content="text/html;
      charset=windows-1252"/>
      <title>Baig International School</title>
      <link rel="stylesheet" type="text/css"
      href="resources/css/BISStyle.css"></link>
      <script src="resources/js/BISScript.js"></script>
</head>

<body>
      <table border="0" cellpadding="0" cellspacing="0" width="100%"
      height="99%">
      <tr bgcolor="White">
      <td>
      <table border="0" cellpadding="0" cellspacing="0" width="100%">
      <tr height="70">
      <td align="left" valign="bottom" width="15%">
          
      <%= new Date() %>
      </td>
      <td align="center" valign="middle" width="*">
      Baig International School
      </td>
      <td align="right" valign="bottom" width="15%">
      <%
            out.println(request.getRemoteUser());
      %>
        |  
      <a href="bissecurityservlet"> Logout </a>
          
      </td>
      </tr>
      </table>
      </td>
      </tr>
      <tr valign="top">
      <td>
      <table border="0" cellpadding="0" cellspacing="0" width="100%">
      <tr>
      <td rowspan="3" align="left">
      <div id="cssmenu">
```

```
<ul>
<li class='has-sub'>
<a href='BisControllerServlet?ParameterActionCommand=BisDashboard'>
<span>Home</span>
</a>
</li>
<li class='has-sub'>
<a href='#'>
<span>Students</span>
</a>
<ul>
<li>
<a href="BisControllerServlet?ParameterActionCommand=
GetStudentDetails">
<span>Details</span></a>
</li>
<li>
<a href="BisControllerServlet?ParameterActionCommand=
GetStudentAcademics&sem=1">
<span>Sem-I Results</span></a>
</li>
<li>
<a href="BisControllerServlet?ParameterActionCommand=
GetStudentAcademics&sem=2">
<span>Sem-II Results</span></a>
</li>
<li>
<a href="BisControllerServlet?ParameterActionCommand=
GetStudentAttendance&sem=1">
<span>Sem-I Attendance</span></a>
</li>
<li>
<a href="BisControllerServlet?ParameterActionCommand=
GetStudentAttendance&sem=2">
<span>Sem-II Attendance</span></a>
</li>
<li>
<a href="BisControllerServlet?ParameterActionCommand=
GetStudentFees">
<span>Fees</span></a>
</li>
</ul>
</li>
<li class='has-sub'>
<a href='#'>
<span>Admin</span></a>
<ul>
<li>
<a href="BisControllerServlet?ParameterActionCommand=AddStudent">
```

```
<span>Add Student</span></a>
</li>
<li class='last'>
<a href="BisControllerServlet?ParameterActionCommand=EditStudent">
<span>Edit Student</span></a>
</li>
<li class='last'>
<a href="BisControllerServlet?ParameterActionCommand=ManageResult">
<span>Manage Result</span></a>
</li>
<li class='last'>
<a href="BisControllerServlet?ParameterActionCommand=
ManageAttendance">
<span>Manage Attendance</span></a>
</li>
<li class='last'>
<a href='\bis\jsp\ManageStudentFees.html'>
<span>Manage Fees</span></a>
</li>
</ul>
</li>
<li class='has-sub'>
<a href='#'>
<span>Reports</span></a>
<ul>
<li>
<a href="BisControllerServlet?ParameterActionCommand=
GetReportByClass">
<span>Class</span></a>
</li>
<li>
<a href='\bis\jsp\ReportsBus.html'>
<span>Bus</span></a>
</li>
<li>
<a href='\bis\jsp\ReportsFees.html'>
<span>Fees</span></a>
</li>
</ul>
</li>
<li class='has-sub'>
<a href='#'>
<span>Help</span></a>
<ul>
<li>
<a href='\bis\jsp\ResultsLegend.html'>
<span>Legend</span></a>
</li>
<li>
```

```
        <a href='#'>
        <span>FAQs</span></a>
        </li>
        <li>
        <a href='#'>
        <span>Holiday Calender</span></a>
        </li>
        <li>
        <a href='#'>
        <span>Escalation Matrix</span></a>
        </li>
        <li>
        <a href='#'>
        <span>Fee Structure</span></a>
        </li>
        </ul>
        </li>
        </ul>
        </div>
        </td>
        </tr>
        </table>
        </td>
        </tr>
        <tr>
        <td>
              <jsp:include page="<%= strDynIncPage %>" flush="true" />
        </td>
        </tr>
        <tr>
        <td colspan="2">
         
        </td>
        </tr>
        <tr><td> </td></tr>
        <tr id="trbgred">
        <td align="center" colspan="2">
              ©copyright: 2015, Mirza Yousuf Ahmed Baig, Build Web
              Applications with Java
        </td>
        </tr>
        </table>
</body>
</html>
```

All the other jsp pages used in the application are detailed in the chapter for use cases implementation.

Log4j

Logging is a mechanism to record the activities performed by an executing software program. When a software program is executed line by line it accomplishes certain intended tasks. During the execution, the program logs the success, failures, important action or any other significant information into a file. This file known as a log file is used to monitor the health as well as the job of the software. The most common usage of logging is to identify system and business errors and it helps in fixing them. Logging helps in smoothly running the software system by providing the required information to the support team. In a broader sense, logging helps a lot in software system governance.

In our sample application we are using Log4j. Apache log4j is a logging utility and it provides ready made mechanism to enable logging in java applications with little configurations.

For more details on logging implementation in our sample application, please refer the chapter on logging.

15

IMPLEMENTING USE CASES

A use case is an end to end scenario for a particular actor interaction with the system in order to accomplish a task. This is a list of one or more steps between an actor with a particular role(s) and the system to achieve a specific task. The actor is generally a human but it could also be an external system or an event triggered by time.

With respect to our application, a use case is an interaction between the user and BIS-SMS web application in order to achieve a particular goal. The user in our case could be a teacher, admin or a clerk. For e.g. the user with admin role can add a new student to the application. The goal in this case is to add a new student to the system. The actor is a human user who holds the admin role. This use case has many steps: first identify the role of the authenticated user then authorize him/her with the privilege to add a student to the system. The next step includes providing the user a form to add the new student details. And finally, validate the form contents entered by the user and then insert the data to the database. Hence, in the above example use case we have seen the actor, the steps, the goal. In order to add more clarity this use case can be supported with a use case diagram which conveys the requirement pictorially for easier understanding and clarity for the use case.

A software application consists of "n" number of use cases. These use cases (with a UML use case diagram) provide clarity for requirements. Help in designing and building the software. Help in testing the software. Use cases help through out the life cycle of software development.

In this chapter, we will define and detail all the use cases of our sample application. We will then implement these use cases and finally we will unit test them. Lets begin with the list of all the use cases for our application.

1. Authenticate user.
2. Authorize user and render dashboard based on role.
3. Load student.
4. Get student details.
5. Get student results.
6. Get student attendance.
7. Get student fees status.
8. Manage student attendance.
9. Add student.
10. Get report by class.

Use Case: Authentication.

Requirements Specification Reference: R1

Prototype Reference: P1

Prerequisite: The user must have an account to access the system.

As per the user requirement specifications and prototype we need to build a login page for this use case. This falls under the category called form based authentication. In this category, a form with user id and password is submitted to authenticate a user. The UI is very simple for this use case with just one page having two fields and a login button. Please refer chapter 16 for more details on securing applications with Apache Tomcat. We have only one jsp page for this use case.

BisLogin.jsp

In order to use container managed security with Apache Tomcat 8 we need to use the following field names and form action. Other than this, the login page is mere a html document with the UI as per the prototype.

```
<form id="frmBisLogin" method="POST" action="j_security_check">
```
The action attribute must be "j_security_check".

```
<input type="password" name="j_password" size="20">
```
The password tag must be named "j_ password ".

```
<input type="text" name="j_username" size="20">
```
The user text field must be named "j_ username".

```
<!DOCTYPE HTML PUBLIC "-//W3C//DTD HTML 4.01 Transitional//EN"
"http://www.w3.org/TR/html4/loose.dtd">

<%@ page contentType="text/html;charset=windows-1252"%>

<html>

<head>

<title> BIS Login </title>
<style>

body {
background-color: #BBBBBB;
}

#dashboardlink {
color: Blue;
font-size: large;
}

#trbgred {
color: white;
background-color: red;
}

#bigwhtxt {
color: White;
```

```
font-size: x-large;
}

#regfont {
color: white;
}

#headingfont {
color: Red;
font-size: xx-large;
font-style: bold;
}

#headingtxt {
color: Red;
font-size: large;
}

#redFontWhiteBg {
color: red;
background-color: White;
}

#whiteBg    {
background-color: White;
font-size: large;
}

#submitButton    {
color: red;
background-color: White;
font-size: large;
}

#clred {
color: red;
}

</style>

</head>

<body bgcolor="#BBBBBB">

      <form id="frmBisLogin" method="POST" action="j_security_check">
      <table border="1" cellpadding="0" cellspacing="0" width="100%">
      <tr bgcolor="White">
      <td>
```

```
<table border="0" cellpadding="0" cellspacing="0" width="100%"
bgcolor="White">
<tr height="70">
<td rowspan="3" align="center">
<font id="headingfont" size="7">
      Baig International School
</font>
</td>
</tr>
</table>
</td>
</tr>
<tr>
<td>
<table border="0" cellpadding="1" cellspacing="1" width="100%">
<tr height="60"><td colspan="3"> </td></tr>
<tr>
<td width="25%">
 
</td>
<td widht="*">
<table border="0" cellpadding="5" cellspacing="5" width="100%"
bgcolor="White">
<tr>
<td colspan="2" id="trbgred" align="left">
  
      Sign in
</td>
<tr>
<td colspan="2" align="left">
 
</td>
</tr>
<tr>
<td align="right" width="50%">
      User Id
</td>
<td width="*">
<input type="text" name="j_username" size="20">
</td>
</tr>
<tr>
<td align="right">
      Password
</td>
<td>
<input type="password" name="j_password" size="20">
</td>
</tr>
```

```
        <tr>
        <td align="center" colspan="2" height="50">
        <input type="submit"  value="   Login    " id="sbmt">
        </td>
        </tr>
        <tr>
        <td colspan="2" align="right">
        <a href="">
              Forgot password
        </a>
          
        </td>
        </tr>
        <tr>
        <td align="right" colspan="2" id="trbgred"> </td>
        </tr>
        </table>
        </td>
        <td width="25%">
         
        </td>
        </tr>
        <tr height="30"><td colspan="3"> </td></tr>
        </table>
        </td>
        </tr>
        <tr id="trbgred">
        <td rowspan="3" align="center">
        <font id="regfont">
              ©copyright: 2015, Mirza Yousuf Ahmed Baig, Build Web
              Applications with Java
        </font>
        </td>
        </tr>
        </table>
        </form>
</body>
</html>
```

This concludes the implementation of this use case. In form based authentication mechanism, the implementers have the luxury to have whatever UI client wants. The only compulsion is having the above described field names and form action point. Note that for using container managed security we need to follow the documentation of the particular server being used. Here, we have used Apache Tomcat and hence we have used j_username, j_password and j_security_check.

Use Case: Authorization.

Requirements Specification Reference: R2

Prototype Reference: P2

Prerequisite: The user must be authenticated and must have at least one assigned role.

Please refer chapter 16 for details on the configuration part. In this use case implementation our objective is to render access links in the dashboard page and global navigation menu based on the role. For this we will have a closer look at the source code of two jsp pages BisHome.jsp and BisDashboard.jsp.

BisDashboard.jsp

This is the landing page of the sample web application post successful authentication. In this dashboard page the links are displayed based on the role(s) of the logged in user.

```
<!DOCTYPE HTML PUBLIC "-//W3C//DTD HTML 4.01 Transitional//EN"
"http://www.w3.org/TR/html4/loose.dtd">

<%@ page contentType="text/html;charset=windows-1252"%>
<%@ page import="com.bis.beans.StudentDetailsBean"%>
<%@ page import="java.util.Hashtable, java.util.Enumeration"%>

<%
StudentDetailsBean studentDetailsBean = null;
if (session != null) {
    studentDetailsBean = (StudentDetailsBean)
session.getAttribute("studentDetailsBean");
}
%>

<html>

<head>

<meta http-equiv="Content-Type" content="text/html; charset=windows-
1252"/>
<title>Baig International School - Dashboard</title>
```

```
<link rel="stylesheet" type="text/css"
href="resources/css/BISStyle.css"></link>
<script src="resources/js/BISScript.js"></script>

</head>

<body>
      <form id="frmDashboard" name="frmDashboard"
      action="BisControllerServlet" method="POST">
      <input type="hidden" name="ParameterActionCommand"
      value="BisDashboard"></input>
      <table border="0" cellpadding="0" cellspacing="0" width="100%">
      <tr><td> </td></tr>
      <tr>
      <td>
      <table border="0" cellpadding="0" cellspacing="0" width="100%">
      <tr>
      <td width="33%" align="center" valign="middle">
      <table border="0" cellpadding="5" cellspacing="0" width="90%"
      bgcolor="White">
      <tr>
      <td align="center" id="trbgred">Find Student</td>
      </tr>
      <tr><td> </td></tr>
      <tr>
      <td align="center">
      Student ID
        
      <input type="text" name="txtStdId" id="txtStdId" size="20"></input>
        
      <input type="button" value="Load Student" id="btnStdDtls"
      onclick="getStudentAJAX()"></input>
      </td>
      </tr>
      <tr><td> </td></tr>
      <tr><td id="trbgred" align="center">Student in Context</td></tr>
      <tr><td> </td></tr>
      <tr>
      <td align="center" id="headingtxt">
      <div id="dvStdSmry">
      <%
      if (studentDetailsBean != null)    {
      out.print(studentDetailsBean.getFullName());
      out.print("   |");
      }
      %>
        
      <%
      if (studentDetailsBean != null)    {
```

```
out.print(studentDetailsBean.getGrade());
out.print(" - ");
out.print(studentDetailsBean.getSection());
out.print("   |");
}
%>
  
<%
if (studentDetailsBean != null)   {
out.print(studentDetailsBean.getStudentId());
}
%>
</div>
</td>
</tr>
<tr><td> </td></tr>
</table>
</td>
<td widht="*" align="center" valign="middle">
<table border="0" cellpadding="7" cellspacing="7" width="95%">
<tr valign="top">
<td align="left" width="50%">
<table border="0" cellpadding="5" cellspacing="0" width="100%"
bgcolor="White">
<tr>
<td align="center" id="trbgred">Student Information</td>
</tr>
<tr>
<td align="left">
<a href="#" id="dashboardlink">
Student details
</a>
</td>
</tr>
<tr>
<td align="left">
<%
if (request.isUserInRole("BisTeacher") ||
request.isUserInRole("BisAdmin")) {
%>
<a href="BisControllerServlet?ParameterActionCommand=
GetStudentAcademics&sem=1" id="dashboardlink">
Semester - I results
</a>
<%
}
else {
%>
<a id="dashboardlink">
```

```
Semester - I results
</a>
<%
}
%>
</td>
</tr>
<tr>
<td align="left">
<%
if (request.isUserInRole("BisTeacher")  ||
request.isUserInRole("BisAdmin")) {
%>
<a href="BisControllerServlet?ParameterActionCommand=
GetStudentAcademics&sem=2" id="dashboardlink">
      Semester - II results
</a>
<%
}
else {
%>
<a  id="dashboardlink">
      Semester - II results
</a>
<%
}
%>
</td>
</tr>
<tr>
<td align="left">
<a href="#" id="dashboardlink">
      Semester-I Attendance
</a>
</td>
</tr>
<tr>
<td align="left">
<a href="#" id="dashboardlink">
      Semester-II Attendance
</a>
</td>
</tr>
<tr>
<td align="left">
<%
if (request.isUserInRole("BisClerk")  ||
      request.isUserInRole("BisAdmin")) {
%>
```

```
<a href="BisControllerServlet?ParameterActionCommand=
GetStudentFees" id="dashboardlink">
      Fees
</a>
<%
}
else {
%>
<a  id="dashboardlink">
      Fees
</a>
<%
}
%>
</td>
</tr>
</table>
</td>
<td align="left" width="*" colspan="2">
<table border="0" cellpadding="5" cellspacing="0" width="100%"
bgcolor="White">
<tr>
<td align="center" id="trbgred">Administration</td>
</tr>
<tr>
<td align="left">
<a href="#" id="dashboardlink">
      Add Student
</a>
</td>
</tr>
<tr>
<td align="left">
<a href="#" id="dashboardlink">
      Edit Student
</a>
</td>
</tr>
<tr>
<td align="left">
<a href="#" id="dashboardlink">
      Manage Result
</a>
</td>
</tr>
<tr>
<td align="left">
<a href="#" id="dashboardlink">
      Manage Attendance
```

```
</a>
</td>
</tr>
<tr>
<td align="left">
<a href="#" id="dashboardlink">
      Manage Fees
</a>
</td>
</tr>
<tr>
<td align="left">
 
</td>
</tr>
</table>
</td>
</tr>
<tr valign="top">
<td align="left" width="50%">
<table border="0" cellpadding="5" cellspacing="0" width="100%"
bgcolor="White">
<tr>
<td align="center" id="trbgred">Reports</td>
</tr>
<tr>
<td align="left">
<a href="BisControllerServlet?ParameterActionCommand=
GetReportByClass" id="dashboardlink">
      Class
</a>
</td>
</tr>
<tr>
<td align="left">
<a href="#" id="dashboardlink">
      Bus
</a>
</td>
</tr>
<tr>
<td align="left">
<a href="#" id="dashboardlink">
      Fees
</a>
</td>
</tr>
<tr>
<td align="left">
```

```
 
</td>
</tr>
<tr>
<td align="left">
 
</td>
</tr>
<tr>
<td align="left" height="27px">
 
</td>
</tr>
</table>
</td>
<td width="*" valign="top">
<table border="0" cellpadding="5" cellspacing="0" width="100%"
bgcolor="White">
<tr>
<td align="center" id="trbgred">Help</td>
</tr>
<tr>
<td align="left">
<a href="#" id="dashboardlink">
      Academics Legend
</a>
</td>
</tr>
<tr>
<td align="left">
<a href="#" id="dashboardlink">
      FAQs
</a>
</td>
</tr>
<tr>
<td align="left">
<a href="#" id="dashboardlink">
      Holiday Calender
</a>
</td>
</tr>
<tr>
<td align="left">
<a href="#" id="dashboardlink">
      Escalation Matrix
</a>
</td>
</tr>
```

```
<tr>
<td align="left">
<a href="#" id="dashboardlink">
      Fee Structure
</a>
</td>
</tr>
<tr>
<td align="left">
<a href="#" id="dashboardlink">
      Events
</a>
</td>
</tr>
</table>
</td>
</tr>
</table>
</td>
</tr>
<tr><td> </td></tr>
<tr>
<td colspan="2" align="center">
<table border="0" cellpadding="5" cellspacing="0" width="100%"
bgcolor="White">
<tr>
<td align="center" id="trbgred">Announcement</td>
</tr>
<tr><td> </td></tr>
<tr>
<td align="center">
      The annual day event is scheduled for Jan 26, 2015.
</td>
</tr>
<tr><td> </td></tr>
<tr><td> </td></tr>
</table>
</td>
</tr>
</table>
</td>
</tr>
<tr><td> </td></tr>
</table>
</form>
</body>
</html>
```

Let us have a closer look at the code snippet which renders links based on the role.

```
<tr>
<td align="left">

<%
      if (request.isUserInRole("BisTeacher") ||
      request.isUserInRole("BisAdmin")) {
%>

<a href="BisControllerServlet?ParameterActionCommand=
GetStudentAcademics&sem=1" id="dashboardlink">
Semester - I results
</a>

<%
}
else {
%>

<a id="dashboardlink">
Semester - I results
</a>

<%
}
%>

</td>
</tr>
```

In the above code snippet, request.isUserInRole("BisTeacher") checks whether the logged in user has the role BisTeacher. If yes, the code renders link for the results. If no, the user only sees a label. We are displaying a label here just to demonstrate for learning purpose. In real applications, the label is generally not shown. That is, the user only sees those links whose access the role has and no labels are shown for those functionalities which the role does not have.

BisHome.jsp

This page is the placeholder page for all other pages. This page has all the commons that belong to the view. The menu, the header and the footer belong to this page. In this page the dynamic region displays various other pages based on user interaction. Please refer chapter 14 for the source code and details about BisHome.jsp page.

This concludes the implementation of this use case. For applications that demand higher level of security, the role can be verified at the server side code implementation as a pre-condition before the execution of each use case.

Use Case: Load Student.

Requirements Specification Reference: R3

Prototype Reference: P3

Prerequisite: The user has to be logged in.

This use case needs to be implemented as per the requirements specification reference above. The UI needs to be as per the prototype reference above. Now that we have complete clarity on use case requirements and UI we will now proceed to implement this use case.

In order to implement this use case, we need to follow the architecture and leverage the framework. To achieve this we will first come up with detailed design and then code it.

The prerequisite for this use case is that the use has to be signed in. The objective of this use case is to load a student into context. Once a student is loaded into context it is available in the http session. All the other use cases use the student id from the http session. This is the prerequisite use case for many use cases in this application. On the dashboard page, the user enters the student id and clicks load student. This use case needs to perform two action. First, it must display the student context information on the load student region within the dashboard page. Second, on the server side it must add the student id to the http session.

In this use case, we are sending the student id and getting back the basic information about the student (name, grade, section and id) for the display. The other action is adding the student id to the session on the server side. On the browser, it does not make sense to submit the entire form and reload the entire dashboard page. Once the user clicks load student button by entering the student id, we need to only send the student id to the server. For sending such selective values to the server and performing action on the server side and also receiving a subset of data for the page without submitting the entire page form or without reloading the entire page we use AJAX. Please go through chapter 20 now for more details on AJAX. That is the prerequisite now to proceed further on this use case implementation.

The user enters student id and clicks load student.

This invokes the javascript function getStudentAJAX() in the BisScript.js.

The BisAjaxControllerServlet is invoked on the server.

In the service method the action command parameter value is read which is LoadStudent

The execute method for the command processor pertaining to LoadStudent is invoked.

The business logic pertaining to this command processor is executed and a response text is returned.

The server returns the Ajax response and that results in the invocation of the AJAX call back function on the browser. Also, the student id is added to the http session.

The call back function sets the response text and the user sees the updated region with student context info. Note that this is just a region refresh and the entire page is not reloaded.

Lets now design this use case with AJAX. Please refer the class diagrams in chapter 14 for more details about the classes used. In our BIS Framework, we have a separate controller to hand all AJAX requests. This is called AJAXControllerServlet. Lets see the sequence diagram for load student use case implemented using AJAX.

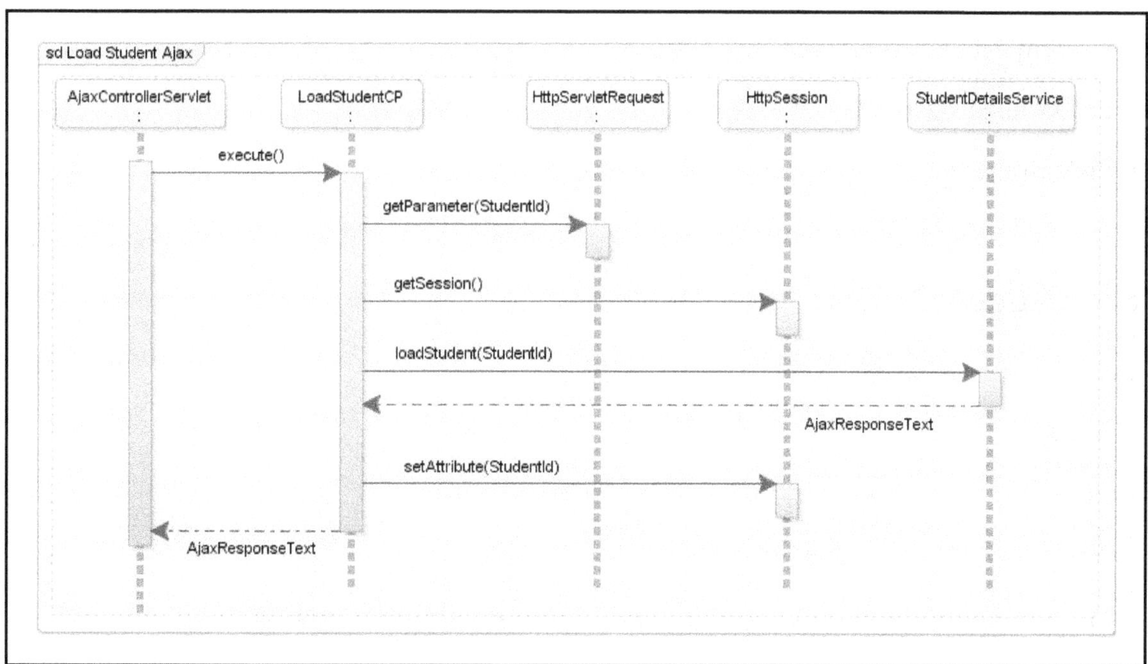

When the user clicks load student after entering the student id. The AjaxControllerServlet is invoked, this servlet then invokes the execute method of LoadStudentCP. Within the execute method, we read the student id entered by the user as a parameter. The StudentDetailsService is than leveraged to load the student. The loadStudent method within StudentDetailsService uses DatabaseService class and queries the database for the given student id. The returned value is composed as a single string with student name, student id, class and section. This forms the AjaxResponseText which is returned back to the browser. Before sending back the AjaxResponseText, the student id is add to the Http session. The browser displays the student context once it receives the AjaxResponseText.

We now have the student in context on the dashboard page and student id in http session. The purpose of load student use case is now achieved using AJAX. Lets now have a closer look into the source code for the artifacts used in this use case.

1. LoadStudentCP.java
2. StudentDetailsService.java
3. BisDashboard.jsp
4. BisScript.js

LoadStudentCP.java

```
package com.bis.cp;

import com.bis.session.StudentDetailsService;
import javax.servlet.http.HttpServletRequest;
import javax.servlet.http.HttpServletResponse;
import javax.servlet.http.HttpSession;
import org.apache.log4j.Logger;

public class LoadStudentCP extends BisCP implements BisCommand {

      static Logger logger = Logger.getLogger(LoadStudentCP.class);

      public LoadStudentCP() {
            super();
      }

      public String execute(HttpServletRequest request,
                                          HttpServletResponse response) {
            String strStudentId = null;
            HttpSession session = null;
            strStudentId = request.getParameter("txtStdId");
            session = request.getSession();
            if (strStudentId != null)   {
            try {
            StudentDetailsService studentDetailsService = new
            StudentDetailsService();
            strAjaxResponseText =
            studentDetailsService.loadStudent(strStudentId);
            session.setAttribute("StudentId", strStudentId);
```

```
                } catch (Exception e) {
                    logger.error(e.getMessage());
                }
            }
        return strAjaxResponseText;
        }
}
```

The execute method performs the following tasks:

⇒ Gets the student id from the request parameter.

⇒ Gets the http session from the request object.

⇒ Creates an instance of StudentDetailsService and calls loadStudent method.

⇒ Adds the student id to the http session.

⇒ Returns the Ajax response text.

StudentDetailsService.java

Let us focus only on the loadStudent method of this java class. Rest of this java class is detailed in the get student details use case.

```
public String loadStudent(String strStudentId)    {

String strStudentSummary="";
String strFirstName = "";
String strMiddleName = "";
String strLastName = "";
String strFullName = "";
String strGrade = "";
String strSection = "";
Connection connection = null;
Statement statement = null ;
ResultSet resultSet = null;

if (strStudentId != null)    {
      StringBuffer sbQuery = new StringBuffer("SELECT FIRST_NAME,
      MIDDLE_NAME, LAST_NAME, GRADE, SECTION FROM STUDENT_DETAILS WHERE
      STUDENT_ID='");
      sbQuery.append(strStudentId+"'");
      DatabaseService databaseService = new DatabaseService();
      connection = databaseService.getDBConnection();
```

```
        try {
        statement = connection.createStatement();
        resultSet = statement.executeQuery(sbQuery.toString());
        resultSet.next(); // Expecting only one record.
        strFirstName = resultSet.getString("FIRST_NAME");
        strMiddleName = resultSet.getString("MIDDLE_NAME");
        strLastName = resultSet.getString("LAST_NAME");
        strGrade = resultSet.getString("GRADE");
        strSection = resultSet.getString("SECTION");
        if (strFirstName != null) {
        strFullName = strFirstName;
        }
        if (strMiddleName != null) {
        strFullName = strFullName + "  " + strMiddleName;
        }
        if (strLastName != null) {
        strFullName = strFullName + "  " + strLastName;
        }
        strStudentSummary = strFullName + "  |  " +
        strGrade + "-" + strSection + "  |  " +
        strStudentId;
              } catch (SQLException sqle) {
                    logger.error(sqle.getMessage());
              } finally {
                    databaseService.closeDBResouces(statement, resultSet);
                    databaseService.releaseDBConnection();  // Releasing
        database          connection.
              }
              }
        else {
              logger.error("Student id is null");
        }
return strStudentSummary;
}
```

The loadStudent method performs the following tasks:

- ⇒ Cooks up a dynamic query for a given student id.
- ⇒ Queries the database for basic student details. The DatabaseService class is leveraged to achieve this.
- ⇒ Builds a string comprising of student summary. This holds name, id, class and section.
- ⇒ Returns the student summary string as Ajax response text.

BisDashboard.jsp

This jsp page is described in detail under the Authorization use case. Here, we will look into only the snippet which deals with the Ajax refresh region.

```
<tr>
      <td align="center" id="headingtxt">
            <div id="dvStdSmry">
            </div>
      </td>
</tr>
```

Once the Ajax based javascript call back function is invoked the div tag with id dvStdSmry is assigned a value for display. This value holding the student summary sent from the Ajax response is dynamically displayed to the region.

Lets look into the javascript part for this use case.

BisScript.js

```
var xmlHttpReq=false;

function getStudentAJAX() {

var stdId = document.getElementById("txtStdId").value;
var url="BisAjaxControllerServlet?ParameterActionCommand=
LoadStudent&txtStdId=";
url = url + stdId;
xmlHttpReq = new XMLHttpRequest();
xmlHttpReq.open("GET",url, true);
xmlHttpReq.send();
xmlHttpReq.onreadystatechange=getStudentAjaxCallBack;

}

function getStudentAjaxCallBack()     {

      if (xmlHttpReq.readyState == 4 && xmlHttpReq.status == 200) {
      document.getElementById("dvStdSmry").innerHTML=xmlHttpReq.
      responseText;
      }
}
```

We have two Javascript functions and one variable for the load student via Ajax use case.

The getStudentAJAX function performs the following tasks:

⇒ Reads the student id entered by the user in the text field.

⇒ Initializes a URL for Ajax controller servlet along with the parameters for load student action command and student id.

⇒ Creates an instance of XMLHttpRequest for making an Ajax call to the server.

⇒ Opens a get request for the given URL.

⇒ Assigns a call back function to the XMLHttpRequest instance to be invoked upon a change in ready state.

⇒ And finally sends the Ajax request to the server.

The getStudentAJAXCallBack function performs the following tasks:

⇒ Validates the ready state for XMLHttpRequest instance.

⇒ Assigns the response text to inner html using the div tag.

This concludes the use case for load student. In this use case we saw how Ajax can be employed to set a student context into the session on server side and the student in question context on the client side.

We have seen that a separate controller servlet is employed for this purpose and that comes with the BIS framework. For Ajax, XMLHttpRequest is used on the client side. We used two javascript functions to achieve this functionality. When the user entered student id and clicked load student button, we invoked the javascript function to make an Ajax call. This javascript function leveraged XMLHttpRequest object and issue an Ajax call for a given URL with given parameters. On the server side, the Ajax controller servlet invoked the execute method for load student command processor. In this method we leveraged student service class which in turn interacted with the database using the database service class. Finally we got the response text as a single string. This response text is returned to the client. Upon receiving the response, the browser invoked the Ajax call back function which in turn refreshed the region using div tag. With this we achieved setting a student in context both on the server side as well as the client side.

Use Case: Get student details.

Requirements Specification Reference: R5

Prototype Reference: P4

Prerequisite: The student has to be loaded into context first.

This use case needs to be implemented as per the requirements specification reference above. The UI needs to be as per the prototype reference above. Now that we have complete clarity on use case requirements and UI we will now proceed to implement this use case.

In order to implement this use case, we need to follow the architecture and leverage the framework. To achieve this we will first come up with detailed design and then code it.

The prerequisite for this use case is that a student must already be existing in the context, for this the user must have loaded the student through the load student use case. When the student is loaded, the student id of a particular student is added to the session. You can refer the load student use case for details on this. Lets assume as of now that the student id is existing in the http session. When the user clicks on get student details link either on dashboard or via the menu, the following flow is triggered.

The user clicks the get student details link

↓

The href for this link is
BisControllerServlet?ParameterActionCommand=GetStudentDetails

↓

The ControllerServlet is invoked on the server

↓

In the service method the action command parameter value is read which is GetStudentDetails

↓

The execute method for the command processor pertaining to GetStudentDetails is invoked

↓

The business logic pertaining to this command processor is executed and a view is returned

↓

The response is returned to the browser with this view

↓

The user sees the student details page

The command processor class pertaining to GetStudentDetails command is GetStudentDetailsCP. The view pertaining to student detail page is StudentDetails.jsp. Now, lets see the sequence of method calls once the execute method of GetStudentDetailsCP is called. Below are the sequence diagrams from this use case.

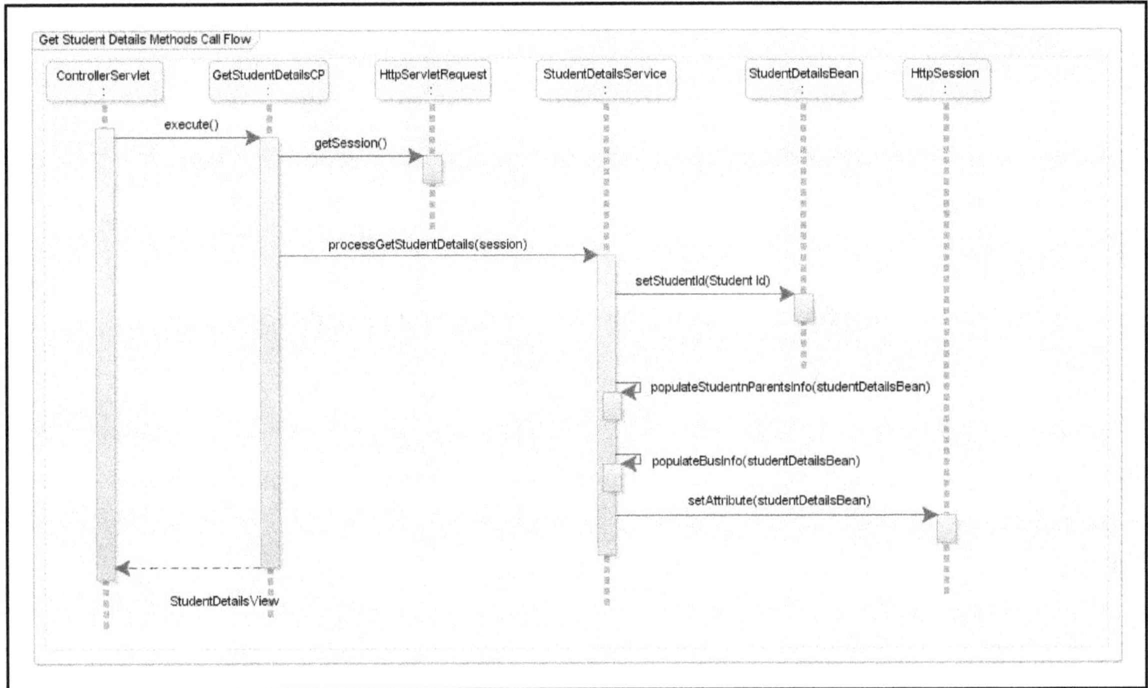

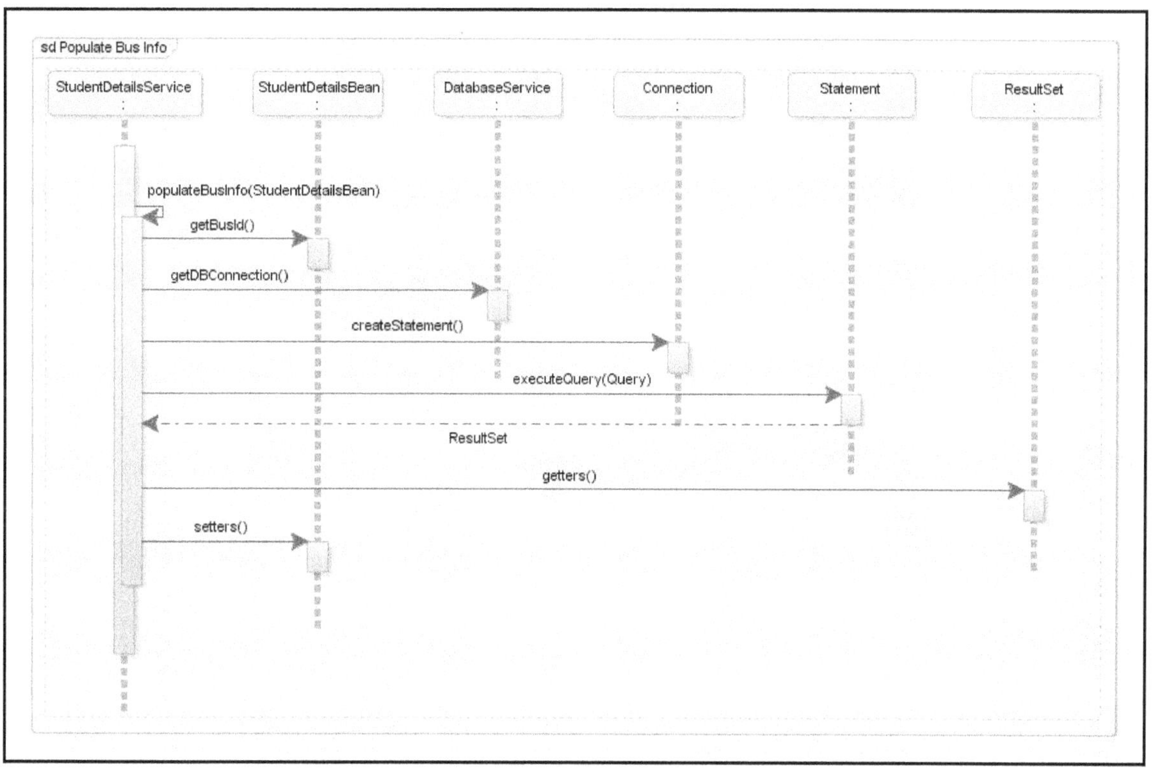

As shown in the above sequence diagrams, the GetStudentDetailsCP invokes the processGetStudentDetails method in the StudentDetailsService class. This method orchestrates the business logic for this use case. The private methods populateStudentnParentsInfo and populateBusInfo within the StudentDetailsService class are invoked. These methods run the appropriate query on the database and fetch the student, parents and bus details from the database tables. In order to interact with the database, the DatabaseService class is leveraged. This data is then populated to a bean called StudentDetailsBean and this bean is then added to the session. The command processor upon success returns the view as a string. This view identifies the jsp to be responded. The jsp reads this bean from the session and presents this data to the user.

At this stage we have the requirements, prototype, architecture, framework and detailed design for the get student details use case in the form of sequence and class diagrams. The next and the most interesting part is coding this use case. In the earlier chapter, we have already created the database tables and added some test data there. Lets identify all the artifacts first. For this use case we need the following files.

- BisHome.jsp
- StudentDetails.jsp
- BISScript.js
- BISStyle.css
- GetStudentDetailsCP.java
- StudentDetailsService.java
- StudentDetailsBean.java
- DatabaseService.java

We will look into BisHome.jsp, BISScript.js, BISStyle.css and DatabaseService.java under commons section as these artifacts are common for all the use cases. Please refer chapter 14 for details about these shared artifacts.

GetStudentDetailsCP.java

Please refer chapter 14 (The BIS-SMS Project Components) for class diagram once before we proceed with this class. This class implements BisCommand interface which has only one method execute. This class extends BisCP which has few variables. We have to implement execute method in this class for get student details use case. Lets look into the actual source code for this class now.

```
package com.bis.cp;

import com.bis.session.StudentDetailsService;
import javax.servlet.http.HttpServletRequest;
import javax.servlet.http.HttpServletResponse;
import javax.servlet.http.HttpSession;
import org.apache.log4j.Logger;

public class GetStudentDetailsCP extends BisCP implements BisCommand {

      static Logger logger = Logger.getLogger(GetStudentDetailsCP.class);

      public GetStudentDetailsCP() {
            super();
      }

      public String execute(HttpServletRequest request,
                                         HttpServletResponse response) {
            HttpSession session = request.getSession();
            String strStudentId;
            if (session != null)    {
            strStudentId = (String) session.getAttribute("StudentId");
            if (strStudentId != null)     {
            StudentDetailsService studentDetailsService
            = new StudentDetailsService();
            try {
            studentDetailsService.processGetStudentDetails(session);
            strNextNavigation = "StudentDetails";
            //The next navigation page upon successful processing.

      } catch (Exception e) {
            logger.error(e.getMessage());
            strNextNavigation = "Error";
            //The next navigation page upon failed processing.
      }
      }
      else {
```

```
                    // strStudentId is null, first entry to the page.
                    strNextNavigation = "StudentDetails";
              }
              }
              else {
                    //Session is null. Valid session doesn't exist.
                    Redirect to Login page.
                    strNextNavigation = "Login";
              }
        return strNextNavigation;
        }
}
```

The execute method of GetStudentDetailsCP Class.

The execute method is called from the controller servlet. This is the job of the framework. The framework gets the command from UI and based on the command loads and executes a specific command processor exploiting the polymorphic feature of java. In this case, the command from UI is "GetStudentDetails". Within the service method of controller servlet, the GetStudentDetailsCP class is loaded and instantiated and the execute method is invoked.

In the execute method, the http session is fetched from the HttpServletRequest object. From the session, the student id is fetched. This is the id of the student which is already loaded into the context. The execute method further instantiates the StudentDetailsService class and invokes the processGetStudentDetails method.

StudentDetailsService.java

Now lets see the StudentDetailsService class source code.

```
package com.bis.session;

import com.bis.beans.StudentDetailsBean;
import com.bis.db.DatabaseService;
import java.sql.Connection;
import java.sql.Date;
import java.sql.ResultSet;
import java.sql.SQLException;
import java.sql.Statement;
import java.text.SimpleDateFormat;
import java.util.Hashtable;
```

```
import java.util.StringTokenizer;
import javax.servlet.http.HttpSession;
import org.apache.log4j.Logger;

public class StudentDetailsService implements BisService {

	static Logger logger =
	Logger.getLogger(StudentDetailsService.class);

	public StudentDetailsService() {
		super();
	}

public void processGetStudentDetails(HttpSession session) {

	String strStudentId = (String) session.getAttribute("StudentId");
	StudentDetailsBean studentDetailsBean;
	studentDetailsBean = new StudentDetailsBean();
	if (strStudentId != null) {
	// This is mandatory before calling the next method.
	studentDetailsBean.setStudentId(strStudentId);
	populateStudentnParentsInfo(studentDetailsBean);
	populateBusInfo(studentDetailsBean);
	if (studentDetailsBean.getSiblings() != null) {
	populateSiblings(studentDetailsBean);
	}
	session.setAttribute("studentDetailsBean", studentDetailsBean);
	} else {
	logger.error("Student id is null");
	}
}

private void populateBusInfo(StudentDetailsBean studentDetailsBean)	{

	String strBusId;
	strBusId = studentDetailsBean.getBusId();
	String strDriverFirstName;
	String strDriverLastName;
	String strDriverFullName;
	String strHelperFirstName;
	String strHelperLastName;
	String strHelperFullName;
	String strDesignation;
	Connection connection = null;
	Statement statement = null;
	ResultSet resultSet = null;
	StringBuffer sbQuery = new StringBuffer();
```

```
sbQuery.append("SELECT ED.DESIGNATION, ED.FIRST_NAME, ED.MIDDLE_NAME,
ED.LAST_NAME, ED.MOBILE_NUMBER, TD.TRANSPORTATION_TYPE, TD.BUS_NUMBER
FROM EMPLOYEE_DETAILS ED, TRANSPORTATION_DETAILS TD WHERE TD.BUS_ID=");
sbQuery.append(strBusId);
sbQuery.append(" AND (ED.EMPLOYEE_ID=TD.DRIVER_EMPLOYEE_ID OR
ED.EMPLOYEE_ID=TD.HELPER_EMPLOYEE_ID) ");
if (strBusId != null) {
connection = DatabaseService.getDBConnection();
try {
statement = connection.createStatement();
      resultSet = statement.executeQuery(sbQuery.toString());
while (resultSet.next()) { // Expecting two records.
      strDesignation = resultSet.getString("DESIGNATION");
      studentDetailsBean.setTransType(resultSet.getString("TRANSPORTATION
_     TYPE"));
      studentDetailsBean.setBusNubmer(resultSet.getString("BUS_NUMBER"));
if (strDesignation != null) {
if (strDesignation.equalsIgnoreCase("Driver")) {
strDriverFirstName = resultSet.getString("FIRST_NAME");
strDriverLastName = resultSet.getString("LAST_NAME");
strDriverFullName = strDriverFirstName + " " + strDriverLastName;
studentDetailsBean.setDriver(strDriverFullName);
studentDetailsBean.setDriverMobile(resultSet.getString("MOBILE_NUMBER"));
}
else if (strDesignation.equalsIgnoreCase("Helper")) {
strHelperFirstName = resultSet.getString("FIRST_NAME");
strHelperLastName = resultSet.getString("LAST_NAME");
strHelperFullName = strHelperFirstName + " " + strHelperLastName;
studentDetailsBean.setHelper(strHelperFullName);
studentDetailsBean.setHelperMobile(resultSet.getString("MOBILE_NUMBER"));
}
else {
logger.debug("Unknown designation.");
}
} else {
logger.debug("Designation is null");
}
}
} catch (SQLException sqle) {
logger.debug(sqle.getMessage());
} finally {
DatabaseService.closeDBResouces(statement, resultSet);
DatabaseService.releaseDBConnection();// Releasing database connection.
}
} else {
logger.debug("Bus id is null");
}
}
```

```
private void populateStudentnParentsInfo(StudentDetailsBean
                                                        studentDetailsBean) {
      String strStudentId;
      strStudentId = studentDetailsBean.getStudentId();
      Connection connection = null;
      Statement statement = null;
      ResultSet resultSet = null;
      StringBuffer sbQuery = new StringBuffer();
      String strFirstName = "";
      String strMiddleName = "";
      String strLastName = "";
      String strFullName = "";
      String strTeacherFirstName = "";
      String strTeacherMiddleName = "";
      String strTeacherLastName = "";
      String strTeacherFullName = "";

sbQuery.append("SELECT\n" +
" studentDetails.FIRST_NAME AS STUDENT_FIRST_NAME,
studentDetails.MIDDLE_NAME AS STUDENT_MIDDLE_NAME,
studentDetails.LAST_NAME AS STUDENT_LAST_NAME,\n" +
" studentDetails.GENDER_CODE, studentDetails.BIRTH_DATE,
studentDetails.BLOOD_GROUP, studentDetails.BUS_ID, studentDetails.GRADE,
studentDetails.SECTION, \n" +
" studentDetails.HEIGHT,studentDetails.WEIGHT, \n" +
" parentDetails.FATHER_NAME, parentDetails.MOTHER_NAME,
parentDetails.FATHER_MOBILE, parentDetails.MOTHER_MOBILE,  \n" +
" parentDetails.ADDRESS, \n" +
" employeeDetails.FIRST_NAME AS TEACHER_FIRST_NAME,
employeeDetails.MIDDLE_NAME AS TEACHER_MIDDLE_NAME,
employeeDetails.LAST_NAME AS TEACHER_LAST_NAME \n" +
" FROM STUDENT_DETAILS studentDetails, PARENT_DETAILS parentDetails,
EMPLOYEE_DETAILS employeeDetails, CLASS_TEACHER_MAPPING CTM \n" +
" WHERE studentDetails.STUDENT_ID=");
sbQuery.append("'" + strStudentId + "' ");
sbQuery.append("AND parentDetails.STUDENT_ID=studentDetails.STUDENT_ID
AND CTM.GRADE=studentDetails.GRADE AND CTM.SECTION=studentDetails.SECTION
AND employeeDetails.EMPLOYEE_ID=CTM.EMPLOYEE_ID");
if (strStudentId != null) {
connection = DatabaseService.getDBConnection();
try {
statement = connection.createStatement();
resultSet = statement.executeQuery(sbQuery.toString());
resultSet.next(); // Expecting only one record.
strFirstName = resultSet.getString("STUDENT_FIRST_NAME");
strMiddleName = resultSet.getString("STUDENT_MIDDLE_NAME");
strLastName = resultSet.getString("STUDENT_LAST_NAME");
if (strFirstName != null) {
strFullName = strFirstName;
```

```
}
if (strMiddleName != null) {
strFullName = strFullName + " " + strMiddleName;
}
if (strLastName != null) {
strFullName = strFullName + " " + strLastName;
}
studentDetailsBean.setFullName(strFullName);
strTeacherFirstName = resultSet.getString("TEACHER_FIRST_NAME");
strTeacherMiddleName = resultSet.getString("TEACHER_MIDDLE_NAME");
strTeacherLastName = resultSet.getString("TEACHER_LAST_NAME");
if (strTeacherFirstName != null) {
strTeacherFullName = strTeacherFirstName;
}
if (strTeacherMiddleName != null) {
strTeacherFullName = strTeacherFullName + " " + strTeacherMiddleName;
}
if (strTeacherLastName != null) {
strTeacherFullName = strTeacherFullName + " " + strTeacherLastName;
}
studentDetailsBean.setClassTeacher(strTeacherFullName);
String strGenderCode = resultSet.getString("GENDER_CODE");
if (strGenderCode != null &&
!(strGenderCode.trim()).equalsIgnoreCase("")) {
if (strGenderCode.equalsIgnoreCase("F")) {
studentDetailsBean.setGender("Female");
} else {
studentDetailsBean.setGender("Male");
}
}
SimpleDateFormat simpleDateFormat = new SimpleDateFormat("dd-MMM-yyyy");
Date birthDate = resultSet.getDate("BIRTH_DATE");
if (birthDate != null) {
studentDetailsBean.setDob(simpleDateFormat.format(birthDate));
} else {
logger.info("DOB is null");
studentDetailsBean.setDob("Please update DOB");
}
String strBloodGroup = resultSet.getString("BLOOD_GROUP");
if (strBloodGroup != null &&
!(strBloodGroup.trim()).equalsIgnoreCase("")) {
if (strBloodGroup.equalsIgnoreCase("AP")) {
studentDetailsBean.setBloodGroup("A +ve");
} else if (strBloodGroup.equalsIgnoreCase("AN")) {
studentDetailsBean.setBloodGroup("A -ve");
} else if (strBloodGroup.equalsIgnoreCase("BP")) {
studentDetailsBean.setBloodGroup("B +ve");
} else if (strBloodGroup.equalsIgnoreCase("BN")) {
studentDetailsBean.setBloodGroup("B -ve");
```

```
} else if (strBloodGroup.equalsIgnoreCase("OP")) {
studentDetailsBean.setBloodGroup("O +ve");
} else if (strBloodGroup.equalsIgnoreCase("ON")) {
studentDetailsBean.setBloodGroup("O -ve");
} else if (strBloodGroup.equalsIgnoreCase("ABP")) {
studentDetailsBean.setBloodGroup("AB +ve");
} else if (strBloodGroup.equalsIgnoreCase("ABN")) {
studentDetailsBean.setBloodGroup("AB -ve");
}
else {
// Invalid Blood Group
studentDetailsBean.setBloodGroup("Please update Blood Group");
logger.info("Invalid Blood Group");
}
} else {
// Blood group is null
studentDetailsBean.setBloodGroup("Please update Blood Group");
logger.info("Blood group is null");
}
studentDetailsBean.setFather(resultSet.getString("FATHER_NAME"));
studentDetailsBean.setFatherMobile(resultSet.getString("FATHER_MOBILE"));
studentDetailsBean.setMother(resultSet.getString("MOTHER_NAME"));
studentDetailsBean.setMotherMobile(resultSet.getString("MOTHER_MOBILE"));
studentDetailsBean.setAddress(resultSet.getString("ADDRESS"));
studentDetailsBean.setBusId(resultSet.getString("BUS_ID"));
studentDetailsBean.setGrade(resultSet.getString("GRADE"));
studentDetailsBean.setSection(resultSet.getString("SECTION"));
studentDetailsBean.setHeight(resultSet.getString("HEIGHT"));
studentDetailsBean.setWeight(resultSet.getInt("WEIGHT")+"");
studentDetailsBean.setSiblings(resultSet.getString("SIBLINGS_STUDENT_IDS"
));
} catch (SQLException sqle) {
logger.error(sqle.getMessage());
} finally {
DatabaseService.closeDBResouces(statement, resultSet);
DatabaseService.releaseDBConnection();  // Releasing database connection.
}
} else {
logger.error("Student id is null");
}
}

public String loadStudent(String strStudentId)    {

      String strStudentSummary="";
      String strFirstName = "";
      String strMiddleName = "";
      String strLastName = "";
      String strFullName = "";
```

```
	String strGrade = "";
	String strSection = "";
	Connection connection = null;
	Statement statement = null ;
	ResultSet resultSet = null;

if (strStudentId != null)   {
StringBuffer sbQuery = new StringBuffer("SELECT FIRST_NAME, MIDDLE_NAME,
LAST_NAME, GRADE, SECTION FROM STUDENT_DETAILS WHERE STUDENT_ID='");
sbQuery.append(strStudentId+"'");
DatabaseService databaseService = new DatabaseService();
connection = databaseService.getDBConnection();
try {
statement = connection.createStatement();
resultSet = statement.executeQuery(sbQuery.toString());
resultSet.next(); // Expecting only one record.
strFirstName = resultSet.getString("FIRST_NAME");
strMiddleName = resultSet.getString("MIDDLE_NAME");
strLastName = resultSet.getString("LAST_NAME");
strGrade = resultSet.getString("GRADE");
strSection = resultSet.getString("SECTION");
if (strFirstName != null) {
strFullName = strFirstName;
}
if (strMiddleName != null) {
strFullName = strFullName + " " + strMiddleName;
}
if (strLastName != null) {
strFullName = strFullName + " " + strLastName;
}
strStudentSummary = strFullName + "  |  " + strGrade
+ "-" + strSection + "  |  " + strStudentId;
} catch (SQLException sqle) {
logger.error(sqle.getMessage());
} finally {
databaseService.closeDBResouces(statement, resultSet);
databaseService.releaseDBConnection();  // Releasing database connection.
}
}
else {
logger.error("Student id is null");
}
return strStudentSummary;
}

	public String getServiceName() {
		return this.getClass().getName();
	}
}
```

The processGetStudentDetails method performs the following tasks:

⇒ Gets the student id from the session.

⇒ Creates an instance of StudenDetailBean and sets the student id.

⇒ Calls populateStudentnParentsInfo and populateBusInfo methods to populate the data from database into StudenDetailBean.

⇒ Adds StudenDetailBean to the session which is consumed by the jsp.

The populateStudentnParentsInfo method performs the following tasks:

⇒ Cooks up the dynamic select query for a given student id.

⇒ Gets the database connection from DatabaseService class.

⇒ Creates the statement and executes the query.

⇒ Populates the StudeneDetailsBean instance from the ResultSet and adds data related to student and parents.

The populateBusInfo method performs the following tasks:

⇒ Cooks up the dynamic select query for a given bus id.

⇒ Gets the database connection from DatabaseService class.

⇒ Creates the statement and executes the query.

⇒ Populates the StudeneDetailsBean instance from the ResultSet and adds data related to bus or transportation.

StudentDetailsBean.java

The StudentDetailsBean class is just a simple java bean with private fields with their getters and setters. Please refer the class diagram and below source code for understanding this class.

```
package com.bis.beans;

import java.util.Hashtable;

public class StudentDetailsBean extends StudentBean {

      public StudentDetailsBean() {
            super();
      }

      private java.lang.String gender;
      private java.lang.String dob;
      private java.lang.String classTeacher;
      private java.lang.String height;
      private java.lang.String weight;
      private java.lang.String bloodGroup;
      private java.lang.String siblings;
      private java.lang.String birthCity;
      private java.lang.String birthStateCode;
      private java.lang.String birthCountryCode;
      private java.lang.String father;
      private java.lang.String mother;
      private java.lang.String fatherMobile;
      private java.lang.String motherMobile;
      private java.lang.String address;
      private java.lang.String busId;
      private java.lang.String fatherQual;
      private java.lang.String motherQual;
      private java.lang.String annualIncome;
      private java.lang.String driver;
      private java.lang.String driverMobile;
      private java.lang.String helper;
      private java.lang.String helperMobile;
      private java.lang.String busNubmer;
      private java.lang.String transType;
      private java.util.Hashtable siblingsHash;

      public void setGender(String gender) {
            this.gender = gender;
      }
```

```
public String getGender() {
      return gender;
}

public void setDob(String dob) {
      this.dob = dob;
}

public String getDob() {
      return dob;
}

public void setClassTeacher(String classTeacher) {
      this.classTeacher = classTeacher;
}

public String getClassTeacher() {
      return classTeacher;
}

public void setHeight(String height) {
      this.height = height;
}

public String getHeight() {
      return height;
}

public void setWeight(String weight) {
      this.weight = weight;
}

public String getWeight() {
      return weight;
}

public void setBloodGroup(String bloodGroup) {
      this.bloodGroup = bloodGroup;
}

public String getBloodGroup() {
      return bloodGroup;
}

public void setSiblings(String siblings) {
      this.siblings = siblings;
}

public String getSiblings() {
```

```
        return siblings;
    }

    public void setBirthCity(String birthCity) {
        this.birthCity = birthCity;
    }

    public String getBirthCity() {
        return birthCity;
    }

    public void setBirthStateCode(String birthStateCode) {
        this.birthStateCode = birthStateCode;
    }

    public String getBirthStateCode() {
        return birthStateCode;
    }

    public void setBirthCountryCode(String birthCountryCode) {
        this.birthCountryCode = birthCountryCode;
    }

    public String getBirthCountryCode() {
        return birthCountryCode;
    }

    public void setFather(String father) {
        this.father = father;
    }

    public String getFather() {
        return father;
    }

    public void setMother(String mother) {
        this.mother = mother;
    }

    public String getMother() {
        return mother;
    }

    public void setFatherMobile(String fatherMobile) {
        this.fatherMobile = fatherMobile;
    }

    public String getFatherMobile() {
        return fatherMobile;
```

```
}

public void setMotherMobile(String motherMobile) {
      this.motherMobile = motherMobile;
}

public String getMotherMobile() {
      return motherMobile;
}

public void setAddress(String address) {
      this.address = address;
}

public String getAddress() {
      return address;
}

public void setBusId(String busId) {
      this.busId = busId;
}

public String getBusId() {
      return busId;
}

public void setFatherQual(String fatherQual) {
      this.fatherQual = fatherQual;
}

public String getFatherQual() {
      return fatherQual;
}

public void setMotherQual(String motherQual) {
      this.motherQual = motherQual;
}

public String getMotherQual() {
      return motherQual;
}

public void setAnnualIncome(String annualIncome) {
      this.annualIncome = annualIncome;
}

public String getAnnualIncome() {
      return annualIncome;
}
```

```
public void setDriver(String driver) {
      this.driver = driver;
}

public String getDriver() {
      return driver;
}

public void setDriverMobile(String driverMobile) {
      this.driverMobile = driverMobile;
}

public String getDriverMobile() {
      return driverMobile;
}

public void setHelper(String helper) {
      this.helper = helper;
}

public String getHelper() {
      return helper;
}

public void setHelperMobile(String helperMobile) {
      this.helperMobile = helperMobile;
}

public String getHelperMobile() {
      return helperMobile;
}

public void setBusNubmer(String busNubmer) {
      this.busNubmer = busNubmer;
}

public String getBusNubmer() {
      return busNubmer;
}

public void setTransType(String transType) {
      this.transType = transType;
}

public String getTransType() {
      return transType;
}
```

```
	public void setSiblingsHash(Hashtable siblingsHash) {
		this.siblingsHash = siblingsHash;
	}

	public Hashtable getSiblingsHash() {
		return siblingsHash;
	}

}
```

StudentDetails.jsp

This jsp is dynamically included in BisHome.jsp as a result for get student details use case invocation through user interaction with the UI..

Till now we have seen that the command for student details goes form UI as a result of user interaction. Then the controller servlet calls get student details command processor and then the student details service is leveraged. Finally, we get the results packaged as an instance of StudentDetailsBean. This bean is now available in the session. In the StudentDetails.jsp file we fetch this bean from the session. And from this bean we fetch all the information related to student details using the getters. The static part of the jsp remains the same as that of the prototype page. Only the dynamic part is added using the bean from the session. Hence, the end user sees the view for a given student with all his/her details.

Here is the source code for the StudentDetails.jsp file.

```
<%@ page import="com.bis.beans.StudentDetailsBean"%>
<%@ page import="java.util.Hashtable, java.util.Enumeration"%>

	<%
		StudentDetailsBean studentDetailsBean = null;
		if (session != null) {
			studentDetailsBean = (StudentDetailsBean)
			session.getAttribute("studentDetailsBean");
		}
	%>

	<form id="frmStdDtls" name="frmStdDtls"
	action="BisControllerServlet" method="POST">
	<input type="hidden" name="ParameterActionCommand"
	value="GetStudentDetails"></input>
```

```
<table border="0" cellpadding="0" cellspacing="0" width="100%"
height="99%">
<tr><td> </td></tr>
<tr><td> </td></tr>
<tr>
<td bgcolor="White" align="center" colspan="3" height="30">
<font size="4">
<%
if (studentDetailsBean != null)    {
out.print(studentDetailsBean.getFullName());
}
%>
   |   
<%
if (studentDetailsBean != null)    {
out.print(studentDetailsBean.getGrade());
out.print(" - ");
out.print(studentDetailsBean.getSection());
}
%>
   |   
<%
if (studentDetailsBean != null)    {
out.print(studentDetailsBean.getStudentId());
}
%>
  
</font>
</td>
</tr>
<tr><td> </td></tr>
<tr><td> </td></tr>
<tr><td> </td></tr>
<tr>
<td widht="*" align="center" valign="top">
<table border="0" cellpadding="10" cellspacing="0" width="100%">
<tr valign="top">
<td width="33%" align="center">
<table border="0" cellpadding="3" cellspacing="0" width="90%"
bgcolor="White">
<tr>
<td colspan="2" align="center" id="trbgred">
Student
</td>
</tr>
<tr>
<td colspan="2"> </td>
</tr>
<tr>
```

```
<td width="25%" align="right" id="clred">Student ID
  </td>
<td width="*" align="left">
  
<%
if (studentDetailsBean != null)   {
out.print(studentDetailsBean.getStudentId());
}
%>
</td>
</tr>
<tr>
<td width="25%" align="right" id="clred">Name   </td>
<td width="*" align="left">
  
<%
if (studentDetailsBean != null)   {
out.print(studentDetailsBean.getFullName());
}
%>
</td>
</tr>
<tr>
<td colspan="2"> </td>
</tr>
<tr>
<td width="*" align="right" id="clred">Gender   </td>
<td width="*" align="left">
  
<%
if (studentDetailsBean != null)   {
out.print(studentDetailsBean.getGender());
}
%>
</td>
</tr>

<tr>
<td align="right" id="clred">Date of birth   </td>
<td width="*" align="left">
  
<%
if (studentDetailsBean != null)   {
out.print(studentDetailsBean.getDob());
}
%>
</td>
</tr>
<tr>
```

```
<td colspan="2"> </td>
</tr>
<tr>
<td align="right" id="clred">Grade   </td>
<td width="*" align="left">
  
<%
if (studentDetailsBean != null)   {
out.print(studentDetailsBean.getGrade());
}
%>
</td>
</tr>
<tr>
<td align="right" id="clred">Section   </td>
<td width="*" align="left">
  
<%
if (studentDetailsBean != null)   {
out.print(studentDetailsBean.getSection());
}
%>
</td>
</tr>
<tr>
<td colspan="2"> </td>
</tr>
<tr>
<td align="right" id="clred">Class Teacher   </td>
<td width="*" align="left">
  
<%
if (studentDetailsBean != null)   {
out.print(studentDetailsBean.getClassTeacher());
}
%>
</td>
</tr>
<tr>
<td colspan="2"> </td>
</tr>
<tr>
<td align="right" id="clred">Height   </td>
<td width="*" align="left">
  
<%
if (studentDetailsBean != null)   {
out.print(studentDetailsBean.getHeight());
}
```

```
%>
</td>
</tr>
<tr>
<td align="right" id="clred">Weight   </td>
<td width="*" align="left">
  
<%
if (studentDetailsBean != null)   {
out.print(studentDetailsBean.getWeight());
}
%>
</td>
</tr>
<tr>
<td colspan="2"> </td>
</tr>
<tr>
<td align="right" id="clred">Blood Group   </td>
<td width="*" align="left">
  
<%
if (studentDetailsBean != null)   {
out.print(studentDetailsBean.getBloodGroup());
}
%>
</td>
</tr>
<tr>
<td colspan="2"> </td>
</tr>
</table>
</td>
<td width="33%" align="center">
<table border="0" cellpadding="3" cellspacing="0" width="90%"
bgcolor="White">
<tr>
<td colspan="2" align="center" id="trbgred">
Parents
</td>
</tr>
<tr>
<td colspan="2"> </td>
</tr>
<tr>
<td width="25%" align="right" id="clred">Father   </td>
<td width="*" align="left">
  
<%
```

```
if (studentDetailsBean != null)   {
out.print(studentDetailsBean.getFather());
}
%>
</td>
</tr>
<tr>
<td colspan="2"> </td>
</tr>
<tr>
<td width="25%" align="right" id="clred">Mobile   </td>
<td width="*" align="left">
  
<%
if (studentDetailsBean != null)   {
out.print(studentDetailsBean.getFatherMobile());
}
%>
</td>
</tr>
<tr>
<td colspan="2"> </td>
</tr>
<tr>
<td width="*" align="right" id="clred">Mother   </td>
<td width="*" align="left">
  
<%
if (studentDetailsBean != null)   {
out.print(studentDetailsBean.getMother());
}
%>
</td>
</tr>
<tr>
<td colspan="2"> </td>
</tr>
<tr>
<td align="right" id="clred">Mobile   </td>
<td width="*" align="left">
  
<%
if (studentDetailsBean != null)   {
out.print(studentDetailsBean.getMotherMobile());
}
%>
</td>
</tr>
<tr>
```

```
<td colspan="2"> </td>
</tr>
<tr height="75">
<td align="right" id="clred">Address   </td>
<td width="*" align="left">
  
<%
if (studentDetailsBean != null)    {
out.print(studentDetailsBean.getAddress());
}
%>
</td>
</tr>
<tr>
<td colspan="2"> </td>
</tr>
<tr>
<td colspan="2"> </td>
</tr>
<tr>
<td colspan="2"> </td>
</tr>
<tr>
<td colspan="2"> </td>
</tr>
<tr>
<td colspan="2"> </td>
</tr>
</table>
</td>
<td width="*" align="center">
<table border="0" cellpadding="3" cellspacing="0" width="90%"
bgcolor="White">
<tr>
<td colspan="2" align="center" id="trbgred">
Bus
</td>
</tr>
<tr>
<td colspan="2"> </td>
</tr>
<tr>
<td width="25%" align="right" id="clred">Bus Id   </td>
<td width="*" align="left">
  
<%
if (studentDetailsBean != null)    {
out.print(studentDetailsBean.getBusId());
}
```

```
%>
</td>
</tr>
<tr>
<td colspan="2"> </td>
</tr>
<tr>
<td width="25%" align="right" id="clred">Driver   </td>
<td width="*" align="left">
  
<%
if (studentDetailsBean != null)    {
out.print(studentDetailsBean.getDriver());
}
%>
</td>
</tr>
<tr>
<td colspan="2"> </td>
</tr>
<tr>
<td width="*" align="right" id="clred">Mobile   </td>
<td width="*" align="left">
  
<%
if (studentDetailsBean != null)    {
out.print(studentDetailsBean.getDriverMobile());
}
%>
</td>
</tr>
<tr>
<td colspan="2"> </td>
</tr>
<tr>
<td align="right" id="clred">Helper   </td>
<td width="*" align="left">
  
<%
if (studentDetailsBean != null)    {
out.print(studentDetailsBean.getHelper());
}
%>
</td>
</tr>
<tr>
<td colspan="2"> </td>
</tr>
<tr>
```

```
<td align="right" id="clred">Mobile   </td>
<td width="*" align="left">
  
<%
if (studentDetailsBean != null)    {
out.print(studentDetailsBean.getHelperMobile());
}
%>
</td>
</tr>
<tr>
<td colspan="2"> </td>
</tr>
<tr>
<td align="right" id="clred">Bus Number   </td>
<td width="*" align="left">
  
<%
if (studentDetailsBean != null)    {
out.print(studentDetailsBean.getBusNubmer());
}
%>
</td>
</tr>
<tr>
<td colspan="2"> </td>
</tr>
<tr>
<td align="right" id="clred">Transportation   </td>
<td width="*" align="left">
  
<%
if (studentDetailsBean != null)    {
out.print(studentDetailsBean.getTransType());
}
%>
</td>
</tr>
<tr>
<td colspan="2"> </td>
</tr>
<tr>
<td colspan="2"> </td>
</tr>
<tr>
<td colspan="2"> </td>
</tr>
</table>
</td>
```

```
</tr>
</table>
</td>
</tr>
<tr><td> </td></tr>
</table>
</form>
```

This concludes the get student details use case implementation from end to end. We composed the requirement specifications, we built the prototype, we followed the architecture for the solution, we leveraged the framework, we developed the various java classes, we used the common components like DatabaseService.java, BISStyle.css etc and we built the view with the jsp page.

Use Case: Get student attendance.

Requirements Specification Reference: R7

Prototype Reference: P6

Prerequisite: The student has to be loaded into context first.

This use case needs to be implemented as per the requirements specification reference above. The UI needs to be as per the prototype reference above. Now that we have complete clarity on use case requirements and UI we will now proceed to implement this use case.

In order to implement this use case, we need to follow the architecture and leverage the framework. To achieve this we will first come up with detailed design and then code it.

The prerequisite for this use case is that a student must already be existing in the context, for this the user must have loaded the student through the load student use case. When the student is loaded, the student id of a particular student is added to the session. You can refer the load student use case for details on this. Lets assume as of now that the student id is existing in the http session. When the user clicks on get student attendance (either for semester I or for semester II) link either on dashboard or via the menu, the following flow is triggered.

Get student attendance link is clicked

The href for these links are

BisControllerServlet?ParameterActionCommand=GetStudentAttendance&sem=1

and

BisControllerServlet?ParameterActionCommand=GetStudentAttendance&sem=2

The ControllerServlet is invoked on the server

In the service method the action command parameter value is read which is GetStudentAttendance

The execute method for the command processor pertaining to GetStudentAttendance is invoked

The business logic pertaining to this command processor is executed and a view is returned

The response is returned to the browser with this view

The user sees the student attendance page for a given semester

The command processor class pertaining to GetStudentAttendance command is GetStudentAttendanceCP. The view pertaining to student detail page is StudentAttendance.jsp. Refer the code below to see the sequence of method calls once the execute method of GetStudentAttendanceCP is invoked.

For this use case we need the following files.

1. GetStudentAttendanceCP.java

2. StudentAttendanceService.java

3. StudentAttendanceBean.java

4. StudentAttendance.jsp

GetStudentAttendanceCP.java

```
package com.bis.cp;

import com.bis.session.StudentAttendanceService;
import javax.servlet.http.HttpServletRequest;
import javax.servlet.http.HttpServletResponse;
import javax.servlet.http.HttpSession;
import org.apache.log4j.Logger;

public class GetStudentAttendanceCP extends BisCP implements BisCommand {

      static Logger logger =
                        Logger.getLogger(GetStudentAttendanceCP.class);

      public GetStudentAttendanceCP() {
            super();
      }

      public String execute(HttpServletRequest request,
                                          HttpServletResponse response) {
      HttpSession session = request.getSession();
      String strStudentId;
      String strSemester = "1";
      // Defaulting semester to first.
      strSemester = request.getParameter("sem");
      if (session != null)    {
      strStudentId = (String) session.getAttribute("StudentId");
```

```
        if (strStudentId != null &&
        !(strStudentId.trim().equalsIgnoreCase("")) )    {
        StudentAttendanceService studentAttendanceService = new
        StudentAttendanceService();
        try {
        studentAttendanceService.processGetStudentAttendance(session,
        strSemester);
        strNextNavigation = "StudentAttendance";
        //The next navigation page upon successful processing.
        } catch (Exception e) {
              logger.error(e.getMessage());
              strNextNavigation = "Error";
              //The next navigation page upon failed processing.
              }
        }
        else {
              // strStudentId is null, first entry to the page.
              strNextNavigation = "StudentAttendance";
        }
        }
        else {
              // session is null. Valid session does not exists. Redirect
              to Login page.
              strNextNavigation = "Login";
              }
        return strNextNavigation;
        }
}
```

The execute method performs the following actions:

⇒ Gets the Http session for the logged in user.

⇒ Gets the semester the user has selected as a parameter value.

⇒ Gets the student id from the session.

⇒ Creates an instance of StudentAttendanceService and invokes processGetStudentAttendance method.

⇒ Sets the next navigation to StudentAttendance.

StudentAttendanceService.java

```
package com.bis.session;
```

```
import com.bis.beans.StudentAttendanceBean;
import com.bis.db.DatabaseService;
import java.sql.Connection;
import java.sql.PreparedStatement;
import java.sql.ResultSet;
import java.sql.SQLException;
import java.sql.Statement;
import javax.servlet.http.HttpServletRequest;
import javax.servlet.http.HttpSession;
import org.apache.log4j.Logger;

public class StudentAttendanceService implements BisService {

	static Logger logger =
			Logger.getLogger(StudentAttendanceService.class);

	public StudentAttendanceService() {
		super();
	}

	public void processGetStudentAttendance(HttpSession session, String
								strSemester) {
		String strStudentId =
		(String)session.getAttribute("StudentId");
		StudentAttendanceBean studentAttendanceBean;
		studentAttendanceBean = new StudentAttendanceBean();

		if (strStudentId != null) {
		studentAttendanceBean.setStudentId(strStudentId); // This is
		mandatory before calling the next method.
		populateStudentAttendance(studentAttendanceBean,
		strSemester);
		populateWorkingDaysforSem(studentAttendanceBean,
		strSemester);
		session.setAttribute("studentAttendanceBean",
		studentAttendanceBean);
		} else {
			logger.error("Student Id is null");
		}
	}

private void populateStudentAttendance(StudentAttendanceBean
			studentAttendanceBean, String strSemester) {
String strStudentId;
strStudentId = studentAttendanceBean.getStudentId();
Connection connection = null;
Statement statement = null;
ResultSet resultSet = null;
```

```
StringBuffer sbQuery = new StringBuffer();
sbQuery.append("SELECT ATTENDANCE FROM STUDENT_ATTENDANCE WHERE
STUDENT_ID=");
sbQuery.append("'" + strStudentId + "' ");
sbQuery.append("AND SEMESTER = '");
sbQuery.append(strSemester);
sbQuery.append("'");

if (strStudentId != null) {
connection = DatabaseService.getDBConnection();
try {
statement = connection.createStatement();
resultSet = statement.executeQuery(sbQuery.toString());
resultSet.next(); // Expecting only one record.
studentAttendanceBean.setAttendance(resultSet.getInt("ATTENDANCE"));
} catch (SQLException sqle) {
logger.error(sqle.getMessage());
} finally {
DatabaseService.closeDBResouces(statement, resultSet);
DatabaseService.releaseDBConnection(); // Releasing database connection.
}
} else {
logger.error("Student id is null");
}
}

private void populateWorkingDaysforSem(StudentAttendanceBean
                        studentAttendanceBean, String strSemester) {
Connection connection = null;
Statement statement = null;
ResultSet resultSet = null;
StringBuffer sbQuery = new StringBuffer();
sbQuery.append("SELECT VALUE FROM BIS_CONSTANTS WHERE PROPERTY='");

if (strSemester.equalsIgnoreCase("1")) {
sbQuery.append("SEM_ONE_WORKING_DAYS'");
} else if (strSemester.equalsIgnoreCase("2")) {
sbQuery.append("SEM_TWO_WORKING_DAYS'");
} else {
logger.debug("Invalid semester returned");
}
DatabaseService databaseService = new DatabaseService();
connection = databaseService.getDBConnection();
try {
statement = connection.createStatement();
resultSet = statement.executeQuery(sbQuery.toString());
resultSet.next(); // Expecting only one record.
studentAttendanceBean.setTotalWorkingDays(Integer.parseInt(resultSet.getS
tring("VALUE")));
```

```
} catch (SQLException sqle) {
logger.error(sqle.getMessage());
} finally {
databaseService.closeDBResouces(statement, resultSet);
databaseService.releaseDBConnection(); // Releasing database connection.
}
}

// Gets student attendance for Manage attendance page. This includes
attendance for both the semesters.
public void processGetStudentAttendance(HttpSession session) throws
                                                            Exception {
String strStudentId = (String)session.getAttribute("StudentId");
StudentAttendanceBean studentAttendanceBean;
studentAttendanceBean = new StudentAttendanceBean();
if (strStudentId != null) {
studentAttendanceBean.setStudentId(strStudentId); // This is mandatory
before calling the next method.
populateStudentAttendance(studentAttendanceBean);
populateWorkingDaysforBothSem(studentAttendanceBean);
session.setAttribute("studentAttendanceBean", studentAttendanceBean);
} else {
logger.error("Student id is null");
}
}

// Populates attendance for both the semesters for a given student.
private void populateStudentAttendance(StudentAttendanceBean
                                            studentAttendanceBean) {
String strStudentId;
String strSem;
strStudentId = studentAttendanceBean.getStudentId();
Connection connection = null;
Statement statement = null;
ResultSet resultSet = null;
StringBuffer sbQuery = new StringBuffer();
sbQuery.append("SELECT ATTENDANCE, SEMESTER FROM STUDENT_ATTENDANCE WHERE
STUDENT_ID=");
sbQuery.append("'" + strStudentId + "' ");
if (strStudentId != null) {
DatabaseService databaseService = new DatabaseService();
connection = databaseService.getDBConnection();
try {
statement = connection.createStatement();
resultSet = statement.executeQuery(sbQuery.toString());
// Expecting two records. One for each semester.
while (resultSet.next()) {
strSem = resultSet.getString("SEMESTER");
if (strSem != null) {
```

```
if (strSem.equalsIgnoreCase("1")) {
studentAttendanceBean.setSemOneAttendance(resultSet.getInt("ATTENDANCE"))
;
} else if (strSem.equalsIgnoreCase("2")) {
studentAttendanceBean.setSemTwoAttendance(
                                    resultSet.getInt("ATTENDANCE"));
}
}
}
} catch (SQLException sqle) {
logger.error(sqle.getMessage());
} finally {
databaseService.closeDBResouces(statement, resultSet);
databaseService.releaseDBConnection(); // Releasing database connection.
}
} else {
logger.error("Student id is null");
}
}

private void populateWorkingDaysforBothSem(StudentAttendanceBean
                                                studentAttendanceBean) {
String strSem;
Connection connection = null;
Statement statement = null;
ResultSet resultSet = null;
StringBuffer sbQuery =
new StringBuffer("SELECT PROPERTY, VALUE FROM BIS_CONSTANTS WHERE
PROPERTY='SEM_ONE_WORKING_DAYS' OR PROPERTY='SEM_TWO_WORKING_DAYS'");

DatabaseService databaseService = new DatabaseService();
connection = databaseService.getDBConnection();

try {
statement = connection.createStatement();
resultSet = statement.executeQuery(sbQuery.toString());
// Expecting two records. One for each semester.
while (resultSet.next()) {
strSem = resultSet.getString("PROPERTY");
if (strSem != null) {
if (strSem.equalsIgnoreCase("SEM_ONE_WORKING_DAYS")) {
studentAttendanceBean.setSemOneTotalWorkingDays(Integer.parseInt(resultSe
t.getString("VALUE")));
} else if (strSem.equalsIgnoreCase("SEM_TWO_WORKING_DAYS")) {
studentAttendanceBean.setSemTwoTotalWorkingDays(Integer.parseInt(resultSe
t.getString("VALUE")));
}
}
}
```

```
} catch (SQLException sqle) {
logger.error(sqle.getMessage());
} finally {
databaseService.closeDBResouces(statement, resultSet);
databaseService.releaseDBConnection(); // Releasing database connection.
}
}

// Updates the student's attendance for the given semester in database.
public void updateStudentAttendance(HttpServletRequest request) {
String strAttendance=null, strUpdateQuery=null, strSem=null,
strStudentId=null;
int updateCount;
Connection connection = null;
PreparedStatement preparedStatement = null;
DatabaseService databaseService = new DatabaseService();
connection = databaseService.getDBConnection();
strUpdateQuery = "UPDATE STUDENT_ATTENDANCE SET ATTENDANCE=? WHERE
STUDENT_ID=? AND SEMESTER=?";
strStudentId = (String)request.getSession().getAttribute("StudentId");
strSem = request.getParameter("ParameterUpdateSemAttendance");
if (strSem != null) {
if (strSem.equalsIgnoreCase("1")) {
strAttendance = request.getParameter("txtPresentSemOne");
} else if (strSem.equalsIgnoreCase("2")) {
strAttendance = request.getParameter("txtPresentSemTwo");
}
}
else {
logger.debug("Semester is null");
}
if (strAttendance != null && strStudentId != null) {
logger.info("strAttendance : "+strAttendance);
logger.info("strStudentId : "+strStudentId);
try {
preparedStatement = connection.prepareStatement(strUpdateQuery);
preparedStatement.setInt(1, Integer.parseInt(strAttendance));
preparedStatement.setString(2, strStudentId);
preparedStatement.setString(3, strSem);
updateCount = preparedStatement.executeUpdate();
logger.info("The udate count for attendanc update is : "+updateCount);
} catch (SQLException sqle) {
logger.error(sqle.getMessage());
} catch (NumberFormatException nfe) {
logger.error(nfe.getMessage());
} finally {
databaseService.closeDBResouces(preparedStatement, null);
databaseService.releaseDBConnection(); // Releasing database connection.
}
```

```
} else {
logger.error("Attendance or student id is null");
}
}

      public String getServiceName() {
            return this.getClass().getName();
      }
}
```

The processGetStudentAttendance method performs the following tasks:

⇒ Gets the student id from the session.

⇒ Creates an instance of StudentAttendanceBean.

⇒ Calls setter of StudentAttendanceBean instance for setting student id.

⇒ Invokes the private methods populateStudentAttendance and populateWorkingDaysforSem.

⇒ Adds the populated StudentAttendanceBean instance to session to be consumed by the view.

The populateStudentAttendance method performs the following tasks:

⇒ Cooks up a dynamic query for a given student and semester to fetch the attendance from the database.

⇒ Leverages the DatabaseService class to get the database connection.

⇒ Calls setter of StudentAttendanceBean instance for setting the attendance.

⇒ Uses the finally block to close all the resources related to database.

The populateWorkingDaysforSem method performs the following tasks:

⇒ Queries BIS_CONSTANTS table for the property based on semester requested by the user. SEM_ONE_WORKING_DAYS for semester one and SEM_TWO_WORKING_DAYS for semester two.

⇒ Leverages the DatabaseService class to get the database connection.

⇒ Calls setter of StudentAttendanceBean instance for setting the total number of working days for the given semester.

⇒ Uses the finally block to close all the resources related to database.

StudentAttendanceBean.java

The StudentAttendanceBean class is just a simple java bean with private fields with their getters and setters. Please refer the class diagram and below source code for understanding this class.

```
package com.bis.beans;

public class StudentAttendanceBean extends StudentBean {

	public StudentAttendanceBean() {
		super();
	}

	private int attendance;
	private int totalWorkingDays;
	private int semOneAttendance;
	private int semTwoAttendance;
	private int semOneTotalWorkingDays;
	private int semTwoTotalWorkingDays;

	public void setAttendance(int attendance) {
		this.attendance = attendance;
	}

	public int getAttendance() {
		return attendance;
	}

	public void setTotalWorkingDays(int totalWorkingDays) {
		this.totalWorkingDays = totalWorkingDays;
	}

	public int getTotalWorkingDays() {
		return totalWorkingDays;
	}
```

```
	public void setSemOneAttendance(int semOneAttendance) {
		this.semOneAttendance = semOneAttendance;
	}

	public int getSemOneAttendance() {
		return semOneAttendance;
	}

	public void setSemTwoAttendance(int semTwoAttendance) {
		this.semTwoAttendance = semTwoAttendance;
	}

	public int getSemTwoAttendance() {
		return semTwoAttendance;
	}

	public void setSemOneTotalWorkingDays(int semOneTotalWorkingDays) {
		this.semOneTotalWorkingDays = semOneTotalWorkingDays;
	}

	public int getSemOneTotalWorkingDays() {
		return semOneTotalWorkingDays;
	}

	public void setSemTwoTotalWorkingDays(int semTwoTotalWorkingDays) {
		this.semTwoTotalWorkingDays = semTwoTotalWorkingDays;
	}

	public int getSemTwoTotalWorkingDays() {
		return semTwoTotalWorkingDays;
	}
}
```

StudentAttendance.jsp

This jsp is dynamically included in BisHome.jsp as a result for get student attendance use case invocation through user interaction with the UI.

Till now we have seen that the command for student attendance goes form UI as a result of user interaction. Then the controller servlet calls get student attendance command processor and then the student attendance service is leveraged. Finally, we get the results packaged as an instance of StudentAttendanceBean. This bean is now available in the session. In the StudentAttendance.jsp file we fetch this bean from the session. And from this bean we fetch all the information related to student attendance using the getters. The static part of the jsp remains the same as that of the prototype page. Only the dynamic part is added using the bean from the session. Hence, the end user sees the view for a given student and semester with all the attendance related details.

Here is the source code for the StudentAttendance.jsp file.

```
<%@ page import="com.bis.beans.StudentResultsBean,
                        com.bis.beans.StudentAttendanceBean"%>
<%@ page import="java.util.Hashtable, java.util.Enumeration"%>

<%
      StudentResultsBean studentResultsBean = null;
      int inPresentPercentage=0;
      int inTotal=0;
      int inPresent=0;
      StudentAttendanceBean studentAttendanceBean = null;

      if (session != null) {
            studentResultsBean = (StudentResultsBean)
            session.getAttribute("studentResultsBean");
            studentAttendanceBean = (StudentAttendanceBean)
            session.getAttribute("studentAttendanceBean");
      }

      if (studentAttendanceBean != null)    {
            inTotal = studentAttendanceBean.getTotalWorkingDays();
            inPresent = studentAttendanceBean.getAttendance();
            if (inTotal > 0 && inPresent >0) {
            inPresentPercentage = Math.abs(100 * inPresent/inTotal);
            }
      }
%>

<form id="frmStudentAttendance">
<table border="0" cellpadding="10" cellspacing="0" width="100%">
<tr><td> </td></tr>
<tr>
<td bgcolor="White" align="center" colspan="3">
<font size="4">
<%
if (studentResultsBean != null)    {
out.print(studentResultsBean.getFullName());
}
%>
   |   
<%
String strSem=request.getParameter("sem");
if ( strSem != null )    {
```

```
if (strSem.equalsIgnoreCase("1"))    {
strSem = "Semester - I";
}
else {
strSem = "Semester - II";
}
}
else {
strSem = "Semester - I";
}
out.print(strSem);
%>
   |   
<%
if (studentResultsBean != null)    {
out.print(studentResultsBean.getGrade());
out.print(" - ");
out.print(studentResultsBean.getSection());
}
%>
   |   
<%
if (studentResultsBean != null)    {
out.print(studentResultsBean.getStudentId());
}
%>
  
</font>
</td>
</tr>
<tr><td> </td></tr>
<tr align="center">
<td height="250px">
<table border="1" cellpadding="5" cellspacing="0" width="70%">
<tr valign="middle" bgcolor="White">
<td bgcolor="White" align="center" height="100px" width="100%"
colspan="2">
Total -
<%
if (studentAttendanceBean != null)    {
out.print(studentAttendanceBean.getTotalWorkingDays());
}
%>
Days.
</td>
</tr>
<tr valign="middle" bgcolor="White" id="bigwhtxt">
<td bgcolor="Green" align="center" height="200px"
width="<%=inPresentPercentage%>%">
```

```
Present - <%=inPresentPercentage%>%
</td>
<td bgcolor="Red" align="center" height="200px" width="*">Absent -
<%=(100-inPresentPercentage)%>%</td>
</tr>
<tr valign="middle" bgcolor="White">
<td bgcolor="White" align="center" height="100px" width="100%"
colspan="2">
|   
Present -
<%
if (studentAttendanceBean != null)    {
out.print(studentAttendanceBean.getAttendance());
}
%>
   |   
Absent -
<%
if (studentAttendanceBean != null)    {
int intAbsent = studentAttendanceBean.getTotalWorkingDays() -
studentAttendanceBean.getAttendance();
out.print(intAbsent);
}
%>
   |
</td>
</tr>
</table>
</td>
</tr>
<tr><td> </td></tr>
</table>
</form>
```

This concludes the get attendance details use case implementation from end to end. We composed the requirement specifications, we built the prototype, we followed the architecture for the solution, we leveraged the framework, we developed the various java classes, we used the common components like DatabaseService.java, BISStyle.css etc and we built the view with the jsp page.

Use Case: Get student fees.

Requirements Specification Reference: R8

Prototype Reference: P7

Prerequisite: The student has to be loaded into context first.

This use case needs to be implemented as per the requirements specification reference above. The UI needs to be as per the prototype reference above. Now that we have complete clarity on use case requirements and UI we will now proceed to implement this use case.

In order to implement this use case, we need to follow the architecture and leverage the framework. To achieve this we will first come up with detailed design and then code it.

The prerequisite for this use case is that a student must already be existing in the context, for this the user must have loaded the student through the load student use case. When the student is loaded, the student id of a particular student is added to the session. You can refer the load student use case for details on this. Lets assume as of now that the student id is existing in the http session. When the user clicks the student fees link either on dashboard or via the menu, the following flow is triggered.

Get student fees link is clicked

↓

The href for the link is

BisControllerServlet?ParameterActionCommand=GetStudentFees

↓

The ControllerServlet is invoked on the server

↓

In the service method the action command parameter value is read which is GetStudentFees

↓

The execute method for the command processor pertaining to GetStudentFees is invoked

↓

The business logic pertaining to this command processor is executed and a view is returned

↓

The response is returned to the browser with this view

The user sees the student fees page

The command processor class pertaining to GetStudentFees command is GetStudentFeesCP. The view pertaining to student detail page is StudentFees.jsp. Refer the code below to see the sequence of method calls once the execute method of GetStudentFeesCP is called.

For this use case we need the following files.

1. GetStudentFeesCP.java
2. StudentFeesService.java
3. StudentFeesBean.java
4. StudentFees.jsp

GetStudentFeesCP.java

```
package com.bis.cp;

import com.bis.session.StudentFeesService;
import javax.servlet.http.HttpServletRequest;
import javax.servlet.http.HttpServletResponse;
import javax.servlet.http.HttpSession;
import org.apache.log4j.Logger;

public class GetStudentFeesCP extends BisCP implements BisCommand {

      static Logger logger = Logger.getLogger(GetStudentFeesCP.class);

      public GetStudentFeesCP() {
            super();
      }

      public String execute(HttpServletRequest request,
                                       HttpServletResponse response) {
            HttpSession session = request.getSession();
            String strStudentId;
            if (session != null)    {
            strStudentId = (String) session.getAttribute("StudentId");
            if (strStudentId != null &&
            !(strStudentId.trim().equalsIgnoreCase("")) )    {
```

```
            StudentFeesService studentFeesService = new
            StudentFeesService();
            try {
            studentFeesService.processGetFeesDetails(session);
            strNextNavigation = "StudentFees";  //The next navigation
            page upon successful processing.
            } catch (Exception e) {
            logger.error(e.getMessage());
            strNextNavigation = "Error";  //The next navigation page upon
            failed processing.
            }
            }
            else {
            // strStudentId is null, first entry to the page.
            strNextNavigation = "StudentFees";
            }
            }
            else {
            // session is null. Valid session doesn't exsit. Redirect to
            Login page.
            strNextNavigation = "Login";
            }
      return strNextNavigation;
      }
}
```

The execute method performs the following actions:

⇒ Gets the Http session for the logged in user.

⇒ Gets the student id from the session.

⇒ Creates an instance of StudentFeesService and invokes processGetFeesDetails method.

⇒ Sets the next navigation to StudentFees.

StudentFeesService.java

```
package com.bis.session;

import com.bis.beans.StudentFeesBean;
import com.bis.db.DatabaseService;
import java.sql.Connection;
import java.sql.ResultSet;
```

```
import java.sql.SQLException;
import java.sql.Statement;
import javax.servlet.http.HttpSession;
import org.apache.log4j.Logger;

public class StudentFeesService implements BisService {

      static Logger logger = Logger.getLogger(StudentFeesService.class);

      public StudentFeesService() {
            super();
      }

      public void processGetFeesDetails(HttpSession session) {
            String strStudentId = (String)
            session.getAttribute("StudentId");
            StudentFeesBean studentFeesBean;
            studentFeesBean = new StudentFeesBean();
            if (strStudentId != null) {
            studentFeesBean.setStudentId(strStudentId); // This is
            mandatory before calling the next method.
            populateFeesInfo(studentFeesBean);
            session.setAttribute("studentFeesBean", studentFeesBean);
            } else {
            logger.error("Student id is null");
            }
      }

      private void populateFeesInfo(StudentFeesBean studentFeesBean) {

      String strStudentId;
      strStudentId = studentFeesBean.getStudentId();
      Connection connection = null;
      Statement statement = null;
      ResultSet resultSet = null;
      StringBuffer sbQuery = new StringBuffer();

      sbQuery.append("SELECT JAN_ACAD, FEB_ACAD, MAR_ACAD, APR_ACAD,
      MAY_ACAD, JUN_ACAD,\n" +
      "             JUL_ACAD, AUG_ACAD, SEP_ACAD, OCT_ACAD, NOV_ACAD,
      DEC_ACAD,\n" +
      "             JAN_BUS, FEB_BUS, MAR_BUS, APR_BUS, MAY_BUS,
      JUN_BUS,\n" +
      "             JUL_BUS, AUG_BUS, SEP_BUS, OCT_BUS, NOV_BUS,
      DEC_BUS\n" +
      "FROM STUDENT_FEES\n" +
      "WHERE STUDENT_ID=");
      sbQuery.append(" '"+strStudentId+"'");
      if (strStudentId != null) {
```

```
        connection = DatabaseService.getDBConnection();
        try {
        statement = connection.createStatement();
        resultSet = statement.executeQuery(sbQuery.toString());
        resultSet.next(); // Expecting only one record.
        studentFeesBean.setJanAcad(resultSet.getString("JAN_ACAD"));
        studentFeesBean.setFebAcad(resultSet.getString("FEB_ACAD"));
        studentFeesBean.setMarAcad(resultSet.getString("MAR_ACAD"));
        studentFeesBean.setAprAcad(resultSet.getString("APR_ACAD"));
        studentFeesBean.setMayAcad(resultSet.getString("MAY_ACAD"));
        studentFeesBean.setJunAcad(resultSet.getString("JUN_ACAD"));
        studentFeesBean.setJulAcad(resultSet.getString("JUL_ACAD"));
        studentFeesBean.setAugAcad(resultSet.getString("AUG_ACAD"));
        studentFeesBean.setSepAcad(resultSet.getString("SEP_ACAD"));
        studentFeesBean.setOctAcad(resultSet.getString("OCT_ACAD"));
        studentFeesBean.setNovAcad(resultSet.getString("NOV_ACAD"));
        studentFeesBean.setDecAcad(resultSet.getString("DEC_ACAD"));
        studentFeesBean.setJanBus(resultSet.getString("JAN_BUS"));
        studentFeesBean.setFebBus(resultSet.getString("FEB_BUS"));
        studentFeesBean.setMarBus(resultSet.getString("MAR_BUS"));
        studentFeesBean.setAprBus(resultSet.getString("APR_BUS"));
        studentFeesBean.setMayBus(resultSet.getString("MAY_BUS"));
        studentFeesBean.setJunBus(resultSet.getString("JUN_BUS"));
        studentFeesBean.setJulBus(resultSet.getString("JUL_BUS"));
        studentFeesBean.setAugBus(resultSet.getString("AUG_BUS"));
        studentFeesBean.setSepBus(resultSet.getString("SEP_BUS"));
        studentFeesBean.setOctBus(resultSet.getString("OCT_BUS"));
        studentFeesBean.setNovBus(resultSet.getString("NOV_BUS"));
        studentFeesBean.setDecBus(resultSet.getString("DEC_BUS"));
        }  catch (SQLException sqle) {
        logger.error(sqle.getMessage());
        }
        finally {
        DatabaseService.closeDBResouces(statement, resultSet);
        DatabaseService.releaseDBConnection();  // Releasing database
        connection.
        }
        } else {
        logger.error("Student id is null");
        }
        }

        public String getServiceName() {
              return this.getClass().getName();
        }
}
```

The processGetFeesDetails method performs the following tasks:

⇒ Gets the student id from the session.

⇒ Creates an instance of StudenFeesBean and sets the student id.

⇒ Calls populateFeesInfo method to populate the data from database into StudenFeesBean.

⇒ Adds StudenFeesBean to the session which is consumed by the jsp.

The populateFeesInfo method performs the following tasks:

⇒ Cooks up the dynamic select query for a given student id.

⇒ Gets the database connection from DatabaseService class.

⇒ Creates the statement and executes the query.

⇒ Populates the StudeneFeesBean instance from the ResultSet and adds data related to student fees.

StudentFeesBean.java

The StudentFeessBean class is just a simple java bean with private fields with their getters and setters. Please refer the class diagram and below source code for understanding this class.

```
package com.bis.beans;

public class StudentFeesBean extends StudentBean {

      public StudentFeesBean() {
            super();
      }

      private java.lang.String janAcad;
      private java.lang.String febAcad;
      private java.lang.String marAcad;
      private java.lang.String aprAcad;
      private java.lang.String mayAcad;
      private java.lang.String junAcad;
      private java.lang.String julAcad;
```

```
    private java.lang.String augAcad;
    private java.lang.String sepAcad;
    private java.lang.String octAcad;
    private java.lang.String novAcad;
    private java.lang.String decAcad;
    private java.lang.String janBus;
    private java.lang.String febBus;
    private java.lang.String marBus;
    private java.lang.String aprBus;
    private java.lang.String mayBus;
    private java.lang.String junBus;
    private java.lang.String julBus;
    private java.lang.String augBus;
    private java.lang.String sepBus;
    private java.lang.String octBus;
    private java.lang.String novBus;
    private java.lang.String decBus;

    public void setJanAcad(String janAcad) {
          this.janAcad = janAcad;
    }

    public String getJanAcad() {
          return janAcad;
    }

    public void setFebAcad(String febAcad) {
          this.febAcad = febAcad;
    }

    public String getFebAcad() {
          return febAcad;
    }

    public void setMarAcad(String marAcad) {
          this.marAcad = marAcad;
    }

    public String getMarAcad() {
          return marAcad;
    }

    public void setAprAcad(String aprAcad) {
          this.aprAcad = aprAcad;
    }

    public String getAprAcad() {
          return aprAcad;
    }
```

```
public void setMayAcad(String mayAcad) {
      this.mayAcad = mayAcad;
}

public String getMayAcad() {
      return mayAcad;
}

public void setJunAcad(String junAcad) {
      this.junAcad = junAcad;
}

public String getJunAcad() {
      return junAcad;
}

public void setJulAcad(String julAcad) {
      this.julAcad = julAcad;
}

public String getJulAcad() {
      return julAcad;
}

public void setAugAcad(String augAcad) {
      this.augAcad = augAcad;
}

public String getAugAcad() {
      return augAcad;
}

public void setSepAcad(String sepAcad) {
      this.sepAcad = sepAcad;
}

public String getSepAcad() {
      return sepAcad;
}

public void setOctAcad(String octAcad) {
      this.octAcad = octAcad;
}

public String getOctAcad() {
      return octAcad;
}
```

```
	public void setNovAcad(String novAcad) {
		this.novAcad = novAcad;
	}

	public String getNovAcad() {
		return novAcad;
	}

	public void setDecAcad(String decAcad) {
		this.decAcad = decAcad;
	}

	public String getDecAcad() {
		return decAcad;
	}

	public void setJanBus(String janBus) {
		this.janBus = janBus;
	}

	public String getJanBus() {
		return janBus;
	}

	public void setFebBus(String febBus) {
		this.febBus = febBus;
	}

	public String getFebBus() {
		return febBus;
	}

	public void setMarBus(String marBus) {
		this.marBus = marBus;
	}

	public String getMarBus() {
		return marBus;
	}

	public void setAprBus(String aprBus) {
		this.aprBus = aprBus;
	}

	public String getAprBus() {
		return aprBus;
	}

	public void setMayBus(String mayBus) {
```

```
        this.mayBus = mayBus;
    }

    public String getMayBus() {
        return mayBus;
    }

    public void setJunBus(String junBus) {
        this.junBus = junBus;
    }

    public String getJunBus() {
        return junBus;
    }

    public void setJulBus(String julBus) {
        this.julBus = julBus;
    }

    public String getJulBus() {
        return julBus;
    }

    public void setAugBus(String augBus) {
        this.augBus = augBus;
    }

    public String getAugBus() {
        return augBus;
    }

    public void setSepBus(String sepBus) {
        this.sepBus = sepBus;
    }

    public String getSepBus() {
        return sepBus;
    }

    public void setOctBus(String octBus) {
        this.octBus = octBus;
    }

    public String getOctBus() {
        return octBus;
    }

    public void setNovBus(String novBus) {
        this.novBus = novBus;
```

```
        }

        public String getNovBus() {
                return novBus;
        }

        public void setDecBus(String decBus) {
                this.decBus = decBus;
        }

        public String getDecBus() {
                return decBus;
        }
}
```

StudentFees.jsp

This jsp is dynamically included in BisHome.jsp as a result for get student fees use case invocation through user interaction with the UI.

Till now we have seen that the command for student fees goes form UI as a result of user interaction. Then the controller servlet calls get student fees command processor and then the student fees service is leveraged. Finally, we get the results packaged as an instance of StudentFeesBean. This bean is now available in the session. In the StudentFees.jsp file we fetch this bean from the session. And from this bean we fetch all the information related to student fees using the getters. The static part of the jsp remains the same as that of the prototype page. Only the dynamic part is added using the bean from the session. Hence, the end user sees the view with the fees details for a given student.

Here is the source code for the StudentFees.jsp file.

```
<%@ page import="com.bis.beans.StudentFeesBean,
                              com.bis.beans.StudentResultsBean"%>
<%@ page import="java.util.Hashtable, java.util.Enumeration"%>

<%
        StudentFeesBean studentFeesBean = null;
        StudentResultsBean studentResultsBean = null;

        if (session != null) {
                studentFeesBean = (StudentFeesBean)
                session.getAttribute("studentFeesBean");
                studentResultsBean = (StudentResultsBean)
                session.getAttribute("studentResultsBean");
```

```
      }
%>

<form id="frmStudentFees">
<table border="0" cellpadding="0" cellspacing="0" width="100%"
height="99%">
<tr>
<td widht="*" align="center" valign="top">
<table border="0" cellpadding="10" cellspacing="0" width="100%">
<tr><td> </td></tr>
<tr>
<td bgcolor="White" align="center" colspan="3">
<%
if (studentResultsBean != null)   {
out.print(studentResultsBean.getFullName());
}
%>
   |   
<%
if (studentResultsBean != null)   {
out.print(studentResultsBean.getGrade());
out.print(" - ");
out.print(studentResultsBean.getSection());
}
%>
   |   
<%
if (studentResultsBean != null)   {
out.print(studentFeesBean.getStudentId());
}
%>
  
</td>
</tr>
<tr><td> </td></tr>
<tr valign="middle">
<td align="center">
<table border="1" cellpadding="10" cellspacing="0" width="80%"
bgcolor="White">
<tr id="trbgred">
<td colspan="12" align="left">
  Academic Fees
</td>
</tr>
<tr id="clred">
<td colspan="3" align="center">
      Term One
</td>
<td colspan="3" align="center">
```

```
      Term Two
</td>
<td colspan="3" align="center">
      Term Three
</td>
<td colspan="3" align="center">
      Term Four
</td>
</tr>
<tr id="clred">
<td align="center" width="8%">
      April
</td>
<td align="center" width="8%">
      May
</td>
<td align="center" width="8%">
      June
</td>
<td align="center" width="8%">
      July
</td>
<td align="center" width="8%">
      August
</td>
<td align="center" width="8%">
      September
</td>
<td align="center" width="8%">
      October
</td>
<td align="center" width="8%">
      November
</td>
<td align="center" width="8%">
      December
</td>
<td align="center" width="8%">
      January
</td>
<td align="center" width="8%">
      February
</td>
<td align="center" width="8%">
      March
</td>
</tr>
<tr>
<td align="center">
```

```
<%
if (studentFeesBean != null)   {
out.print(studentFeesBean.getAprAcad());
}
%>
</td>
<td align="center">
<%
if (studentFeesBean != null)   {
out.print(studentFeesBean.getMayAcad());
}
%>
</td>
<td align="center">
<%
if (studentFeesBean != null)   {
out.print(studentFeesBean.getJunAcad());
}
%>
</td>
<td align="center">
<%
if (studentFeesBean != null)   {
out.print(studentFeesBean.getJulAcad());
}
%>
</td>
<td align="center">
<%
if (studentFeesBean != null)   {
out.print(studentFeesBean.getAugAcad());
}
%>
</td>
<td align="center">
<%
if (studentFeesBean != null)   {
out.print(studentFeesBean.getSepAcad());
}
%>
</td>
<td align="center">
<%
if (studentFeesBean != null)   {
out.print(studentFeesBean.getOctAcad());
}
%>
</td>
<td align="center">
```

```
<%
if (studentFeesBean != null)   {
out.print(studentFeesBean.getNovAcad());
}
%>
</td>
<td align="center">
<%
if (studentFeesBean != null)   {
out.print(studentFeesBean.getDecAcad());
}
%>
</td>
<td align="center">
<%
if (studentFeesBean != null)   {
out.print(studentFeesBean.getJanAcad());
}
%>
</td>
<td align="center">
<%
if (studentFeesBean != null)   {
out.print(studentFeesBean.getFebAcad());
}
%>
</td>
<td align="center">
<%
if (studentFeesBean != null)   {
out.print(studentFeesBean.getMarAcad());
}
%>
</td>
</tr>
</table>
</td>
</tr>
<tr valign="middle">
<td align="center">
<table border="1" cellpadding="10" cellspacing="0" width="80%"
                                                      bgcolor="White">
<tr id="trbgred">
<td colspan="12" align="left">
<font size="4">
  Bus Fees
</font>
</td>
</tr>
```

```
<tr id="clred">
<td align="center" width="8%">
      April
</td>
<td align="center" width="8%">
      May
</td>
<td align="center" width="8%">
      June
</td>
<td align="center" width="8%">
      July
</td>
<td align="center" width="8%">
      August
</td>
<td align="center" width="8%">
      September
</td>
<td align="center" width="8%">
      October
</td>
<td align="center" width="8%">
      November
</td>
<td align="center" width="8%">
      December
</td>
<td align="center" width="8%">
      January
</td>
<td align="center" width="8%">
      February
</td>
<td align="center" width="8%">
      March
</td>
</tr>
<tr>
<td align="center">
<%
if (studentFeesBean != null)   {
out.print(studentFeesBean.getAprBus());
}
%>
</td>
<td align="center">
<%
if (studentFeesBean != null)   {
```

```
out.print(studentFeesBean.getMayBus());
}
%>
</td>
<td align="center">
<%
if (studentFeesBean != null)   {
out.print(studentFeesBean.getJunBus());
}
%>
</td>
<td align="center">
<%
if (studentFeesBean != null)   {
out.print(studentFeesBean.getJulBus());
}
%>
</td>
<td align="center">
<%
if (studentFeesBean != null)   {
out.print(studentFeesBean.getAugBus());
}
%>
</td>
<td align="center">
<%
if (studentFeesBean != null)   {
out.print(studentFeesBean.getSepBus());
}
%>
</td>
<td align="center">
<%
if (studentFeesBean != null)   {
out.print(studentFeesBean.getOctBus());
}
%>
</td>
<td align="center">
<%
if (studentFeesBean != null)   {
out.print(studentFeesBean.getNovBus());
}
%>
</td>
<td align="center">
<%
if (studentFeesBean != null)   {
```

```
out.print(studentFeesBean.getDecBus());
}
%>
</td>
<td align="center">
<%
if (studentFeesBean != null)   {
out.print(studentFeesBean.getJanBus());
}
%>
</td>
<td align="center">
<%
if (studentFeesBean != null)   {
out.print(studentFeesBean.getFebBus());
}
%>
</td>
<td align="center">
<%
if (studentFeesBean != null)   {
out.print(studentFeesBean.getMarBus());
}
%>
</td>
</tr>
</table>
</td>
</tr>
<tr valign="middle">
<td align="center">
<table border="1" cellpadding="10" cellspacing="0" width="80%"
                                                      bgcolor="White">
<tr id="trbgred">
<td align="left">
  Other Fees
</td>
</tr>
<tr>
<td align="left">
 
</td>
</tr>
</table>
</td>
</tr>
<tr><td> </td></tr>
</table>
</td>
```

```
</tr>
</table>
</form>
```

This concludes the get student fees use case implementation from end to end. We composed the requirement specifications, we built the prototype, we followed the architecture for the solution, we leveraged the framework, we developed the various java classes, we used the common components like DatabaseService.java, BISStyle.css etc and we built the view with the jsp page.

Use Case: Get student results.

Requirements Specification Reference: R6

Prototype Reference: P5

Prerequisite: The student has to be loaded into context first.

This use case needs to be implemented as per the requirements specification reference above. The UI needs to be as per the prototype reference above. Now that we have complete clarity on use case requirements and UI we will now proceed to implement this use case.

In order to implement this use case, we need to follow the architecture and leverage the framework. To achieve this we will first come up with detailed design and then code it.

The prerequisite for this use case is that a student must already be existing in the context, for this the user must have loaded the student through the load student use case. When the student is loaded, the student id of a particular student is added to the session. You can refer the load student use case for details on this. Lets assume as of now that the student id is existing in the http session. When the user clicks on get student result (either for semester I or for semester II) link either on dashboard or via the menu, the following flow is triggered.

Get student result link is clicked.

The href for these links are

BisControllerServlet?ParameterActionCommand=GetStudentAcademics&sem=1

and

BisControllerServlet?ParameterActionCommand=GetStudentAcademics&sem=2

The ControllerServlet is invoked on the server

In the service method the action command parameter value is read which is GetStudentAcademics.

The execute method for the command processor pertaining to GetStudentAcademics is invoked.

The business logic pertaining to this command processor is executed and a view is returned.

The response is returned to the browser with this view.

The user sees the student results page for a given semester.

The command processor class pertaining to GetStudentAcademics command is GetStudentAcademicsCP. The view pertaining to student detail page is StudentAcademics.jsp. Refer the code below to see the sequence of method calls once the execute method of GetStudentAcademicsCP is called.

For this use case we need the following files.

1. GetStudentAcademicsCP.java
2. StudentAcademicsService.java
3. StudentResultsBean.java
4. StudentAcademics.jsp

GetStudentAcademicsCP.java

```
package com.bis.cp;

import com.bis.session.StudentAcademicsService;
import javax.servlet.http.HttpServletRequest;
import javax.servlet.http.HttpServletResponse;
import javax.servlet.http.HttpSession;
import org.apache.log4j.Logger;

public class GetStudentAcademicsCP extends BisCP implements BisCommand {

      static Logger logger =
      Logger.getLogger(GetStudentAcademicsCP.class);

      public GetStudentAcademicsCP() {
            super();
      }

      public String execute(HttpServletRequest request,
                                    HttpServletResponse response) {
            HttpSession session = request.getSession();
            String strStudentId;
            String strSemester = "1";
            // Defaulting semester to first.
            strSemester = request.getParameter("sem");
            if (session != null)    {
```

```
            strStudentId = (String) session.getAttribute("StudentId");
            if (strStudentId != null &&
            !(strStudentId.trim().equalsIgnoreCase("")) )    {
            StudentAcademicsService studentAcademicsService = new
            StudentAcademicsService();
            try {
            studentAcademicsService.processGetStudentResults(session,
            strSemester);
            strNextNavigation = "StudentAcademics";      //The next
            navigation page upon successful processing.
            } catch (Exception e) {
            logger.error(e.getMessage());
            strNextNavigation = "Error";      //The next navigation page
            upon failed processing.
            }
            }
            else {
            // strStudentId is null, first entry to the page.
            strNextNavigation = "StudentAcademics";
            }
            }
            else {
            // session is null. Valid session doesn't exsit. Redirect to
            Login page.
            strNextNavigation = "Login";
            }
        return strNextNavigation;
        }
}
```

The execute method performs the following actions:

⇒ Gets the Http session for the logged in user.

⇒ Gets the semester the user has selected as a parameter value.

⇒ Gets the student id from the session.

⇒ Creates an instance of StudentAcademicsService and invokes processGetStudentResults method.

⇒ Sets the next navigation to StudentAcademics.

StudentAcademicsService.java

```
package com.bis.session;

import com.bis.beans.StudentResultsBean;
import com.bis.db.DatabaseService;
import java.sql.Connection;
import java.sql.ResultSet;
import java.sql.SQLException;
import java.sql.Statement;
import javax.servlet.http.HttpSession;
import org.apache.log4j.Logger;

public class StudentAcademicsService implements BisService {

      static Logger logger =
      Logger.getLogger(StudentAcademicsService.class);

      public StudentAcademicsService() {
            super();
      }

      public void processGetStudentResults(HttpSession session,
                                                String strSemester) {
            String strStudentId = (String)
            session.getAttribute("StudentId");
            StudentResultsBean studentResultsBean;
            studentResultsBean = new StudentResultsBean();

            if (strStudentId != null) {
                  studentResultsBean.setStudentId(strStudentId); // This
                  is mandatory before calling the next method.
                  populateStudentResults(studentResultsBean,
                  strSemester);
                  session.setAttribute("studentResultsBean",
                  studentResultsBean);
            } else {
                  logger.error("Student Id is null");
            }
      }

      private void populateStudentResults(StudentResultsBean
                              studentResultsBean, String strSemester) {
            String strStudentId;
            strStudentId = studentResultsBean.getStudentId();
            Connection connection = null;
            Statement statement = null;
            ResultSet resultSet = null;
```

```
      StringBuffer sbQuery = new StringBuffer();
      String strFirstName = "";
      String strMiddleName = "";
      String strLastName = "";
      String strFullName = "";

sbQuery.append("SELECT \n" +
"             SD.FIRST_NAME, SD.MIDDLE_NAME, SD.LAST_NAME, SD.GRADE,
SD.SECTION, \n" +
"             SR.ENGLISH_GRADE, SR.MATHS_GRADE, SR.SCIENCE_GRADE,
SR.SOCIAL_GRADE, \n" +
"             SR.LANG2_GRADE, SR.LANG3_GRADE, SR.COMPSC_GRADE,
SR.ARTS_GRADE, \n" +
"             SR.MUSIC_GRADE, SR.DANCE_GRADE, SR.PHYSICALEDU_GRADE,
SR.VALUEEDU_GRADE,\n" +
"             SR.SCHOOLPROJECT_GRADE,\n" +
"             SR.ENGLISH_REM, SR.MATHS_REM, SR.SCIENCE_REM,
SR.SOCIAL_REM, \n" +
"             SR.LANG2_REM, SR.LANG3_REM, SR.COMPSC_REM,
SR.ARTS_REM, \n" +
"             SR.MUSIC_REM, SR.DANCE_REM, SR.PHYSICALEDU_REM,
SR.VALUEEDU_REM,\n" +
"             SR.SCHOOLPROJECT_REM,            \n" +
"             CSR.COLLAB_LEARNING, CSR.COMMUNICATION_SKILLS,
CSR.COMMUNITY_CONSC, \n" +
"             CSR.COMPREHENSIVE_GROWTH, CSR.CREATIVE_THINKING,
CSR.CRITICAL_THINKING,\n" +
"             CSR.EMO_QUO, CSR.HEALTH_QUO, CSR.INTELLI_QUO,
CSR.SOCIAL_QUO, \n" +
"             CSR.SCHOLASTICPERFORMANCE_REM,
CSR.COSCHOLASTICPERFORMANCE_REM\n" +
"FROM \n" +
"             STUDENT_DETAILS SD, SCHOLASTIC_RESULTS SR,
COSCHOLASTIC_RESULTS CSR\n" +
"             \n" +
"WHERE \n" +
"             SD.STUDENT_ID = ");
sbQuery.append(" '"+strStudentId+"' ");
sbQuery.append("AND SR.STUDENT_ID = ");
sbQuery.append(" '"+strStudentId+"' ");
sbQuery.append(" AND SR.SEMESTER = ");
sbQuery.append(" '"+strSemester+"' ");
sbQuery.append("AND CSR.STUDENT_ID = ");
sbQuery.append(" '"+strStudentId+"' ");
sbQuery.append(" AND CSR.SEMESTER = ");
sbQuery.append(" '"+strSemester+"' ");
if (strStudentId != null) {
connection = DatabaseService.getDBConnection();
try {
```

```
statement = connection.createStatement();
resultSet = statement.executeQuery(sbQuery.toString());
resultSet.next(); // Expecting only one record.
strFirstName = resultSet.getString("FIRST_NAME");
strMiddleName = resultSet.getString("MIDDLE_NAME");
strLastName = resultSet.getString("LAST_NAME");
if (strFirstName != null) {
strFullName = strFirstName;
}
if (strMiddleName != null) {
strFullName = strFullName + " " + strMiddleName;
}
if (strLastName != null) {
strFullName = strFullName + " " + strLastName;
}
studentResultsBean.setFullName(strFullName);
studentResultsBean.setGrade(resultSet.getString("GRADE"));
studentResultsBean.setSection(resultSet.getString("SECTION"));
studentResultsBean.setEnglishGrade(resultSet.getString("ENGLISH_GRA
DE"));
studentResultsBean.setMathsGrade(resultSet.getString("MATHS_GRADE")
);
studentResultsBean.setScienceGrade(resultSet.getString("SCIENCE_GRA
DE"));
studentResultsBean.setSocialGrade(resultSet.getString("SOCIAL_GRADE
"));
studentResultsBean.setLang2Grade(resultSet.getString("LANG2_GRADE")
);
studentResultsBean.setLang3Grade(resultSet.getString("LANG3_GRADE")
);
studentResultsBean.setCompScGrade(resultSet.getString("COMPSC_GRADE
"));
studentResultsBean.setArtsGrade(resultSet.getString("ARTS_GRADE"));
studentResultsBean.setMusicGrade(resultSet.getString("MUSIC_GRADE")
);
studentResultsBean.setDanceGrade(resultSet.getString("DANCE_GRADE")
);
studentResultsBean.setPhyEduGrade(resultSet.getString("PHYSICALEDU_
GRADE"));
studentResultsBean.setValEduGrade(resultSet.getString("VALUEEDU_GRA
DE"));
studentResultsBean.setSchProjGrade(resultSet.getString("SCHOOLPROJE
CT_GRADE"));
studentResultsBean.setEnglishRem(resultSet.getString("ENGLISH_REM")
);
studentResultsBean.setMathsRem(resultSet.getString("MATHS_REM"));
studentResultsBean.setScienceRem(resultSet.getString("SCIENCE_REM")
);
studentResultsBean.setSocialRem(resultSet.getString("SOCIAL_REM"));
```

```
studentResultsBean.setLang2Rem(resultSet.getString("LANG2_REM"));
studentResultsBean.setLang3Rem(resultSet.getString("LANG3_REM"));
studentResultsBean.setCompScRem(resultSet.getString("COMPSC_REM"));
studentResultsBean.setArtsRem(resultSet.getString("ARTS_REM"));
studentResultsBean.setMusicRem(resultSet.getString("MUSIC_REM"));
studentResultsBean.setDanceRem(resultSet.getString("DANCE_REM"));
studentResultsBean.setPhyEduRem(resultSet.getString("PHYSICALEDU_RE
M"));
studentResultsBean.setValEduRem(resultSet.getString("VALUEEDU_REM")
);
studentResultsBean.setSchProjRem(resultSet.getString("SCHOOLPROJECT
_REM"));
studentResultsBean.setCollabLearning(resultSet.getString("COLLAB_LE
ARNING"));
studentResultsBean.setCommSkills(resultSet.getString("COMMUNICATION
_SKILLS"));
studentResultsBean.setCommunityConsc(resultSet.getString("COMMUNITY
_CONSC"));
studentResultsBean.setCompGrowth(resultSet.getString("COMPREHENSIVE
_GROWTH"));
studentResultsBean.setCreativeThinking(resultSet.getString("CREATIV
E_THINKING"));
studentResultsBean.setCriticalThinking(resultSet.getString("CRITICA
L_THINKING"));
studentResultsBean.setEmoQuo(resultSet.getString("EMO_QUO"));
studentResultsBean.setHealthQuo(resultSet.getString("HEALTH_QUO"));
studentResultsBean.setIntelliQuo(resultSet.getString("INTELLI_QUO")
);
studentResultsBean.setSocialQuo(resultSet.getString("SOCIAL_QUO"));
studentResultsBean.setScholasticPerformanceRem(resultSet.getString(
"SCHOLASTICPERFORMANCE_REM"));
studentResultsBean.setCoScholasticPerformanceRem(resultSet.getStrin
g("COSCHOLASTICPERFORMANCE_REM"));
} catch (SQLException sqle) {
logger.error(sqle.getMessage());
} finally {
DatabaseService.closeDBResouces(statement, resultSet);
DatabaseService.releaseDBConnection();  // Releasing database
connection.
}
} else {
logger.error("Student Id is null");
}
}

      public String getServiceName() {
            return this.getClass().getName();
      }
}
```

The processGetStudentResults method performs the following tasks:

⇒ Gets the student id from the session.

⇒ Creates an instance of StudentResultsBean.

⇒ Calls setter of StudentResultsBean instance for setting student id.

⇒ Invokes the private method populateStudentResults.

⇒ Adds the populated StudentResultsBean instance to session to be consumed by the view.

The populateStudentResults method performs the following tasks:

⇒ Cooks up a dynamic query for a given student and semester to fetch the results from the database.

⇒ Leverages the DatabaseService class to get the database connection.

⇒ Calls setter of StudentResultsBean instance for setting the results fields.

⇒ Uses the finally block to close all the resources related to database.

StudentResultsBean.java

The StudentResultsBean class is just a simple java bean with private fields with their getters and setters. Please refer the class diagram and below source code for understanding this class.

```
package com.bis.beans;

public class StudentResultsBean extends StudentBean {

      public StudentResultsBean() {
            super();
      }

      private java.lang.String englishGrade;
      private java.lang.String mathsGrade;
```

```
private java.lang.String scienceGrade;
private java.lang.String socialGrade;
private java.lang.String lang2Grade;
private java.lang.String lang3Grade;
private java.lang.String compScGrade;
private java.lang.String artsGrade;
private java.lang.String musicGrade;
private java.lang.String danceGrade;
private java.lang.String phyEduGrade;
private java.lang.String valEduGrade;
private java.lang.String schProjGrade;
private java.lang.String englishRem;
private java.lang.String mathsRem;
private java.lang.String scienceRem;
private java.lang.String socialRem;
private java.lang.String lang2Rem;
private java.lang.String lang3Rem;
private java.lang.String compScRem;
private java.lang.String artsRem;
private java.lang.String musicRem;
private java.lang.String danceRem;
private java.lang.String phyEduRem;
private java.lang.String valEduRem;
private java.lang.String schProjRem;
private java.lang.String collabLearning;
private java.lang.String commSkills;
private java.lang.String communityConsc;
private java.lang.String compGrowth;
private java.lang.String creativeThinking;
private java.lang.String criticalThinking;
private java.lang.String emoQuo;
private java.lang.String healthQuo;
private java.lang.String intelliQuo;
private java.lang.String socialQuo;
private java.lang.String scholasticPerformanceRem;
private java.lang.String coScholasticPerformanceRem;

public void setEnglishGrade(String englishGrade) {
      this.englishGrade = englishGrade;
}

public String getEnglishGrade() {
      return englishGrade;
}

public void setMathsGrade(String mathsGrade) {
      this.mathsGrade = mathsGrade;
}
```

```
	public String getMathsGrade() {
		return mathsGrade;
	}

	public void setScienceGrade(String scienceGrade) {
		this.scienceGrade = scienceGrade;
	}

	public String getScienceGrade() {
		return scienceGrade;
	}

	public void setSocialGrade(String socialGrade) {
		this.socialGrade = socialGrade;
	}

	public String getSocialGrade() {
		return socialGrade;
	}

	public void setLang2Grade(String lang2Grade) {
		this.lang2Grade = lang2Grade;
	}

	public String getLang2Grade() {
		return lang2Grade;
	}

	public void setLang3Grade(String lang3Grade) {
		this.lang3Grade = lang3Grade;
	}

	public String getLang3Grade() {
		return lang3Grade;
	}

	public void setCompScGrade(String compScGrade) {
		this.compScGrade = compScGrade;
	}

	public String getCompScGrade() {
		return compScGrade;
	}

	public void setArtsGrade(String artsGrade) {
		this.artsGrade = artsGrade;
	}

	public String getArtsGrade() {
```

```
        return artsGrade;
    }

    public void setMusicGrade(String musicGrade) {
        this.musicGrade = musicGrade;
    }

    public String getMusicGrade() {
        return musicGrade;
    }

    public void setDanceGrade(String danceGrade) {
        this.danceGrade = danceGrade;
    }

    public String getDanceGrade() {
        return danceGrade;
    }

    public void setPhyEduGrade(String phyEduGrade) {
        this.phyEduGrade = phyEduGrade;
    }

    public String getPhyEduGrade() {
        return phyEduGrade;
    }

    public void setValEduGrade(String valEduGrade) {
        this.valEduGrade = valEduGrade;
    }

    public String getValEduGrade() {
        return valEduGrade;
    }

    public void setSchProjGrade(String schProjGrade) {
        this.schProjGrade = schProjGrade;
    }

    public String getSchProjGrade() {
        return schProjGrade;
    }

    public void setEnglishRem(String englishRem) {
        this.englishRem = englishRem;
    }

    public String getEnglishRem() {
        return englishRem;
```

```
	}

	public void setMathsRem(String mathsRem) {
		this.mathsRem = mathsRem;
	}

	public String getMathsRem() {
		return mathsRem;
	}

	public void setScienceRem(String scienceRem) {
		this.scienceRem = scienceRem;
	}

	public String getScienceRem() {
		return scienceRem;
	}

	public void setSocialRem(String socialRem) {
		this.socialRem = socialRem;
	}

	public String getSocialRem() {
		return socialRem;
	}

	public void setLang2Rem(String lang2Rem) {
		this.lang2Rem = lang2Rem;
	}

	public String getLang2Rem() {
		return lang2Rem;
	}

	public void setLang3Rem(String lang3Rem) {
		this.lang3Rem = lang3Rem;
	}

	public String getLang3Rem() {
		return lang3Rem;
	}

	public void setCompScRem(String compScRem) {
		this.compScRem = compScRem;
	}

	public String getCompScRem() {
		return compScRem;
	}
```

```
public void setArtsRem(String artsRem) {
      this.artsRem = artsRem;
}

public String getArtsRem() {
      return artsRem;
}

public void setMusicRem(String musicRem) {
      this.musicRem = musicRem;
}

public String getMusicRem() {
      return musicRem;
}

public void setDanceRem(String danceRem) {
      this.danceRem = danceRem;
}

public String getDanceRem() {
      return danceRem;
}

public void setPhyEduRem(String phyEduRem) {
      this.phyEduRem = phyEduRem;
}

public String getPhyEduRem() {
      return phyEduRem;
}

public void setValEduRem(String valEduRem) {
      this.valEduRem = valEduRem;
}

public String getValEduRem() {
      return valEduRem;
}

public void setSchProjRem(String schProjRem) {
      this.schProjRem = schProjRem;
}

public String getSchProjRem() {
      return schProjRem;
}
```

```
    public void setCollabLearning(String collabLearning) {
          this.collabLearning = collabLearning;
    }

    public String getCollabLearning() {
          return collabLearning;
    }

    public void setCommSkills(String commSkills) {
          this.commSkills = commSkills;
    }

    public String getCommSkills() {
          return commSkills;
    }

    public void setCommunityConsc(String communityConsc) {
          this.communityConsc = communityConsc;
    }

    public String getCommunityConsc() {
          return communityConsc;
    }

    public void setCompGrowth(String compGrowth) {
          this.compGrowth = compGrowth;
    }

    public String getCompGrowth() {
          return compGrowth;
    }

    public void setCreativeThinking(String creativeThinking) {
          this.creativeThinking = creativeThinking;
    }

    public String getCreativeThinking() {
          return creativeThinking;
    }

    public void setCriticalThinking(String criticalThinking) {
          this.criticalThinking = criticalThinking;
    }

    public String getCriticalThinking() {
          return criticalThinking;
    }

    public void setEmoQuo(String emoQuo) {
```

```
		this.emoQuo = emoQuo;
	}

	public String getEmoQuo() {
		return emoQuo;
	}

	public void setHealthQuo(String healthQuo) {
		this.healthQuo = healthQuo;
	}

	public String getHealthQuo() {
		return healthQuo;
	}

	public void setIntelliQuo(String intelliQuo) {
		this.intelliQuo = intelliQuo;
	}

	public String getIntelliQuo() {
		return intelliQuo;
	}

	public void setSocialQuo(String socialQuo) {
		this.socialQuo = socialQuo;
	}

	public String getSocialQuo() {
		return socialQuo;
	}

	public void setScholasticPerformanceRem(String
	scholasticPerformanceRem) {
		this.scholasticPerformanceRem = scholasticPerformanceRem;
	}

	public String getScholasticPerformanceRem() {
		return scholasticPerformanceRem;
	}

	public void setCoScholasticPerformanceRem(String
	coScholasticPerformanceRem) {
		this.coScholasticPerformanceRem = coScholasticPerformanceRem;
	}

	public String getCoScholasticPerformanceRem() {
		return coScholasticPerformanceRem;
	}
}
```

StudentAcademics.jsp

This jsp is dynamically included in BisHome.jsp as a result for get student results use case invocation through user interaction with the UI.

Till now we have seen that the command for student results goes form UI as a result of user interaction. Then the controller servlet calls get student academics command processor and then the student academics service is leveraged. Finally, we get the results packaged as an instance of StudentResultsBean. This bean is now available in the session. In the StudentAcademics.jsp file we fetch this bean from the session. And from this bean we fetch all the information related to student results using the getters. The static part of the jsp remains the same as that of the prototype page. Only the dynamic part is added using the bean from the session. Hence, the end user sees the view for a given student and semester with all the academic results related details.

Here is the source code for the StudentAcademics.jsp file.

```
<%@ page import="com.bis.beans.StudentResultsBean"%>
<%@ page import="java.util.Hashtable, java.util.Enumeration"%>

<%
      StudentResultsBean studentResultsBean = null;
      if (session != null) {
            studentResultsBean = (StudentResultsBean)
            session.getAttribute("studentResultsBean");
      }
%>

<form id="frmStudAcads" name="frmStudAcads" action="BisControllerServlet"
method="POST">
<input type="hidden" name="ParameterActionCommand"
value="GetStudentAcademics"></input>
<input type="hidden" name="sem" value="<%=
request.getParameter("sem")%>"></input>
<table border="0" cellpadding="0" cellspacing="0" width="100%"
height="99%">
<tr><td> </td></tr>
<tr><td> </td></tr>
<tr>
<td widht="*" align="center" valign="top">
<table border="0" cellpadding="4" cellspacing="0" width="100%">
<tr>
```

```
<td bgcolor="White" align="center" colspan="3">
<font size="4">
<%
if (studentResultsBean != null)   {
out.print(studentResultsBean.getFullName());
}
%>
   |   
<%
String strSem=request.getParameter("sem");
if ( strSem != null )   {
if (strSem.equalsIgnoreCase("1"))   {
strSem = "Semester - I";
}
else {
strSem = "Semester - II";
}
}
else {
strSem = "Semester - I";
}
out.print(strSem);
%>
   |   
<%
if (studentResultsBean != null)   {
out.print(studentResultsBean.getGrade());
out.print(" - ");
out.print(studentResultsBean.getSection());
}
%>
   |   
<%
if (studentResultsBean != null)   {
out.print(studentResultsBean.getStudentId());
}
%>
  
</font>
</td>
</tr>
<tr><td> </td></tr>
<tr><td> </td></tr>
<tr valign="top">
<td align="left" width="50%">
<table border="1" cellpadding="5" cellspacing="0" width="100%"
bgcolor="White">
<tr>
<td colspan="3" align="center" id="trbgred">
```

```
Scholastic Performance - Core Curriculum - Assessment
</td>
</tr>
<tr id="clred">
<td width="20%" align="center">  Subject</td>
<td width="10%" align="center">Grade</td>
<td width="*" align="center">Remarks</td>
</tr>
<tr>
<td align="left" id="clred">  English</td>
<td align="center">
<%
if (studentResultsBean != null)   {
out.print(studentResultsBean.getEnglishGrade());
}
%>
</td>
<td align="left">
<%
if (studentResultsBean != null)   {
out.print(studentResultsBean.getEnglishRem());
}
%>
</td>
</tr>
<tr>
<td align="left" id="clred">  Mathematics</td>
<td align="center">
<%
if (studentResultsBean != null)   {
out.print(studentResultsBean.getMathsGrade());
}
%>
</td>
<td align="left">
<%
if (studentResultsBean != null)   {
out.print(studentResultsBean.getMathsRem());
}
%>
</td>
</tr>
<tr>
<td align="left" id="clred">  Science</td>
<td align="center">
<%
if (studentResultsBean != null)   {
out.print(studentResultsBean.getScienceGrade());
}
```

```
%>
</td>
<td align="left">
<%
if (studentResultsBean != null)   {
out.print(studentResultsBean.getScienceRem());
}
%>
</td>
</tr>
<tr>
<td align="left" id="clred">  Social Science</td>
<td align="center">
<%
if (studentResultsBean != null)   {
out.print(studentResultsBean.getSocialGrade());
}
%>
</td>
<td align="left">
<%
if (studentResultsBean != null)   {
out.print(studentResultsBean.getSocialRem());
}
%>
</td>
</tr>
<tr>
<td align="left" id="clred">  Language II</td>
<td align="center">
<%
if (studentResultsBean != null)   {
out.print(studentResultsBean.getLang2Grade());
}
%>
</td>
<td align="left">
<%
if (studentResultsBean != null)   {
out.print(studentResultsBean.getLang2Rem());
}
%>
</td>
</tr>
<tr>
<td align="left" id="clred">  Language III</td>
<td align="center">
<%
if (studentResultsBean != null)   {
```

```
out.print(studentResultsBean.getLang3Grade());
}
%>
</td>
<td align="left">
<%
if (studentResultsBean != null)   {
out.print(studentResultsBean.getLang3Rem());
}
%>
</td>
</tr>
<tr>
<td align="left" id="clred">  Computer Science</td>
<td align="center">
<%
if (studentResultsBean != null)   {
out.print(studentResultsBean.getCompScGrade());
}
%>
</td>
<td align="left">
<%
if (studentResultsBean != null)   {
out.print(studentResultsBean.getCompScRem());
}
%>
</td>
</tr>
</table>
</td>
<td align="left" width="*" colspan="2">
<table border="1" cellpadding="5" cellspacing="0" width="100%"
bgcolor="White">
<tr>
<td colspan="3" align="center" id="trbgred">Scholastic Performance - Co
Curriculum -
Assessment</td>
</tr>
<tr id="clred">
<td width="20%" align="center">  Subject</td>
<td width="10%" align="center">Grade</td>
<td width="*" align="center">Remarks</td>
</tr>
<tr>
<td align="left" id="clred">  Arts</td>
<td align="center">
<%
if (studentResultsBean != null)   {
```

```
out.print(studentResultsBean.getArtsGrade());
}
%>
</td>
<td align="left">
<%
if (studentResultsBean != null)   {
out.print(studentResultsBean.getArtsRem());
}
%>
</td>
</tr>
<tr>
<td align="left" id="clred">  Music</td>
<td align="center">
<%
if (studentResultsBean != null)   {
out.print(studentResultsBean.getMusicGrade());
}
%>
</td>
<td align="left">
<%
if (studentResultsBean != null)   {
out.print(studentResultsBean.getMusicRem());
}
%>
</td>
</tr>
<tr>
<td align="left" id="clred">  Dance</td>
<td align="center">
<%
if (studentResultsBean != null)   {
out.print(studentResultsBean.getDanceGrade());
}
%>
</td>
<td align="left">
<%
if (studentResultsBean != null)   {
out.print(studentResultsBean.getDanceRem());
}
%>
</td>
</tr>
<tr>
<td align="left" id="clred">  Physical Education</td>
<td align="center">
```

```
<%
if (studentResultsBean != null)   {
out.print(studentResultsBean.getPhyEduGrade());
}
%>
</td>
<td align="left">
<%
if (studentResultsBean != null)   {
out.print(studentResultsBean.getPhyEduRem());
}
%>
</td>
</tr>
<tr>
<td align="left" id="clred">  Value Education</td>
<td align="center">
<%
if (studentResultsBean != null)   {
out.print(studentResultsBean.getValEduGrade());
}
%>
</td>
<td align="left">
<%
if (studentResultsBean != null)   {
out.print(studentResultsBean.getValEduRem());
}
%>
</td>
</tr>
<tr>
<td align="left" id="clred">  School Project</td>
<td align="center">
<%
if (studentResultsBean != null)   {
out.print(studentResultsBean.getSchProjGrade());
}
%>
</td>
<td align="left">
<%
if (studentResultsBean != null)   {
out.print(studentResultsBean.getSchProjRem());
}
%>
</td>
</tr>
<tr>
```

```
<td align="left" id="clred">  Other</td>
<td align="center">-</td>
<td align="left">-</td>
</tr>
</table>
</td>
</tr>
<tr valign="top">
<td align="left" width="50%">
<table border="1" cellpadding="5" cellspacing="0" width="100%"
bgcolor="White">
<tr>
<td colspan="2" align="center" id="trbgred">Co - Scholastic
Activities</td>
</tr>
<tr>
<td align="left" id="clred" width="30%">  Critical
Thinking</td>
<td align="left" width="*">
<%
if (studentResultsBean != null)   {
out.print(studentResultsBean.getCreativeThinking());
}
%>
</td>
</tr>
<tr>
<td align="left" id="clred">  Creative Thinking</td>
<td align="left">
<%
if (studentResultsBean != null)   {
out.print(studentResultsBean.getCreativeThinking());
}
%>
</td>
</tr>
<tr>
<td align="left" id="clred">  Collaborative Learning</td>
<td align="left">
<%
if (studentResultsBean != null)   {
out.print(studentResultsBean.getCollabLearning());
}
%>
</td>
</tr>
<tr>
<td align="left" id="clred">  Communication Skills</td>
<td align="left">
```

```
<%
if (studentResultsBean != null)   {
out.print(studentResultsBean.getCommSkills());
}
%>
</td>
</tr>
<tr>
<td align="left" id="clred">  Comprehensive Growth</td>
<td align="left">
<%
if (studentResultsBean != null)   {
out.print(studentResultsBean.getCompGrowth());
}
%>
</td>
</tr>
<tr>
<td align="left" id="clred">  IQ - Intelligence Quotient</td>
<td align="left">
<%
if (studentResultsBean != null)   {
out.print(studentResultsBean.getIntelliQuo());
}
%>
</td>
</tr>
<tr>
<td align="left" id="clred">  EQ - Emotional Quotient</td>
<td align="left">
<%
if (studentResultsBean != null)   {
out.print(studentResultsBean.getEmoQuo());
}
%>
</td>
</tr>
<tr>
<td align="left" id="clred">  EQ - Social Quotient</td>
<td align="left">
<%
if (studentResultsBean != null)   {
out.print(studentResultsBean.getSocialQuo());
}
%>
</td>
</tr>
<tr>
<td align="left" id="clred">  EQ - Health Quotient</td>
```

```
<td align="left">
<%
if (studentResultsBean != null)    {
out.print(studentResultsBean.getHealthQuo());
}
%>
</td>
</tr>
<tr>
<td align="left" id="clred">  EQ - Community Consciousness</td>
<td align="left">
<%
if (studentResultsBean != null)    {
out.print(studentResultsBean.getCommunityConsc());
}
%>
</td>
</tr>
</table>
</td>
<td width="*" valign="top">
<table border="1" cellpadding="5" cellspacing="0" width="100%"
bgcolor="White">
<tr>
<td colspan="2" align="center" id="trbgred">Synthesis and
Recommendations</td>
</tr>
<tr height="152" valign="top">
<td align="left" width="30%" id="clred">  Scholastic
Performance</td>
<td width="*" align="left">
<%
if (studentResultsBean != null)    {
out.print(studentResultsBean.getScholasticPerformanceRem());
}
%>
</td>
</tr>
<tr height="152" valign="top">
<td align="left" id="clred">  Co - Scholastic Performance</td>
<td align="left">
<%
if (studentResultsBean != null)    {
out.print(studentResultsBean.getCoScholasticPerformanceRem());
}
%>
</td>
</tr>
</table>
```

```
</td>
</tr>
</table>
</td>
</tr>
<tr><td> </td></tr>
<tr><td> </td></tr>
</table>
</form>
```

This concludes the get student results use case implementation from end to end. We composed the requirement specifications, we built the prototype, we followed the architecture for the solution, we leveraged the framework, we developed the various java classes, we used the common components like DatabaseService.java, BISStyle.css etc and we built the view with the jsp page.

Use Case: Help pages.

Requirements Specification Reference: R12

Prototype Reference: P11

Prerequisite: The user has to be logged in.

This use case needs to be implemented as per the requirements specification reference above. The UI needs to be as per the prototype reference above. Now that we have complete clarity on use case requirements and UI we will now proceed to implement this use case.

In order to implement this use case, we just need to add a link to the dashboard page as well has to the global Help menu. These are just plain static html pages and hence we do not trigger any business logic flow on the server side. The html link only loads the requested html page from the public_html folder under the exploded application folder when deployed in Apache Tomcat server. In our sample application we have only one static html page for help module. And this page will be displayed as a pop up window.

Get legends help page link is clicked.

The href for the link is \bis\jsp\ResultsLegend.html

The requested page ResultsLegend.html is displayed as a pop up window.

For this use case we need only one html page and that is ResultsLegend.html

BisHome.jsp code for launching results legend html page pop up window.

```
<a onclick="javascript:void
window.open('ResultsLegend.html','1247','width=1600,height=800,tool
bar=0,menubar=0,location=100,status=0,scrollbars=0,resizable=1,left
=180,top=140');return false;">
<span>Legend</span>
</a>
```

ResultsLegend.html

```
<!DOCTYPE html>
<html>

<head>
	<title>BIS Help Legend</title>
	<link rel="stylesheet" type="text/css"
	href="resources/css/BISStyle.css"></link>
</head>

<body>
	<form id="frmHome">
	<table border="0" cellpadding="0" cellspacing="0" width="100%"
	height="99%">                                 <tr>
	<td widht="*" align="center" valign="top">
	<table border="1" cellpadding="10" cellspacing="0" width="100%">
	<tr>
	<td bgcolor="White" align="center" id="clred" colspan="3">
	<font size="4">Help - Legend</font>
	</td>
	</tr>
	<tr valign="middle">
	<td align="center">
	<table border="1" cellpadding="4" cellspacing="0" width="80%"
	bgcolor="White">
	<tr id="trbgred">
	<td colspan="12" align="left">
	<font size="4">
	  Scholastic Performance - Core Curriculum
	</font>
```

```
</td>
</tr>
<tr>
<td align="center">
Marks Range
</td>
<td align="center">
Absolute Grade
</td>
<td align="center">
Grade Point
</td>
</tr>
<tr>
<td align="center">
81 - 100
</td>
<td align="center">
A
</td>
<td align="center">
10
</td>
</tr>
<tr>
<td align="center">
61 - 80
</td>
<td align="center">
B
</td>
<td align="center">
8
</td>
</tr>
<tr>
<td align="center">
41 - 60
</td>
<td align="center">
C
</td>
<td align="center">
6
</td>
</tr>
<tr>
<td align="center">
21 - 40
```

```
</td>
<td align="center">
D
</td>
<td align="center">
4
</td>
</tr>
<tr>
<td align="center">
00 - 20
</td>
<td align="center">
E
</td>
<td align="center">
-
</td>
</tr>
</table>
</td>
</tr>
<tr valign="middle">
<td align="center">
<table border="1" cellpadding="4" cellspacing="0" width="80%"
bgcolor="White">
<tr id="trbgred">
<td colspan="12" align="left">
<font size="4">
  Scholastic Performance - Co Curriculum
</font>
</td>
</tr>
<tr>
<td align="center" width="*">
Music
</td>
<td align="center" width="15%">
A+
</td>
<td align="center" width="15%">
A
</td>
<td align="center" width="15%">
B+
</td>
<td align="center" width="15%">
B
</td>
```

```
<td align="center" width="15%">
C
</td>
</tr>
<tr>
<td align="center">
Dance
</td>
<td align="center">
A+
</td>
<td align="center">
A
</td>
<td align="center">
B+
</td>
<td align="center">
B
</td>
<td align="center">
C
</td>
</tr>
<tr>
<td align="center">
Arts
</td>
<td align="center">
A+
</td>
<td align="center">
A
</td>
<td align="center">
B+
</td>
<td align="center">
B
</td>
<td align="center">
C
</td>
</tr>
<tr>
<td align="center">
Physical Education
</td>
<td align="center">
```

```
A+
</td>
<td align="center">
A
</td>
<td align="center">
B+
</td>
<td align="center">
B
</td>
<td align="center">
C
</td>
</tr>
<tr>
<td align="center">
Value Education
</td>
<td align="center">
A+
</td>
<td align="center">
A
</td>
<td align="center">
B+
</td>
<td align="center">
B
</td>
<td align="center">
C
</td>
</tr>
</table>
</td>
</tr>
<tr valign="middle">
<td align="center">
<table border="1" cellpadding="4" cellspacing="0" width="80%"
bgcolor="White">
<tr id="trbgred">
<td colspan="12" align="left">
<font size="4">
  Co - Curriculum
</font>
</td>
</tr>
```

```
<tr>
<td align="center">
Code
</td>
<td align="center">
Description
</td>
<td align="center">
Score
</td>
</tr>
<tr>
<td align="center">
LA
</td>
<td align="center">
Latent
</td>
<td align="center">
&lt; 3
</td>
</tr>
<tr>
<td align="center">
EM
</td>
<td align="center">
Emerging
</td>
<td align="center">
4 - 5
</td>
</tr>
<tr>
<td align="center">
DE
</td>
<td align="center">
Developing
</td>
<td align="center">
6 - 8
</td>
</tr>
<tr>
<td align="center">
AP
</td>
<td align="center">
```

```
        Appreciable
        </td>
        <td align="center">
        9 - 11
        </td>
        </tr>
        <tr>
        <td align="center">
        AC
        </td>
        <td align="center">
        Accelerating
        </td>
        <td align="center">
        12 - 13
        </td>
        </tr>
        <tr>
        <td align="center">
        OS
        </td>
        <td align="center">
        Outstanding
        </td>
        <td align="center">
        14 - 15
        </td>
        </tr>
        </table>
        </td>
        </tr>
        <tr>
        <td bgcolor="White" colspan="3"> </td>
        </tr>
        </table>
        </td>
        </tr>
        </table>
        </form>
</body>
</html>
```

Use Case: Report by class.

Requirements Specification Reference: R11

Prototype Reference: P10

Prerequisite: The user has to be logged in and must have the role which has the privilege to access report by class functionality.

This use case needs to be implemented as per the requirements specification reference above. The UI needs to be as per the prototype reference above. Now that we have complete clarity on use case requirements and UI we will now proceed to implement this use case.

In order to implement this use case, we need to follow the architecture and leverage the framework. To achieve this we will first come up with detailed design and then code it.

The prerequisite for this use case is that the user must logged in and belong to the role which has access to reports. When the user clicks on reports by class link either on dashboard or via the menu, the following flow is triggered.

The user clicks the report by class link

↓

The href for this link is

BisControllerServlet?ParameterActionCommand=GetReportByClass

↓

The ControllerServlet is invoked on the server

↓

In the service method the action command parameter value is read which is GetReportByClass

↓

The execute method for the command processor pertaining to GetReportByClass is invoked

↓

The business logic pertaining to this command processor is executed and a view is returned

↓

The response is returned to the browser with this view

↓

The user sees the report by class page

↓

The users selects the report criteria and clicks generate report.

The command processor class pertaining to GetReportByClass command is GetReportByClass CP. The view pertaining to student detail page is ReportByClass.jsp. Now, lets see the sequence of method calls once the execute method of GetReportByClassCP is called. Below is the sequence diagram from this use case.

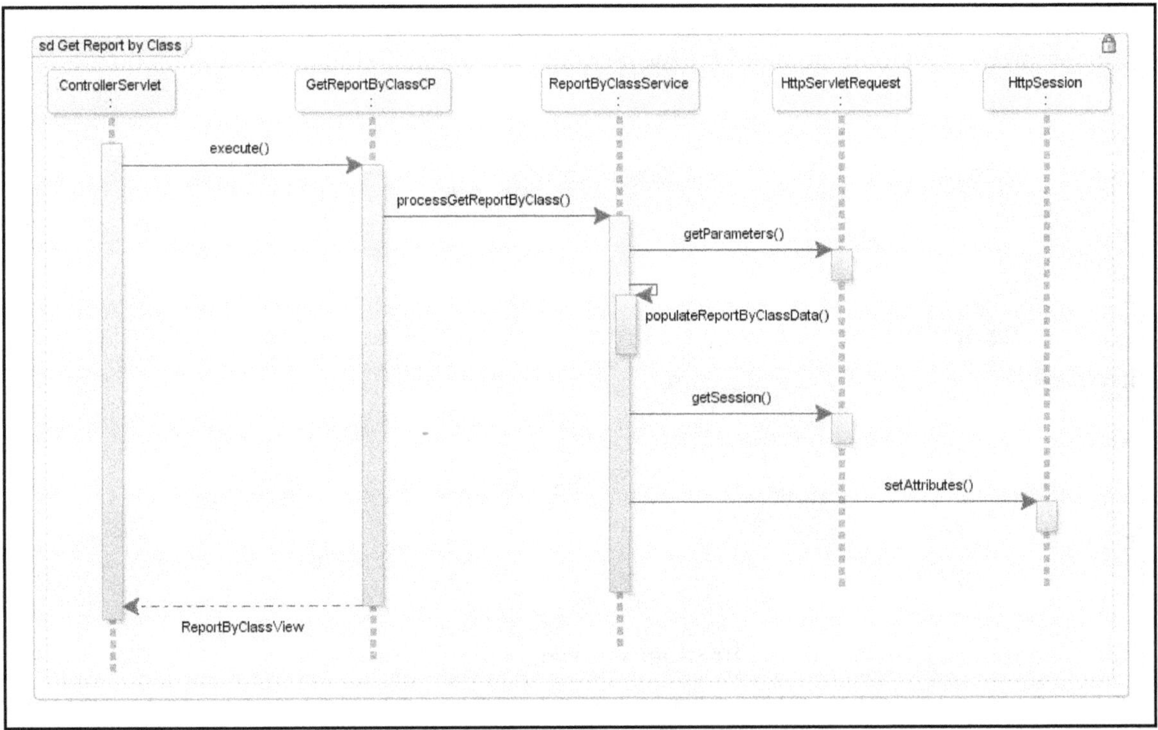

The execute method of get report by class command processor is called from the controller servlet. The execute method calls process get report by class method of the report by class service class. This process method reads the report criteria i.e. the section and the grade from the http request parameter send from the jsp page. Then the process method invokes the private method populate report by class data. In populate report by class data method, a select query is executed at the database for the given criteria (with a where clause for grade and section). This may return one or more records. These records are captured in 'n' number of instances of Student Details Bean. All these instances are then added to an Array List. This array list is then added to the session. The jsp consumes this array list, it gets all the instances and displays them as a record each on the reports results region of the page.

At this stage we have the requirements, prototype, architecture, framework and detailed design for the get report by class use case in the form of sequence and class diagrams. The next and the most interesting part is coding this use case. In the earlier chapter, we have already created the database tables and added some test data there. Lets identify all the artifacts first. For this use case we need the following files.

ReportByClass.jsp

GetReportByClass CP.java

ReportByClass Service.java

ReportByClass Bean.java

GetReportByClassCP.java

Please refer chapter 14 (The BIS-SMS Project Components) for class diagram once before we proceed with this class. This class implements BisCommand interface which has only one method execute. This class extends BisCP which has few variables. We have to implement execute method in this class for get student details use case. Lets look into the actual source code for this class now.

```
package com.bis.cp;

import com.bis.session.reports.ReportByClassService;
import javax.servlet.http.HttpServletRequest;
import javax.servlet.http.HttpServletResponse;
import org.apache.log4j.Logger;

public class GetReportByClassCP extends BisCP implements BisCommand {

      static Logger logger = Logger.getLogger(GetReportByClassCP.class);

      public GetReportByClassCP() {
            super();
      }
```

```
        public String execute(HttpServletRequest request,
                                                    HttpServletResponse response) {
                ReportByClassService reportByClassService = new
                ReportByClassService();
                try {
                reportByClassService.processGetReportByClass(request);
                strNextNavigation = "ReportByClass";
                } catch (Exception excep) {
                logger.error(excep.getMessage());
                strNextNavigation = "Error";  //The next navigation page upon
                failed processing.
                }
        return strNextNavigation;
        }
}
```

The execute method of GetReportByClassCP Class.

The execute method is called from the controller servlet. This is the job of the framework. The framework gets the command from UI and based on the command loads and executes a specific command processor exploiting the polymorphic feature of java. In this case, the command from UI is "GetReportByClass". Within the service method of controller servlet, the GetReportByClassCP class is loaded and instantiated and the execute method is invoked.

The execute method performs the following actions:

⇒ Creates an instance of ReportByClassService and invokes processGetReportByClass method.

⇒ Sets the next navigation to ReportByClass.

ReportByClassService.java

Now let us see the ReportByClassService class source code.

```
package com.bis.session.reports;

import com.bis.beans.reports.ReportByClassBean;
import com.bis.db.DatabaseService;
import com.bis.session.BisService;
import java.sql.Connection;
```

```
import java.sql.ResultSet;
import java.sql.SQLException;
import java.sql.Statement;
import java.util.ArrayList;
import javax.servlet.http.HttpServletRequest;
import javax.servlet.http.HttpSession;
import org.apache.log4j.Logger;

public class ReportByClassService implements BisService {

      static Logger logger =
      Logger.getLogger(ReportByClassService.class);

      public ReportByClassService() {
            super();
      }

      public void processGetReportByClass(HttpServletRequest request) {
            String strClass;
            String strSection;
            strClass = request.getParameter("selClass");
            strSection = request.getParameter("selSection");
            if (strClass != null && strSection != null )    {
            ArrayList reportsBeansList =
            pupulateReportsByClassData(strClass, strSection);
            HttpSession session = request.getSession();
            session.setAttribute("reportsBeansList", reportsBeansList);
            session.setAttribute("grade", strClass);
            session.setAttribute("section", strSection);
            }
            else    {
            logger.error("Section/Class is null");
            }
      }

      private ArrayList pupulateReportsByClassData(String strClass,
                                                    String strSection)      {
            Connection connection = null;
            Statement statement = null ;
            ResultSet resultSet = null;
            String strFirstName = "";
            String strMiddleName = "";
            String strLastName = "";
            String strFullName = "";
            String strStudentId = "";
            String strGender = "";
            String strBusId = "";
            ReportByClassBean reportByClassBean;
```

```
        ArrayList <ReportByClassBean> reportsBeansList = new
        ArrayList<ReportByClassBean>();
        StringBuffer sbQuery = new StringBuffer("SELECT FIRST_NAME,
        MIDDLE_NAME, LAST_NAME, STUDENT_ID, GENDER_CODE, BUS_ID FROM
        STUDENT_DETAILS WHERE GRADE='");
        sbQuery.append(strClass);
        sbQuery.append("' AND SECTION='");
        sbQuery.append(strSection);
        sbQuery.append("'");
        DatabaseService databaseService = new DatabaseService();

connection = databaseService.getDBConnection();
try {
statement = connection.createStatement();
resultSet = statement.executeQuery(sbQuery.toString());
while (resultSet.next()) {
// Prepare full name
strFirstName = resultSet.getString("FIRST_NAME");
strMiddleName = resultSet.getString("MIDDLE_NAME");
strLastName = resultSet.getString("LAST_NAME");
if (strFirstName != null) {
strFullName = strFirstName;
}
if (strMiddleName != null) {
strFullName = strFullName + " " + strMiddleName;
}
if (strLastName != null) {
strFullName = strFullName + " " + strLastName;
}
// prepare gender from code
strGender = resultSet.getString("GENDER_CODE");
if (strGender != null)  {
if (strGender.equalsIgnoreCase("F"))     {
strGender = "Female";
}
else {
strGender = "Male";
}
}
else {
strGender = "";
}
// student id and bus id
strStudentId = resultSet.getString("STUDENT_ID");
strBusId = resultSet.getString("BUS_ID");
// Now we are ready with one compelte record.
reportByClassBean = new ReportByClassBean();
reportByClassBean.setStudentName(strFullName);
reportByClassBean.setStudentId(strStudentId);
```

```
        reportByClassBean.setGender(strGender);
        reportByClassBean.setStudentId(strStudentId);
        reportByClassBean.setBusId(strBusId);
        reportsBeansList.add(reportByClassBean);
        }
        } catch (SQLException sqle) {
        logger.error(sqle.getMessage());
        } finally {
        databaseService.closeDBResouces(statement, resultSet);
        databaseService.releaseDBConnection();  // Releasing database
        connection.
        }
        return reportsBeansList;
        }

        public String getServiceName() {
              return null;
        }
}
```

The processGetReportByClass method performs the following tasks:

⇒ Gets the request parameter value for selected class and section.

⇒ Calls the private method populateReportsByClassData method to populate the data from database into an array list of ReportByClassBean instances.

⇒ Adds this array list of ReportByClassBean instances to the session which is consumed by the jsp.

⇒ Adds the selected class and grade to session which is to be displayed as selected report criteria.

The pupulateReportsByClassData method performs the following tasks:

⇒ Cooks up the dynamic select query for the given class and section.

⇒ Gets the database connection from DatabaseService class.

⇒ Creates the statement and executes the query.

⇒ Populates the ReportByClassBean instance from the ResultSet for each record.

Each ReportByClassBean instance which now represents a record from database query is added to the array list. This array list now holds all the records as number of instances of ReportByClassBean.

For e.g. say the user selected class VI and section A. The dynamic query will add these two conditions in the where clause for section and class. Suppose say, the query returned 11 records for this criteria. An instance of ReportByClassBean is created and populated with setters. This single instance of ReportByClassBean holds data for one record. Similarly 11 such instances of ReportByClassBean are created and in each data pertaining to each record from ResultSet is added. This array list now holds 11 instances of ReportByClassBean. The array list is than added to the session. On the jsp side, the array list is fetched from the session. And from the array list each instance of ReportByClassBean is fetched and the fields from it are displayed as one row. Hence the resultant report jsp page will display 11 records.

ReportByClassBean.java

The ReportByClassBean class is just a simple java bean with private fields with their getters and setters. Please refer the class diagram and below source code for understanding this class.

```
package com.bis.beans.reports;

import com.bis.beans.BisBean;

public class ReportByClassBean extends BisBean  {

      public ReportByClassBean() {
            super();
      }

      private java.lang.String studentName;
      private java.lang.String studentId;
      private java.lang.String gender;
      private java.lang.String busId;

      public void setStudentName(String studentName) {
            this.studentName = studentName;
      }

      public String getStudentName() {
            return studentName;
      }
```

```
	public void setStudentId(String studentId) {
		this.studentId = studentId;
	}

	public String getStudentId() {
		return studentId;
	}

	public void setGender(String gender) {
		this.gender = gender;
	}

	public String getGender() {
		return gender;
	}

	public void setBusId(String busId) {
		this.busId = busId;
	}

	public String getBusId() {
		return busId;
	}
}
```

ReportByClass.jsp

This jsp is dynamically included in BisHome.jsp as a result for get report by class use case invocation through user interaction with the UI. For the initial request to this page we only need to display the reports criteria. This is achieved by checking null for the array list of ReportyByClassBean. Hence, for the first request to this page only the criteria is displayed. Once the user selects the criteria and hits generate report, the resultant report is displayed with "n" number of records as described in the example above.

Till now we have seen that the command for report by class goes form UI as a result of user interaction. Then the controller servlet calls get report by class command processor and then the report by class service is leveraged. Finally, we get the results packaged as an array list of instances of ReportByClassBean. This array list with the n number of bean instances is now available in the session. In the ReportByClass.jsp file we fetch this array list of bean instances from the session. And from each bean we fetch all the information related to student details using the getters. The static part of the jsp remains the same as that of the prototype page. Only the dynamic part is added using the array list of the beans from the session. Hence, the end user sees the view for a given report criteria with all the student records.

Here is the source code for the ReportByClass.jsp file.

```
<%@ page import="com.bis.beans.reports.ReportByClassBean"%>
<%@ page import="java.util.ArrayList"%>
<%@ page import="java.util.Iterator"%>

<%
      ReportByClassBean reportByClassBean;
      Iterator recItr = null;
      if (session != null) {
            ArrayList reportsBeansList = (ArrayList)
            session.getAttribute("reportsBeansList");
            if (reportsBeansList != null)      {
            recItr = reportsBeansList.iterator();
            }
      }
%>

<form id="frmReportByCls" name="frmReportByCls" method="POST"
action="BisControllerServlet">
<input type="hidden" name="ParameterActionCommand"
value="GetReportByClass"></input>
<table border="0" cellpadding="0" cellspacing="0" width="100%"
height="99%">
<tr>
<td widht="*" align="center" valign="top">
<table border="0" cellpadding="10" cellspacing="0" width="100%">
<tr><td> </td></tr>
<tr>
<td bgcolor="White" align="center" id="clred" colspan="3">
Class :
<select name="selClass" id="selClass">
<option selected="true" value="I">
I
</option>
<option value="II">
II
</option>
<option value="III">
III
</option>
<option value="IV">
IV
</option>
<option value="V">
```

```
V
</option>
<option value="VI">
VI
</option>
<option value="VII">
VII
</option>
<option value="VIII">
VIII
</option>
<option value="IX">
IX
</option>
<option value="X">
X
</option>
</select>
  
Section :
<select name="selSection" id="selSection">
<option selected="true" value="A">
A
</option>
<option value="B">
B
</option>
<option value="C">
C
</option>
<option value="D">
D
</option>
<option value="E">
E
</option>
<option value="F">
F
</option>
<option value="G">
G
</option>
</select>
  
<input type="button" value="Generate Report" name="btnGenRepByCls"
id="btnGenRepByCls" onclick="generateRptByCls()">
</td>
</tr>
<tr><td> </td></tr>
```

```
<tr valign="middle">
<td align="center">
<table border="1" cellpadding="4" cellspacing="0" width="80%"
bgcolor="White">
<tr id="clred">
<td colspan="12" align="center">
  Report: Class Wise
  |  
Class :
<%
String strGrade = (String) session.getAttribute("grade");
if (strGrade != null) {
out.print(strGrade);
}
else {
out.print("None");
}
%>
  |  
Section :
<%
String strSection = (String) session.getAttribute("section");
if (strSection != null) {
out.print(strSection);
}
else {
out.print("None");
}
%>
</td>
</tr>
<tr id="trbgred">
<td align="center" width="*">
Name
</td>
<td align="center" width="20%">
Student Id
</td>
<td align="center" width="20%">
Gender
</td>
<td align="center" width="20%">
Bus Id
</td>
</tr>
<%
if (recItr != null) {
while (recItr.hasNext())  {
reportByClassBean = (ReportByClassBean) recItr.next();
```

```
%>
<tr>
<td align="center">
<%=reportByClassBean.getStudentName()%>
</td>
<td align="center">
<%=reportByClassBean.getStudentId()%>
</td>
<td align="center">
<%=reportByClassBean.getGender()%>
</td>
<td align="center">
<%=reportByClassBean.getBusId()%>
</td>
</tr>
<% } } %>
</table>
</td>
</tr>
</table>
</td>
</tr>
</table>
</form>
```

For this use case please study the dynamic part of the jsp code. We fetched the array list from the session. From array list we got the iterator. We used this iterator to dynamically display all the records (with each and every individual fields) in a tabular format.

This concludes the get report by class use case implementation from end to end. We composed the requirement specifications, we built the prototype, we followed the architecture for the solution, we leveraged the framework, we developed the various java classes, we used the common components like DatabaseService.java, BISStyle.css etc and we built the view with the jsp page.

Use Case: Add Student.

Requirements Specification Reference: R10

Prototype Reference: P9

Prerequisite: The user has to be logged in and must have the role which has the privilege to add a new student.

This use case needs to be implemented as per the requirements specification reference above. The UI needs to be as per the prototype reference above. Now that we have complete clarity on use case requirements and UI we will now proceed to implement this use case.

In order to implement this use case, we need to follow the architecture and leverage the framework. To achieve this we will first come up with detailed design and then code it.

The prerequisite for this use case is that the user has to be logged in and must have the role which has the privilege to add a new student. When the user clicks on add student link either on dashboard or via the menu, the following flow is triggered.

The user clicks the add student link

↓

The href for this link is

BisControllerServlet?ParameterActionCommand=AddStudent

↓

The ControllerServlet is invoked on the server

↓

In the service method the action command parameter value is read which is AddStudent

↓

The execute method for the command processor pertaining to AddStudent is invoked

↓

The business logic pertaining to this command processor is executed and a confirmation message is returned.

The command processor class pertaining to AddStudent command is AddStudentCP. The view pertaining to student detail page is AddStudent.jsp. Now, lets see the sequence of method calls once the execute method of AddStudentCP is called. Below is the sequence diagram from this use case.

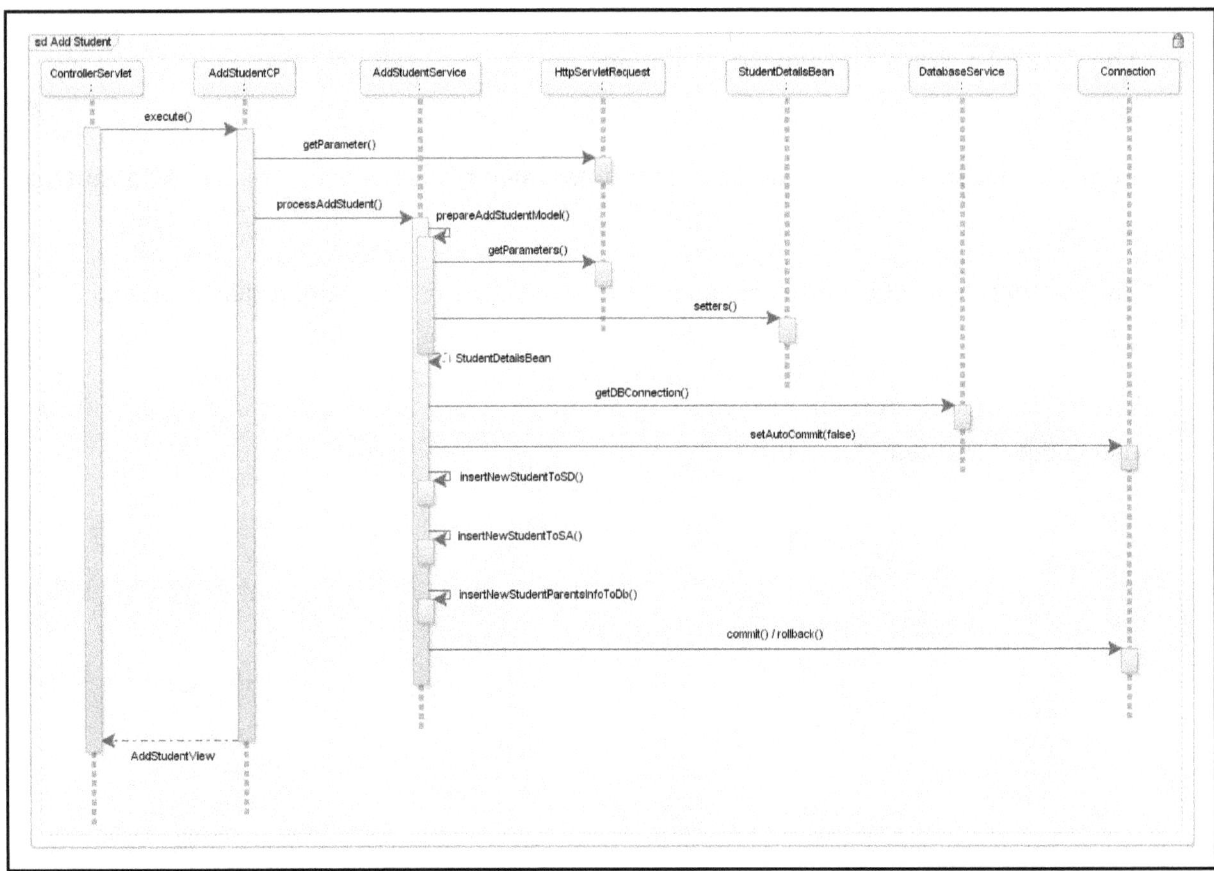

The controller servlet invokes the execute method of the Add Student command processor. The first thing the execute method does is that it checks whether this is a request for blank form or is a filled form submission. This is done via a request parameter which is send by the add student view as a hidden variable. If it is a request for blank form the execute method returns the view. If it is a form submission, the execute method invokes process add student method in the Add Student Service class.

The process add student method calls the private method prepare add student model. The prepare add student model method reads all the http request parameters sent from the jsp form and populates the Student Details Bean. Now, we have all the data from the form in the form of a bean instance. The process method gets the database connection and explicitly turns off the auto commit mode. The process method then invokes three private methods, each of these methods insert one record to respective tables. These three methods return the status of insertion as a Boolean value. All the three Boolean values are checked, if all of them are true than the transaction is committed else the transaction is rolled back. Finally, the add student view is returned to the user.
At this stage we have the requirements, prototype, architecture, framework and detailed design for the add student use case in the form of sequence and class diagrams. The next and the most interesting part is coding this use case. In the earlier chapter, we have already created the database tables and added some test data there. Lets identify all the artifacts first. For this use case we need the following files along with the commons.

AddStudent.jsp

AddStudentCP.java

StudentDetailsBean.java

AddStudentCP.java

Please refer chapter 14 (The BIS-SMS Project Components) for class diagram once before we proceed with this class. This class implements BisCommand interface which has only one method execute. This class extends BisCP which has few variables. We have to implement execute method in this class for get student details use case. Lets look into the actual source code for this class now.

```
package com.bis.cp;

import com.bis.session.AddStudentService;
import javax.servlet.http.HttpServletRequest;
import javax.servlet.http.HttpServletResponse;
import org.apache.log4j.Logger;

public class AddStudentCP extends BisCP implements BisCommand {
```

```
        static Logger logger = Logger.getLogger(AddStudentCP.class);

        public AddStudentCP() {
                super();
        }

        String strAddStdFrmSubmitted = "No";
        // Defaulting add student form submitted hidden value to false.

        public String execute(HttpServletRequest request,
                                                HttpServletResponse response) {
        strAddStdFrmSubmitted =
                        request.getParameter("paramAddStdFrmSubmitted");
        try {
                if (strAddStdFrmSubmitted != null &&
                strAddStdFrmSubmitted.equalsIgnoreCase("Yes"))    {
                AddStudentService addStudentService = new
                AddStudentService();
                addStudentService.processAddStudent(request);
                }
                strNextNavigation = "AddStudent";    //The next navigation
                page upon successful processing.
        } catch (Exception excep) {
                logger.error(excep.getMessage());
                strNextNavigation = "Error";  //The next navigation page upon
                failed processing.
                }
        return strNextNavigation;
        }
}
```

The execute method of AdddentCP Class.

The execute method is called from the controller servlet. This is the job of the framework. The framework gets the command from UI and based on the command loads and executes a specific command processor exploiting the polymorphic feature of java. In this case, the command from UI is "AddStudent". Within the service method of controller servlet, the AddStudentCP class is loaded and instantiated and the execute method is invoked.

The execute method performs the following tasks:

⇒ Gets the new student form submitted flag from the request parameter. This is Yes in case the user has submitted the add new student form using the AddStudent.jsp. This is No in case the user has requested the add new student blank form. That is, the initial load of the add student page in order to fill it and submit it.

⇒ Checks the value for paramAddStdFrmSubmitted parameter.

⇒ If yes, creates an instance of AddStudentService and calls processAddStudent method. This method orchestrates the insertion of new records in the database for the new student. And finally, sets the next navigation view.

⇒ If no, directly sets the next navigation to AddStudent. This loads the blank form on the browser in order to submit a new student. The user sees the add student form page.

AddStudentService.java

Now, let us see the source code of AddStudentService.java class.

```
package com.bis.session;

import com.bis.beans.StudentDetailsBean;
import com.bis.db.DatabaseService;
import com.bis.utility.BisUtility;
import java.sql.Connection;
import java.sql.PreparedStatement;
import java.sql.SQLException;
import java.text.ParseException;
import java.text.SimpleDateFormat;
import javax.servlet.http.HttpServletRequest;
import org.apache.log4j.Logger;

public class AddStudentService implements BisService {

      static Logger logger = Logger.getLogger(AddStudentService.class);

      public AddStudentService() {
            super();
      }

      public void processAddStudent(HttpServletRequest request)   {
            boolean isStudentInfoInsertedToSD = false;
            boolean isStudentInfoInsertedToSA = false;
            boolean isParentsInfoInserted = false;
            StudentDetailsBean studentDetailsBean = null;
```

```
        Connection connection = null;
        studentDetailsBean = prepareAddStudentModel(request);
        connection = DatabaseService.getDBConnection();
try {
connection.setAutoCommit(false);
isStudentInfoInsertedToSD =
insertNewStudentToSD(studentDetailsBean, connection);
isStudentInfoInsertedToSA =
insertNewStudentToSA(studentDetailsBean, connection);
isParentsInfoInserted =
insertNewStudentParentsInfoToDb(studentDetailsBean, connection);
if ( isStudentInfoInsertedToSD && isParentsInfoInserted &&
isStudentInfoInsertedToSA )    {
connection.commit();
BisUtility.sendMail("New student " +
studentDetailsBean.getFirstName() + " " +
studentDetailsBean.getLastName()  + " is added.", "The new student
with the id: "+studentDetailsBean.getStudentId() + " is added.");
}
else {
connection.rollback();
logger.error("New student insertion to database failed.");
}
} catch (SQLException sqle) {
logger.error(sqle.getMessage());
}
finally {
DatabaseService.releaseDBConnection();  // Releasing database
connection.
}
}

private StudentDetailsBean
            prepareAddStudentModel(HttpServletRequest request) {

StudentDetailsBean studentDetailsBean = new StudentDetailsBean();
studentDetailsBean.setFirstName(
request.getParameter("txtFirstName"));
studentDetailsBean.setMiddleName(
request.getParameter("txtMiddleName"));
studentDetailsBean.setLastName(
request.getParameter("txtLastName"));
studentDetailsBean.setFather(
request.getParameter("txtFatherName"));
studentDetailsBean.setFatherMobile(
request.getParameter("txtFatMob"));
studentDetailsBean.setMother(
request.getParameter("txtMotherName"));
studentDetailsBean.setMotherMobile(
```

```
request.getParameter("txtMotMob"));
studentDetailsBean.setAddress(request.getParameter("taAddress"));
studentDetailsBean.setGender(request.getParameter("radSex"));
studentDetailsBean.setDob(request.getParameter("datDob"));
studentDetailsBean.setGrade(request.getParameter("selGrade"));
studentDetailsBean.setSection(request.getParameter("selSection"));
studentDetailsBean.setWeight(request.getParameter("numWeight"));
studentDetailsBean.setHeight(request.getParameter("txtHeight"));
studentDetailsBean.setSiblings(
request.getParameter("txtSiblings"));
studentDetailsBean.setBloodGroup(
request.getParameter("selBldGrp"));
studentDetailsBean.setBusId(request.getParameter("selBusId"));
String strDob = studentDetailsBean.getDob();
StringBuffer sbStudentId =
BisUtility.generateStudentId(studentDetailsBean.getFirstName(),
studentDetailsBean.getLastName(), studentDetailsBean.getMother(),
studentDetailsBean.getFather(), strDob);
studentDetailsBean.setStudentId(sbStudentId.toString());
return studentDetailsBean;
}

private boolean insertNewStudentToSD(StudentDetailsBean
                studentDetailsBean, Connection connection)    {
      boolean isStudentInfoInserted = false;
      int insertCount = 0;
      java.sql.Date datDob = null;
      PreparedStatement preparedStatement = null;
      DatabaseService databaseService = new DatabaseService();

SimpleDateFormat sdFormat = new SimpleDateFormat("yyyy-MM-dd");
String strInsertQuery = "INSERT INTO STUDENT_DETAILS (STUDENT_ID,
ACTIVE_FLAG, FIRST_NAME, MIDDLE_NAME, LAST_NAME, GENDER_CODE,
BIRTH_DATE, GRADE, SECTION, HEIGHT, WEIGHT, BLOOD_GROUP,
SIBLINGS_STUDENT_IDS, BUS_ID) VALUES
(?,?,?,?,?,?,?,?,?,?,?,?,?,?)";

try {
java.util.Date parsedDate =
sdFormat.parse(studentDetailsBean.getDob());
datDob = new java.sql.Date(parsedDate.getTime());
preparedStatement = connection.prepareStatement(strInsertQuery);
preparedStatement.setString(1, studentDetailsBean.getStudentId());
preparedStatement.setString(2, "Y");
preparedStatement.setString(3, studentDetailsBean.getFirstName());
preparedStatement.setString(4, studentDetailsBean.getMiddleName());
preparedStatement.setString(5, studentDetailsBean.getLastName());
preparedStatement.setString(6, studentDetailsBean.getGender());
preparedStatement.setDate(7, datDob);
```

```
preparedStatement.setString(8, studentDetailsBean.getGrade());
preparedStatement.setString(9, studentDetailsBean.getSection());
preparedStatement.setString(10, studentDetailsBean.getHeight());
preparedStatement.setString(11, studentDetailsBean.getWeight());
preparedStatement.setString(12,
studentDetailsBean.getBloodGroup());
preparedStatement.setString(13, studentDetailsBean.getSiblings());
preparedStatement.setString(14, studentDetailsBean.getBusId());
insertCount = preparedStatement.executeUpdate();
if (insertCount == 1)   {
isStudentInfoInserted = true;
}
else {
logger.error("Failed to insert new student record in
Student_Details table");
}
} catch (SQLException sqle) {
isStudentInfoInserted = false;
logger.error(sqle.getMessage());
} catch (ParseException pe) {
logger.error(pe.getMessage());
}
finally {
databaseService.closeDBResouces(preparedStatement,null);
}
return isStudentInfoInserted;
}


// Inserts two rows to Student_Attendance table with zero
attendance for each semester. Provisioning for later update.

private boolean insertNewStudentToSA(StudentDetailsBean
                 studentDetailsBean, Connection connection)    {

      boolean isStudentInfoInsertedToSA = false;
      int insertCountSem1 = 0;
      int insertCountSem2 = 0;
      PreparedStatement preparedStatement = null;
      DatabaseService databaseService = new DatabaseService();

String strInsertQuery = "INSERT INTO STUDENT_ATTENDANCE
(STUDENT_ID, ATTENDANCE, SEMESTER) VALUES (?,?,?)";
try {
preparedStatement = connection.prepareStatement(strInsertQuery);
preparedStatement.setString(1, studentDetailsBean.getStudentId());
preparedStatement.setInt(2, 0);
preparedStatement.setString(3, "1");
insertCountSem1 = preparedStatement.executeUpdate();
```

```
preparedStatement.setString(3, "2");
insertCountSem2 = preparedStatement.executeUpdate();
if (insertCountSem1 == 1 && insertCountSem2 == 1)    {
isStudentInfoInsertedToSA = true;
}
else {
logger.error("Failed to insert new student record in
Student_Attendance table");
}
} catch (SQLException sqle) {
isStudentInfoInsertedToSA = false;
logger.error(sqle.getMessage());
}
finally {
databaseService.closeDBResouces(preparedStatement,null);
}
return isStudentInfoInsertedToSA;
}

private boolean insertNewStudentParentsInfoToDb(StudentDetailsBean
                  studentDetailsBean, Connection connection)    {

      boolean isParentsInfoInserted = false;
      PreparedStatement preparedStatement = null;
      DatabaseService databaseService = new DatabaseService();
      int insertCount=0;

String strInsertQuery = "INSERT INTO PARENT_DETAILS (FATHER_NAME,
MOTHER_NAME, FATHER_MOBILE, MOTHER_MOBILE, ADDRESS,
FATHER_QUALIFICATION, MOTHER_QUALIFICATION, ANNUAL_INCOME,
STUDENT_ID) VALUES (?,?,?,?,?,?,?,?,?)";
try {
preparedStatement = connection.prepareStatement(strInsertQuery);
preparedStatement.setString(1, studentDetailsBean.getFather());
preparedStatement.setString(2, studentDetailsBean.getMother());
preparedStatement.setString(3,
studentDetailsBean.getFatherMobile());
preparedStatement.setString(4,
studentDetailsBean.getMotherMobile());
preparedStatement.setString(5, studentDetailsBean.getAddress());
preparedStatement.setString(6, studentDetailsBean.getFatherQual());
preparedStatement.setString(7, studentDetailsBean.getMotherQual());
preparedStatement.setString(8,
studentDetailsBean.getAnnualIncome());
preparedStatement.setString(9, studentDetailsBean.getStudentId());
insertCount = preparedStatement.executeUpdate();
if (insertCount ==1)    {
isParentsInfoInserted = true;
}
```

```
        else {
        logger.error("Failed to insert new student parent's record in
        Parents_Details table");
        }
        } catch (SQLException sqle) {
        isParentsInfoInserted = false;
        logger.error(sqle.getMessage());
        }
        finally {
        databaseService.closeDBResouces(preparedStatement,null);
        }
        return isParentsInfoInserted;
        }

        public String getServiceName() {
              return this.getClass().getName();
        }
}
```

The processAddStudent method performs the following tasks:

⇒ Creates an instance of StudentDetailsBean and calls prepareAddStudentModel method to populate the data sent via the html form into this bean instance. This instance now holds the client side validated data sent by the user by submitting add student form.

⇒ Leverages DatabaseService class to get database connection.

⇒ Sets auto commit for the database connection to false. In this case we have to explicitly commit or roll back the database insertion operations. We did this in order to manually control the database transaction. For this use case we have to insert a record in three tables. This has to be an either all or none operation. The records for a new student must go in all these three tables, in case of success, we will commit it. If the insertion fails in one or more tables, we perform the roll back which ensures that none of the details about the student are entered to any of the tables. This saves us from inconsistencies of data for a given student.

⇒ Initializes three boolean variables to capture status of insertion to each table.

⇒ For creating a new student, we need to insert one record into each of the following tables: Student_details, Parent_details and Student_attendance. This is achieved via calls to three private methods in the same class. All these methods return a boolean value which is nothing but the status of the operation. Each method return true if the insertion succeeds and false if the insertion fails.

⇒ After calling all the three methods the boolean returned status are checked, if all the tree returned values are true, the transaction is committed and an email is sent using sendEmail method of BisUtility class.

⇒ If one or more returned values are false, the transaction is rolled back. This guarantees that the records are inserted either in all the three tables or none.

The prepareAddStudentModel method performs the following tasks:

⇒ Reads the values of all the form elements sent from the jsp page. All these parameters are read from the request object and the values are populated to the Student Details Bean instance using setter methods.

⇒ Calls the generateStudentId method in BisUtility class in order to generate student id from the values submitted by the user for a given student.

⇒ Calls the setter method of student details bean instance to set this generated student id.

⇒ And finally, returns this populated instance of student details bean.

The insertNewStudentToSD method performs the following tasks:

⇒ Cooks up the dynamic insert query with placeholders for adding a new record to student details table.

⇒ Gets the database connection from DatabaseService class.

⇒ Gets the prepared statement from the connection for the given query.

⇒ Uses setXXX methods of prepared statement to set the values fetched from the student details bean instance.

⇒ Calls execute update method to insert a record to the database table student details.

⇒ The status is captured in a boolean variable and is returned to the calling method.

⇒ Performs the closure of database resources in the finally block.

The insertNewStudentToSA method performs the following tasks:

⇒ Cooks up the dynamic insert query with placeholders for adding a new record to student attendance table.

⇒ Gets the database connection from DatabaseService class.

⇒ Gets the prepared statement from the connection for the given query.

⇒ Uses setXXX methods of prepared statement to set the values fetched from the student details bean instance.

⇒ Calls execute update method to insert a record to the database table student attendance.

⇒ The status is captured in a boolean variable and is returned to the calling method.

⇒ In a finally block, the database resources which were used are closed.

The insertNewStudentParentsInfoToDb method performs the following tasks:

⇒ Cooks up the dynamic insert query with placeholders for adding a new record to parent details table.

⇒ Gets the database connection from DatabaseService class.

⇒ Gets the prepared statement from the connection for the given query.

⇒ Uses setXXX methods of prepared statement to set the values fetched from the student details bean instance.

⇒ Calls execute update method to insert a record to the database table parent details.

⇒ The status is captured in a boolean variable and is returned to the calling method.

⇒ In a finally block, the database resources which were used are closed.

StudentDetailsBean.java

Please refer to the get student details use case for the details about this bean.

AddStudent.jsp

This jsp is dynamically included in BisHome.jsp as a result for add student use case invocation through user interaction with the UI.

Till now we have seen that the command for add student goes form UI as a result of user interaction. Then the controller servlet calls add student command processor. The command processor checks whether it is a request for a blank form to submit a new student or it is a new student form submission. For the former case, the command processor renders the blank form via add student jsp page. And for the later case, the command processor utilizes add student service class to insert a new student to the database.

The add student jsp page provides all the mandatory as well as optional fields in order to create a new student. All the fields are validated at the client side using javascript.

Here is the source code for the AddStudent.jsp file.

```
<form id="frmAddStudent" name="frmAddStudent" method="POST"
action="BisControllerServlet">
<input type="hidden" name="ParameterActionCommand"
value="AddStudent"></input>
<input type="hidden" name="paramAddStdFrmSubmitted"
id="paramAddStdFrmSubmitted" value="No"></input>

<table border="0" cellpadding="10" cellspacing="0" width="100%">
<tr><td colspan="2"> </td></tr>
<tr>
<td align="center" colspan="2" id="whiteBg">
      Add Student
</td>
</tr>
<tr><td colspan="2"> </td></tr>
<tr valign="top">
<td width="50%" align="center">
```

```
<table border="1" cellpadding="5" cellspacing="0" width="90%"
bgcolor="White">
<tr>
<td colspan="2"> </td>
</tr>
<tr>
<td width="25%" align="right" id="clred">First Name   </td>
<td width="*" align="left">
<input type="text" size="30" name="txtFirstName" maxlength="30"></input>
</td>
</tr>
<tr>
<td width="25%" align="right" id="clred">Middle Name   </td>
<td width="*" align="left">
<input type="text" size="30" name="txtMiddleName" maxlength="30"></input>
</td>
</tr>
<tr>
<td width="25%" align="right" id="clred">Last Name   </td>
<td width="*" align="left">
<input type="text" size="30" name="txtLastName" maxlength="30"></input>
</td>
</tr>
<tr>
<td colspan="2"> </td>
</tr>
<tr>
<td width="*" align="right" id="clred">Gender   </td>
<td width="*" align="left">
<input type="radio" name="radSex" value="M">Male</input>
<input type="radio" name="radSex" value="F">Female</input>
</td>
</tr>
<tr>
<td align="right" id="clred">Date of birth   </td>
<td width="*" align="left">
<input type="date" name="datDob"></input>  <!-- HTML5 Element -->
</td>
</tr>
<tr>
<td colspan="2"> </td>
</tr>
<tr>
<td align="right" id="clred">Grade   </td>
<td width="*" align="left">

<select name="selGrade">
<option value="LKG">L.K.G</option>
<option value="UKG">U.K.G</option>
```

```
<option value="I">I - First</option>
<option value="II">II - Second</option>
<option value="III">III - Third</option>
<option value="IV">IV - Fourth</option>
<option value="V">V - Fifth</option>
<option value="VI">VI - Sixth</option>
<option value="VII">VII - Seventh</option>
<option value="VIII">VIII - Eight</option>
<option value="IX">IX - Ninth</option>
<option value="X">X - Tenth</option>
</select>

</td>
</tr>
<tr>
<td align="right" id="clred">Section   </td>
<td width="*" align="left">

<select name="selSection">
<option value="A">A</option>
<option value="B">B</option>
<option value="C">C</option>
<option value="D">D</option>
<option value="E">E</option>
</select>

</td>
</tr>
<tr>
<td colspan="2">  </td>
</tr>
<tr>
<td align="right" id="clred">Height   </td>
<td width="*" align="left">
<!-- HTML5 Element -->
<input type="text" name="txtHeight"></input>
   Foot.Inches
</td>
</tr>
<tr>
<td align="right" id="clred">Weight   </td>
<td width="*" align="left">
<!-- HTML5 Element -->
<input type="number" min="6" max="150" name="numWeight"></input>
   KG
</td>
</tr>
<tr>
<td colspan="2"> </td>
```

```
</tr>
<tr>
<td align="right" id="clred">Blood Group   </td>
<td width="*" align="left">

<select name="selBldGrp">
<option value="AP">A +ve</option>
<option value="BP">B +ve</option>
<option value="ABP">AB +ve</option>
<option value="OP">O +ve</option>
<option value="AN">A -ve</option>
<option value="BN">B -ve</option>
<option value="ABN">AB -ve</option>
<option value="ON">O -ve</option>
</select>

</td>
</tr>
<tr>
<td align="right" id="clred">Siblings   </td>
<td width="*" align="left">
<input type="text" name="txtSiblings" size="40" maxlength="100"></input>
</td>
</tr>
<tr>
<td colspan="2"> </td>
</tr>
</table>
</td>
<td width="*" align="center">
<table border="1" cellpadding="5" cellspacing="0" width="90%"
bgcolor="White">
<tr>
<td colspan="2"> </td>
</tr>
<tr>
<td width="25%" align="right" id="clred">Father   </td>
<td width="*" align="left">
<input type="text" size="30" name="txtFatherName" maxlength="30"></input>
</td>
</tr>
<tr>
<td colspan="2"> </td>
</tr>
<tr>
<td width="25%" align="right" id="clred">Mobile   </td>
<td width="*" align="left">
<input type="text" name="txtFatMob" maxlength="20"></input>
</td>
```

```
</tr>
<tr>
<td colspan="2"> </td>
</tr>
<tr>
<td width="*" align="right" id="clred">Mother   </td>
<td width="*" align="left">
<input type="text" size="30" name="txtMotherName" maxlength="30"></input>
</td>
</tr>
<tr>
<td colspan="2"> </td>
</tr>
<tr>
<td align="right" id="clred">Mobile   </td>
<td width="*" align="left">
<input type="text" name="txtMotMob" maxlength="20"></input>
</td>
</tr>
<tr>
<td colspan="2"> </td>
</tr>
<tr height="130">
<td align="right" id="clred">Address   </td>
<td width="*" align="left">
<textarea name="taAddress" cols="45" rows="6"></textarea>
</td>
</tr>
<tr>
<td colspan="2"> </td>
</tr>
<tr>
<td width="25%" align="right" id="clred">Bus Number   </td>
<td width="*" align="left">

<select name="selBusId">
<option value="01">01</option>
<option value="02">02</option>
<option value="03">03</option>
<option value="04">04</option>
<option value="05">05</option>
<option value="06">06</option>
<option value="07">07</option>
<option value="08">08</option>
<option value="09">09</option>
<option value="10">10</option>
<option value="11">11</option>
<option value="12">12</option>
<option value="13">13</option>
```

```
<option value="14">14</option>
<option value="15">15</option>
<option value="16">16</option>
<option value="17">17</option>
<option value="18">18</option>
<option value="19">19</option>
<option value="20">20</option>
<option value="11">21</option>
<option value="22">22</option>
<option value="23">23</option>
<option value="24">24</option>
<option value="25">25</option>
<option value="26">26</option>
<option value="27">27</option>
<option value="28">28</option>
<option value="29">29</option>
<option value="30">30</option>
<option value="-1">Private</option>
</select>

</td>
</tr>
<tr>
<td colspan="2"> </td>
</tr>
<tr>
<td colspan="2"> </td>
</tr>
</table>
</td>
</tr>
<tr>
<td colspan="3"> </td>
</tr>
<tr valign="middle" align="center">
<td colspan="3">
<input type="submit" name="subAddStd" value="   Submit   "
id="submitButton" onclick="submitAddStdForm()" ></input>
</td>
</tr>
<tr>
<td colspan="3"> </td>
</tr>
</table>
</form>
```

This concludes the add new student use case implementation from end to end. We composed the requirement specifications, we built the prototype, we followed the architecture for the solution, we leveraged the framework, we developed the various java classes, we used the common components like DatabaseService.java, BISStyle.css etc and we built the view with the jsp page.

Use Case: Manage Student Attendance.

Requirements Specification Reference: R9

Prototype Reference: P8

Prerequisite:

1. The user has to be logged in and must have the role which has the privilege to update the attendance of the students.

2. The student whose attendance needs to be updated has to be loaded into context first.

This use case needs to be implemented as per the requirements specification reference above. The UI needs to be as per the prototype reference above. Now that we have complete clarity on use case requirements and UI we will now proceed to implement this use case.

In order to implement this use case, we need to follow the architecture and leverage the framework. To achieve this we will first come up with detailed design and then code it.

The prerequisite for this use case is that the user has to be logged in and must have the role which has the privilege to update the attendance of the students. And the other prerequisite is that the student whose attendance needs to be updated must already be existing in the context, for this the user must have loaded the student following the load student use case. When the student is loaded, the student id of a particular student is added to the session. You can refer the load student use case for details on this. Let us assume as of now that the student id is existing in the http session. When the user clicks on manage attendance link either on dashboard or via the menu, the following flow is triggered.

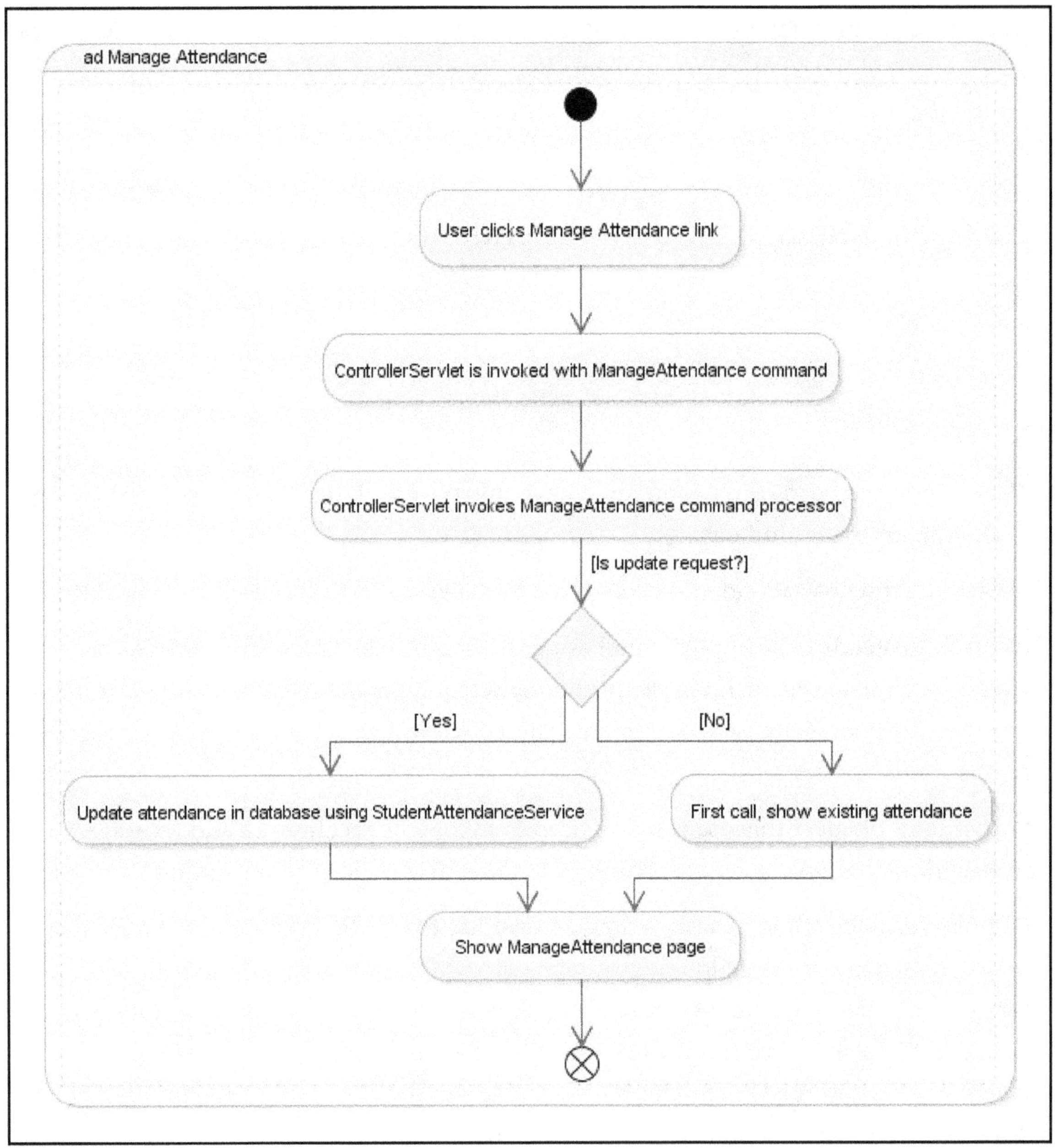
ad Manage Attendance
User clicks Manage Attendance link
ControllerServlet is invoked with ManageAttendance command
ControllerServlet invokes ManageAttendance command processor
[Is update request?]
[Yes]
[No]
Update attendance in database using StudentAttendanceService
First call, show existing attendance
Show ManageAttendance page

The user clicks the manage attendance link

The href for this link is

BisControllerServlet?ParameterActionCommand=ManageAttendance

The ControllerServlet is invoked on the server

In the service method the action command parameter value is read which is ManageAttendance

The execute method for the command processor pertaining to ManageAttendance is invoked

The business logic pertaining to this command processor is executed resulting in an update of the attendance in the database for a given student and semester.

The view pertaining to manage attendance is returned back.

The user sees the updated attendance in the manage attendance page.

The command processor class pertaining to ManageAttendance command is ManageAttendanceCP. The view pertaining to student detail page is ManageAttendance.jsp. Now, lets see the sequence of method calls once the execute method of ManageAttendanceCP is called. Below is the sequence diagram from this use case.

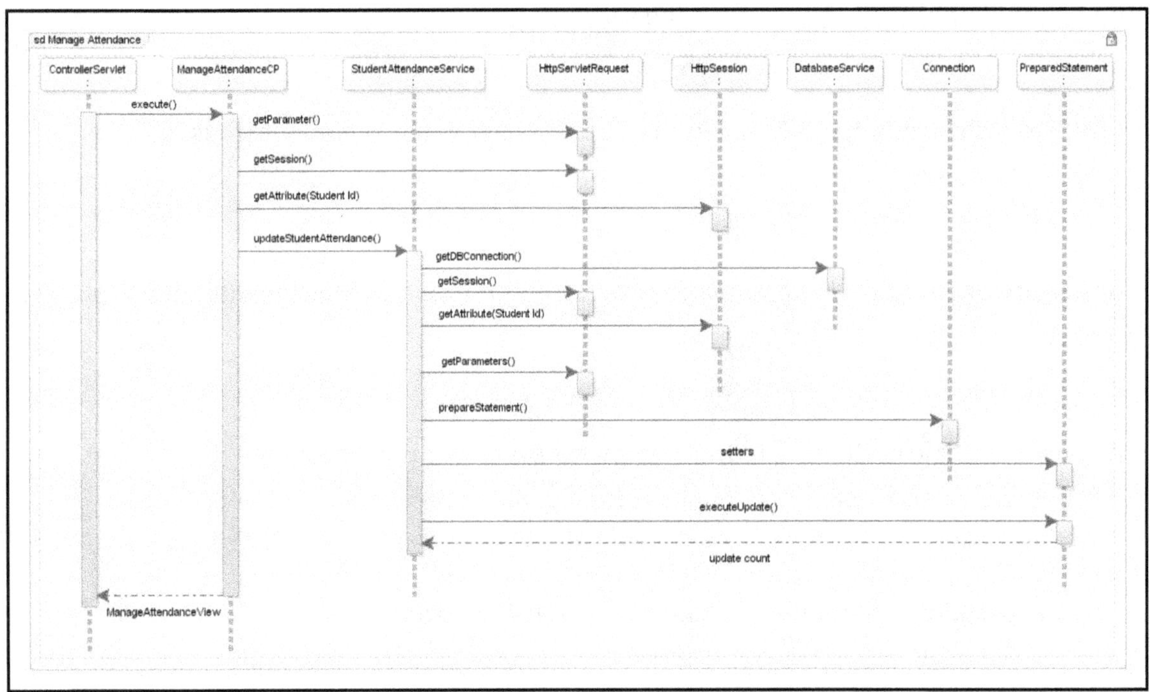

The controller servlet invokes the execute method of the Manage Attendance command processor. From the hidden variable via the request parameter, the execute methods checks whether this is an initial request for manage attendance page. If so, it just returns the view. If this request turns out to be an update request, the execute method invokes the update student attendance method in Student Attendance Service class. The update student attendance method reads the student id from the session and the semester from the request parameter. This method then leverages Database Service class and updates the attendance in the required database table.

At this stage we have the requirements, prototype, architecture, framework and detailed design for the manage attendance use case in the form of sequence and class diagrams. The next and the most interesting part is coding this use case. In the earlier chapter, we have already created the database tables and added some test data there. Lets identify all the artifacts first. For this use case we need the following files along with the commons.

ManageAttendanceCP.java

StudentAttendanceService.java

StudentAttendanceBean.java

ManageAttendance.jsp

ManageAttendanceCP.java

Please refer chapter 14 (The BIS-SMS Project Components) for class diagram once before we proceed with this class. This class implements BisCommand interface which has only one method execute. This class extends BisCP which has few variables. We have to implement execute method in this class for manage attendance use case. Lets look into the actual source code for this class now.

```
package com.bis.cp;

import com.bis.session.StudentAttendanceService;
import javax.servlet.http.HttpServletRequest;
import javax.servlet.http.HttpServletResponse;
import javax.servlet.http.HttpSession;
import org.apache.log4j.Logger;

public class ManageAttendanceCP extends BisCP implements BisCommand {

      static Logger logger = Logger.getLogger(ManageAttendanceCP.class);

      public ManageAttendanceCP() {
            super();
      }

      public String execute(HttpServletRequest request,
                                    HttpServletResponse response) {
```

```
        String strStudentId;
        String strParamUpdateAttFrmSubmitted = "No"; // Defaulting to
        No.
        strParamUpdateAttFrmSubmitted =
        request.getParameter("paramUpdateAttFrmSubmitted");
        HttpSession session = request.getSession();

        if (session != null) {
        strStudentId = (String)session.getAttribute("StudentId");
        if (strStudentId != null) {
        StudentAttendanceService studentAttendanceService = new
        StudentAttendanceService();
        if (strParamUpdateAttFrmSubmitted != null &&
        strParamUpdateAttFrmSubmitted.equalsIgnoreCase("Yes")) {
        studentAttendanceService.updateStudentAttendance(request);
        strNextNavigation = "ManageAttendance";
        }

        try {
              studentAttendanceService.processGetStudentAttendance(
              session);
              // Gets student attendance for Manage attendance page.
              This includes attendance for both the semesters.
              strNextNavigation = "ManageAttendance";
              //The next navigation page upon successful processing.
        } catch (Exception e) {
              logger.error(e.getMessage());
              strNextNavigation = "Error";
              //The next navigation page upon failed processing.
        }
        } else {
              // strStudentId is null, redirect to home page to
              select student.
              strNextNavigation = "BisDashboard";
        }
        } else {
              // session is null. Valid session doesn't exsit.
              Redirect to Login page.
              strNextNavigation = "Login";
        }
    return strNextNavigation;
    }
}
```

The execute method of ManageAttendanceCP Class.

The execute method is called from the controller servlet. This is the job of the framework. The framework gets the command from UI and based on the command loads and executes a specific command processor exploiting the polymorphic feature of java. In this case, the command from UI is "ManageAttendance". Within the service method of controller servlet, the ManageAttendanceCP class is loaded and instantiated and the execute method is invoked.

The execute method performs the following tasks:

⇒ Gets the update attendance form submitted flag from the request parameter. This is Yes in case the user has submitted the update attendance request using the ManageAttendance.jsp. This is No in case the user has requested the manage attendance page for the first time. In this case, the manage page displays existing attendance for a given student for both the semesters.

⇒ Checks the value for paramUpdateAttFrmSubmitted parameter.

⇒ If yes, creates an instance of StudentAttendanceService and calls updateStudentAttendance method. This method orchestrates an update of attendance in the database. And finally, sets the next navigation view.

⇒ The logic here does not require to check for a "No" value. The execute method than calls processGetStudentAttendance. This methods takes the user to manage attendance page view with the existing attendance values in the database. The job of processGetStudentAttendance is to only fetch the attendance from database and display it to the user in the ManageAttendance.jsp page. This ensures that the user sees the latest attendance.

⇒ If its an update request, the updateStudentAttendance method updates the attendance in the database and the user is shown the updated attendance in the view. If its not an update request, that is, if the user has navigated to manage attendance page for the first time. The user is shown the existing attendance in the manage attendance jsp page.

StudentAttendanceService.java

Please refer to get student attendance use case for the source code of this class. Also refer the same use case for the detailed description of processGetStudentAttendance method.

The updateStudentAttendance method performs the following tasks:

⇒ Cooks up the dynamic update query with placeholders for updating the attendance to student attendance table.

⇒ Gets the database connection from DatabaseService class.

⇒ Gets the prepared statement from the connection for the given query.

⇒ The semester and the new attendance values are fetched from the request parameters. The setXXX methods are used to set these values to the prepared statement.

⇒ The student id is fetched from the session and is set to the prepared statement via a setter method.

⇒ Calls execute update method to update the attendance in the student attendance table.

⇒ The database resources which were used are closed in the finally block.

StudentAttendanceBean.java

Please refer to the get student attendance use case for the details about this bean.

ManageAttendance.jsp

This jsp is dynamically included in BisHome.jsp as a result for manage attendance use case invocation through user interaction with the UI.

Till now we have seen that the command for manage attendance goes form UI as a result of user interaction. Then the controller servlet calls manage attendance command processor. The command processor checks whether it is an initial request for the manage attendance page or whether the user has submitted an update request. For the former case, the command processor renders the manage attendance jsp page with the existing attendance. And for the later case, the command processor utilizes manage attendance service class to update the attendance in the database.

The manage attendance jsp page provides two editable text fields for updating attendance for each semester. These text fields display the existing attendance values and once updated these fields display the updated values. The values entered by the user for these text fields are validated at the client side using javascript.

Here is the source code for the ManageAttendance.jsp file.

```
<%@ page import="com.bis.beans.StudentResultsBean,
                        com.bis.beans.StudentAttendanceBean"%>
<%@ page import="java.util.Hashtable, java.util.Enumeration"%>

<%
      StudentResultsBean studentResultsBean = null;
      int inPresentPercentage=0;
      int inTotal=0;
      int inPresent=0;
      StudentAttendanceBean studentAttendanceBean = null;

      if (session != null) {
            studentResultsBean = (StudentResultsBean)
            session.getAttribute("studentResultsBean");
            studentAttendanceBean = (StudentAttendanceBean)
            session.getAttribute("studentAttendanceBean");
      }

      if (studentAttendanceBean != null)    {
            inTotal = studentAttendanceBean.getTotalWorkingDays();
            inPresent = studentAttendanceBean.getAttendance();
            if (inTotal > 0 && inPresent >0) {
            inPresentPercentage = Math.abs(100 * inPresent/inTotal);
            }
      }
%>

<form id="frmManageAttendance" name="frmManageAttendance" method="POST"
action="BisControllerServlet">
<input type="hidden" name="ParameterActionCommand"
value="ManageAttendance"></input>
<input type="hidden" name="ParameterUpdateSemAttendance"
id="ParameterUpdateSemAttendance"></input>
<input type="hidden" name="paramUpdateAttFrmSubmitted"
id="paramUpdateAttFrmSubmitted" value="No"></input>
<table border="0" cellpadding="10" cellspacing="0" width="100%">
<tr><td> </td></tr>
<tr>
<td align="center" colspan="3" id="whiteBg">
      Manage Attendance
```

```
</td>
</tr>
<tr><td> </td></tr>
<tr align="center">
<td height="250px">
<table border="1" cellpadding="10" cellspacing="0" width="80%">
<tr>
<td align="center" colspan="3" id="trbgred">
<%
if (studentResultsBean != null)   {
out.print(studentResultsBean.getFullName());
}
%>
   |   
<%
if (studentResultsBean != null)   {
out.print(studentResultsBean.getGrade());
out.print(" - ");
out.print(studentResultsBean.getSection());
}
%>
   |   
<%
if (studentResultsBean != null)   {
out.print(studentResultsBean.getStudentId());
}
%>
</td>
</tr>
<tr align="center" id="whiteBg">
<td width="50%">
<table border="0" cellpadding="5" cellspacing="0" width="60%">
<tr><td colspan="3"> </td></tr>
<tr><td colspan="3"> </td></tr>
<tr>
<td align="center" colspan="3" id="trbgred">
      Semester - I
</td>
</tr>
<tr valign="middle" >
<td align="right" width="45%">
Total working days
</td>
<td width="10%"> </td>
<td width="*" align="left">
<%
if (studentAttendanceBean != null)   {
out.print(studentAttendanceBean.getSemOneTotalWorkingDays());
}
```

```
%>
</td>
</tr>
<tr valign="middle" >
<td align="right" >
      Present
</td>
<td> </td>
<td>
<input type="text" id="txtPresentSemOne" name="txtPresentSemOne"
size="12"
value="<%
if (studentAttendanceBean != null)   {
out.print(studentAttendanceBean.getSemOneAttendance());
}
%>"/>
</td>
</tr>
<tr valign="middle" >
<td align="right" >
      Absent
</td>
<td> </td>
<td>
<%
if (studentAttendanceBean != null)   {
int intAbsent = studentAttendanceBean.getSemOneTotalWorkingDays() -
studentAttendanceBean.getSemOneAttendance();
out.print(intAbsent);
}
%>
</td>
</tr>
<tr valign="middle" >
<td align="center"  colspan="3" id="trbgred">
<input type="button" name="btnUpdAttSem1" value="    Update    "
id="btnUpdAttSem1" onclick="updateAttendance('1')" />
</td>
</tr>
<tr><td colspan="3"> </td></tr>
<tr><td colspan="3"> </td></tr>
</table>
</td>
<td width="*">
<table border="0" cellpadding="5" cellspacing="0" width="60%">
<tr><td colspan="3"> </td></tr>
<tr><td colspan="3"> </td></tr>
<tr>
<td align="center" colspan="3" id="trbgred">
```

```
      Semester - II
</td>
</tr>
<tr valign="middle" >
<td align="right" width="45%">
Total working days
</td>
<td width="10%"> </td>
<td width="*" align="left">
<%
if (studentAttendanceBean != null)   {
out.print(studentAttendanceBean.getSemTwoTotalWorkingDays());
}
%>
</td>
</tr>
<tr valign="middle" >
<td align="right" >
      Present
</td>
<td> </td>
<td>
<input type="text" id="txtPresentSemTwo" name="txtPresentSemTwo"
size="12"
value="<%
if (studentAttendanceBean != null)   {
out.print(studentAttendanceBean.getSemTwoAttendance());
}
%>"/>
</td>
</tr>
<tr valign="middle" >
<td align="right" >
      Absent
</td>
<td> </td>
<td>
<%
if (studentAttendanceBean != null)   {
int intAbsent = studentAttendanceBean.getSemTwoTotalWorkingDays() -
studentAttendanceBean.getSemTwoAttendance();
out.print(intAbsent);
}
%>
</td>
</tr>
<tr valign="middle" >
<td align="center"  colspan="3" id="trbgred">
```

```
<input type="button" name="btnUpdAttSem2" value="    Update    "
id="btnUpdAttSem2" onclick="updateAttendance('2')"/>
</td>
</tr>
<tr><td colspan="3"> </td></tr>
<tr><td colspan="3"> </td></tr>
</table>
</td>
</tr>
</table>
</td>
</tr>
<tr><td> </td></tr>
</table>
</form>
```

This concludes the manage attendance use case implementation from end to end. We composed the requirement specifications, we built the prototype, we followed the architecture for the solution, we leveraged the framework, we developed the various java classes, we used the common components like DatabaseService.java, BISStyle.css etc and we built the view with the jsp page.

16
SECURING APPLICATION

Security is one of the most important aspect of any application. In our sample application BIS-SMS we need to ensure that only authenticated users are allowed to access the application.

Once authenticated a user can access the application. The next thing that needs to be identified is authorization. An authenticated user may not have privileges to access everything in the application. This is governed by user roles. Roles define the access privilege to a particular service or data. For e.g. a user with administrator role can add a new student whereas a user with teacher role can only view a student. Authorization dictates the roles and roles in turn control the access rights. In our application we will define roles as per the requirements specifications for authentication and authorization.

Configuring data source security realm for Apache Tomcat 8

We will use container managed security for our application. That is, in our case the authentication and authorization is provided out of the box by Apache Tomcat 8 server. We will only configure the security for our application. Following steps are required to configure container managed security for a web application in Apache Tomcat 8 server.

Step 1: Create Tables

We need a storage for user names, passwords and user roles. This is know as a realm. For this we will use database. We are using separate schema for database security realm called BisSecurityRealm. Please refer chapter 9 database design for details about the database design for BisSecurityRealm schema. Once you create this schema and all the tables you may proceed to the next step.

[Note: The scripts to create the database tables is provided in chapter 22 under the appendix section for database scripts.]

Step 2: Create data source

This data source must point to the BisSecurityRealm schema. This data source is used by server to read user name, password and roles.

In order to create the data source, add the following entry to server's context descriptor file located at $CATALINA_BASE/conf/context.xml.

```
<Resource
      name="jdbc/BisSecurityRealmDS"
      auth="Container"
      maxActive="20"
      maxIdle="5"
      maxWait="10000"
      factory="oracle.ucp.jdbc.PoolDataSourceImpl"
      driverClassName="oracle.jdbc.OracleDriver"
      url="jdbc:oracle:thin:BisSecurityRealm/Welcome01@127.1.1.0:1521:XE"
      type="oracle.ucp.jdbc.PoolDataSource"
      connectionFactoryClassName="oracle.jdbc.pool.OracleDataSource"
      connectionPoolName="SecurityUCPPool"
      validateConnectionOnBorrow="true"
      sqlForValidateConnection="select 1 from DUAL"
/>
```

You need to make sure that the value for url attribute points to your database and user.

```
      jdbc:oracle:thin:userId/pwd@host:port:sid

      e.g. jdbc:oracle:thin:BisSecurityRealm/Welcome01@127.1.1.0:1521:XE
```

Restart the server for the availability of the data source.

Step 3: Add <relam> element to server.xml file.

Goto $CATALINA_BASE/conf/ folder and open server.xml file. Add the following realm tag entry to this file.

```
<Realm
      className="org.apache.catalina.realm.DataSourceRealm"
      dataSourceName="jdbc/BisSecurityRealmDS"
```

```
        userTable="users"
        userNameCol="user_name"
        userCredCol="user_pass"
        userRoleTable="user_roles"
        roleNameCol="role_name"
        localDataSource="true"
/>
```

Here's the description of the attributes:

className: Identifies the type of realm.

dataSourceName: The name of the data source whose connections are configured for BisSecurityRealm schema.

userTable: Name of the table which is holding the user names and passwords.

userNameCol: The column within userTable which holds the user names.

userCredCol: The column within userTable which holds the user password.

userRoleTable: The table which holds the user roles.

roleNameCol: The column within userRoleTable which holds the role names.

Save the server.xml file and restart the server.

We made two entries in conf folder. One in the server.xml file for realm configuration and the other in context.xml for data source configuration.

Step 4: Verification

To test insert the user Yousuf.Baig and password Welcome01 to users table. Now, add the role names admin-gui, admin-script and manager-gui to user_roles table for the user Yousuf.Baig.

Go to the server home page and click manager app link on the right hand side. The server will challenge you for a user id and password. Enter Yousuf.Baig as user and Welcome01 as password and press enter. The server will verify the user and password in the database and if validated it will look for the roles. And since we have added the roles for this user it will take you to the manager app page.

Enabling Security for BIS-SMS

Adding entries to application web.xml for security enablement.

To use the container managed security with the above configurations, we now need to configure the application to leverage the container managed security of Apache Tomcat 8. In order to do this we need to add few entries to the web.xml file of the sample application. We will now add the following entries to web.xml located at WEB-INF folder of the sample web application BIS-SMS.

```
<security-constraint>

      <web-resource-collection>
            <web-resource-name>
                  Wildcard means whole application requires
                  authentication
            </web-resource-name>
            <url-pattern>/*</url-pattern>
            <http-method>GET</http-method>
            <http-method>POST</http-method>
      </web-resource-collection>

      <auth-constraint>
            <role-name>BisAdmin</role-name>
            <role-name>BisTeacher</role-name>
            <role-name>BisClerk</role-name>
      </auth-constraint>

      <user-data-constraint>
            <transport-guarantee>NONE</transport-guarantee>
      </user-data-constraint>

</security-constraint>

<login-config>
      <auth-method>FORM</auth-method>
      <form-login-config>
            <form-login-page>/BisLogin.jsp</form-login-page>
            <form-error-page>/BisLogin.jsp</form-error-page>
      </form-login-config>
</login-config>

<welcome-file-list>
      <welcome-file>BisLandingPage.jsp</welcome-file>
</welcome-file-list>
```

The <welcome-file-list> typically has one entry for the landing page upon successful authentication of the user. The server auto navigates the user to this page once authorized.

The <auth-method> with in the <login-config> tag specifies the authentication method. Here we will specify FORM since we have BisLogin.jsp file for form based authentication.

In the <form-login-page> tag we will specify our login page which is BisLogin.jsp

Within the <auth-constraint> tag under <security-constraints> we need to grant access of the application to a list of roles. Note that we have to specify all the roles that we want to use in this application's authorization. You may have many roles in the database. Some of them might be used by other web applications. The database is generally a centralized repository of all the users and roles in an enterprise. Each application will access its own users and roles.

LDAP servers are typically used in large enterprises as single source of information for all the users and roles. Oracle OID and Microsoft AD are the most popular examples of directory services used. We are not using any LDAP services for our application. However, this can be achieved with its specific configurations.

With this we are done with the enablement of container managed security of our sample application. Redeploy the application with the new modified web.xml file.

BIS-SMS Users and Roles

We will now add the following users and roles to the database for our sample application. Please refer to the requirements specification table for the roles details.

Users/Roles	BisAdmin	BisTeacher	BisClerk
Padma.kulkarni	✓	×	×
Guru.nath	×	✓	×
Shamim.banu	×	×	✓

In the authorization use case implementation, we will see how the dashboard and links are rendered to each of this user based on their roles.

17

BUILD AND DEPLOYMENT

Once a web application is ready, it has to be built, packaged and then deployed to the server.

A ready web application is nothing but a set of refined files. These files are typically java, Servlets, jsps, .css, xml and Javascript. All these files have to be packaged as per standards and then finally deployed to the server.

The Web Application Archive

As per JEE deployment specifications, we need to build a ".war" file for our application which can be deployed to the servlet container. war stands for Web Achieve. In our case, we need to build Bis.war file.

The .war file comprises of:

All the HTML/JSP files

All the complied java classes

All the libraries referenced (if any) in the form of .jar files

The deployment description (web.xml file)

The context file

Properties files

All the .css and .js files

Manifest file

A .war file build based on standards can be deployed to any server which is compliant with the standards. The Bis.war file we are building as a part of exercise is based on JEE standards. Since Bis.war is compliant with JEE standards, it can be deployed to any server which is JEE compliant. Hence, we can deploy the web archieve of our application to Weblogic, Websphere, Apache Tomcat or to any JEE complaint server.

Now, we have two things. One, build the Bis.war file and two, deploy it to Apache Tomcat server.

Building the Bis.war file

There are various methods to build the .war file. The simplest and easiest is to use an IDE like jdeveloper. In our case, we will use jdeveloper to build the Bis.war file.

Build Bis.war with jdeveloper

Step 1: Right click BisViewController project and select project properties as shown in the figure below.

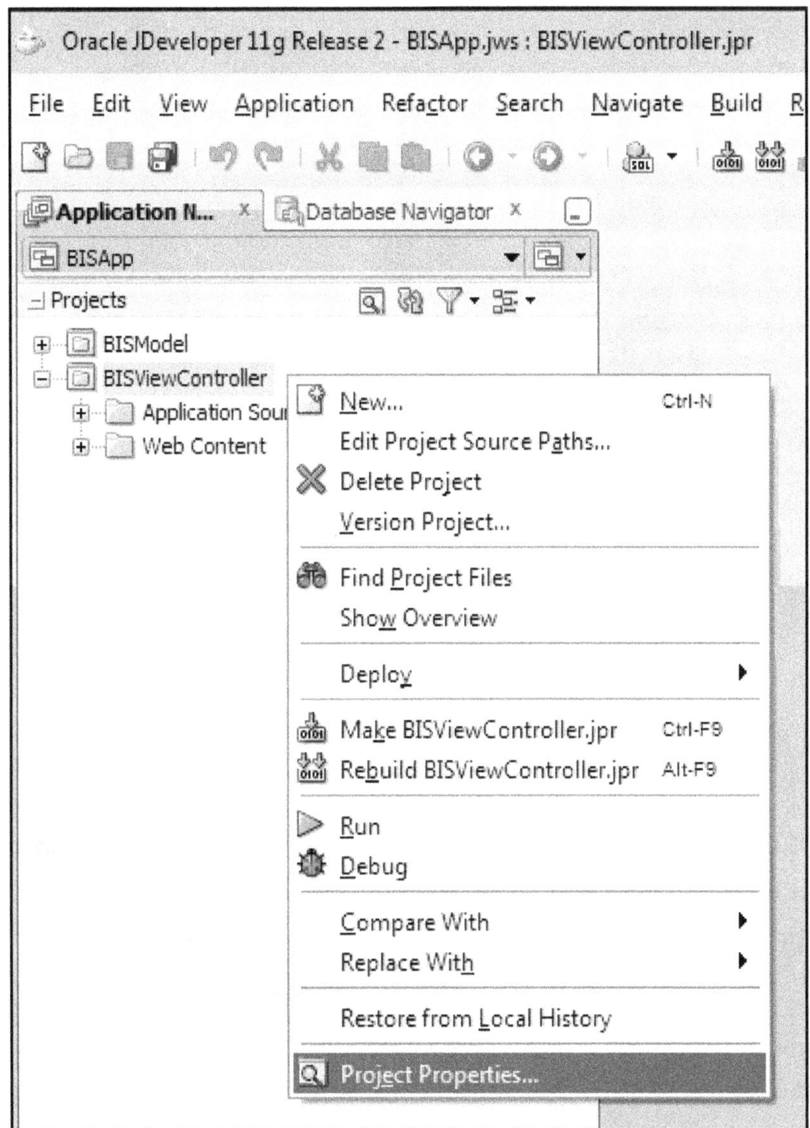

Step 2: On the left hand side, select Deployment and on the right hand side click new as shown in the figure below.

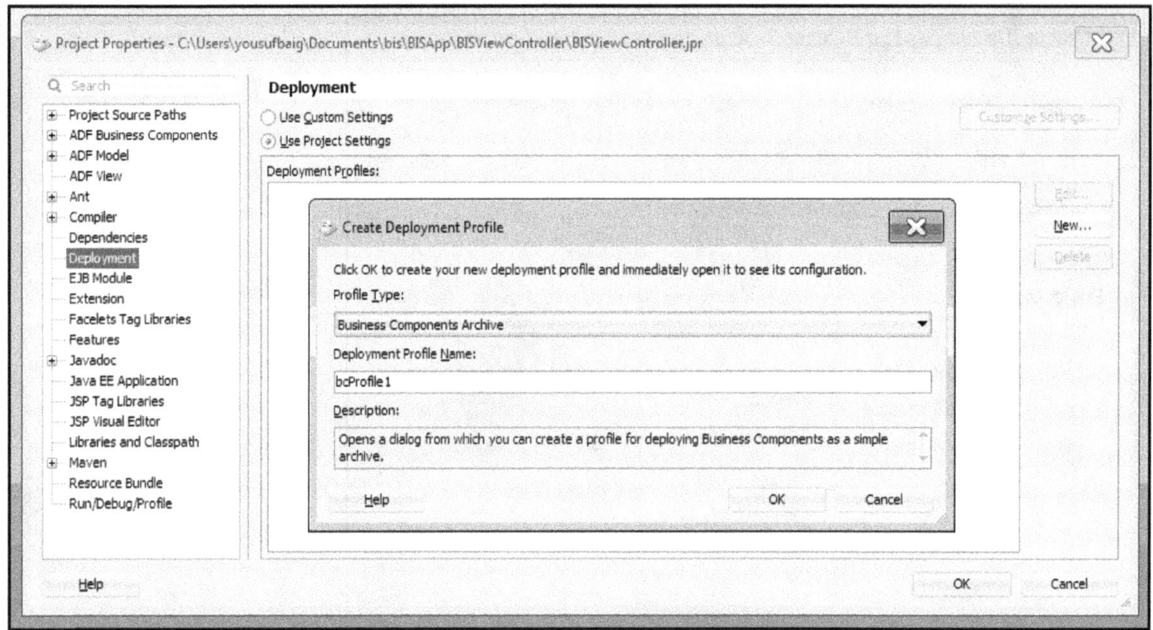

Step 3: Select war file under the profile type drop down menu and provide a name (Bis) for deployment profile. Click ok.

Step 4: Select Specify Java EE Web Context Root radio button and specify the context root as "Bis". Leave everything as it is and click ok. You will now see the deployment profile listed. Click ok to close the project properties dialogue/wizard. Save all and proceed to next steps.

Step 5: Right click the BisViewController project and select Deploy than Bis. In the wizard, select "Deploy to WAR" and click finish.

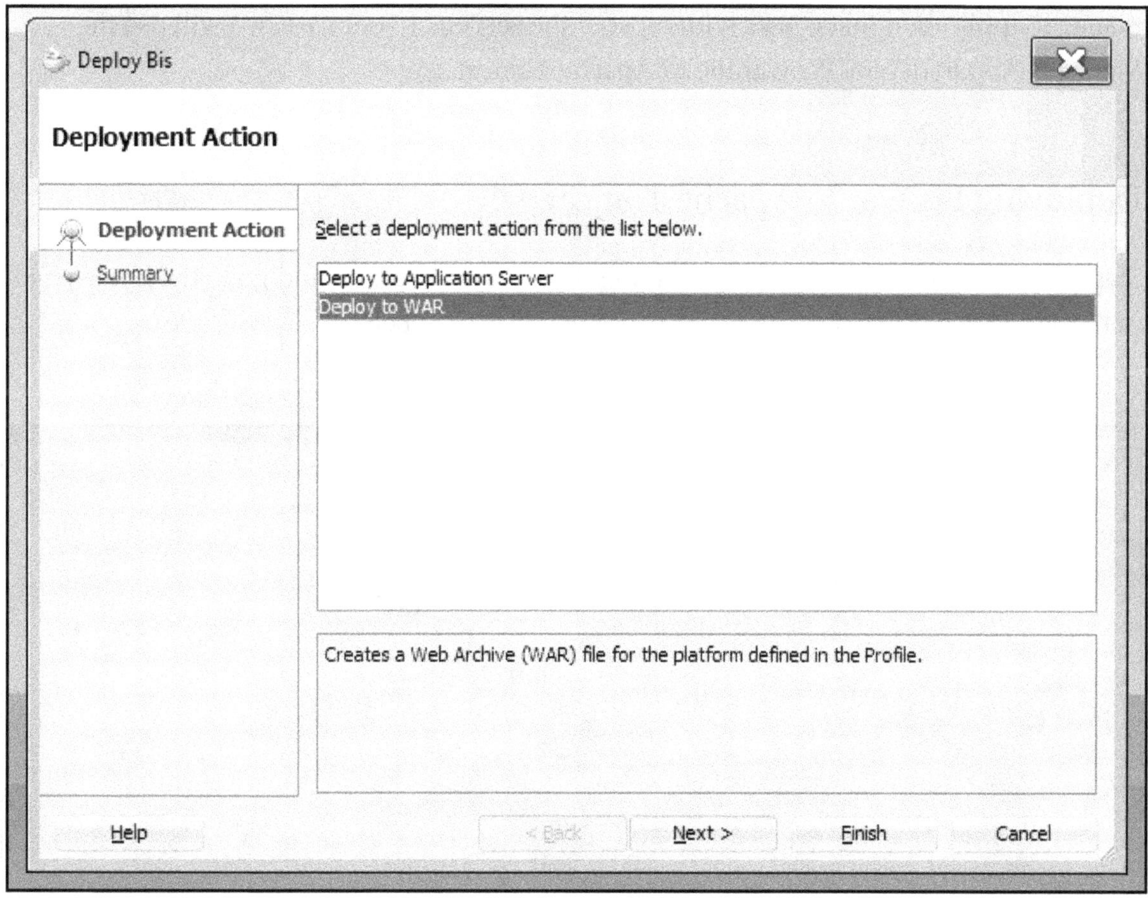

Step 6: Once you click finish, jdeveloper will prepare the Bis.war file for you and the log will tell you where the file is located. Go to the folder and verify the presence of the war file.

This completes the preparation of the war file. Now, lets deploy this war file to Apache Tomcat server.

Deploying the .war file

The war file can be deployed in various ways. The most common practice is to use ant script for deployment. The other easy way of doing it is using the GUI based deployment manager application that comes with most of the servers. In our case, we will use the Manager App to deploy Bis.war file to Apache Tomcat.

Deploying Bis.war to Apache Tomcat

Step 1: Make sure that the server is running. Launch the browser and go to the home page of the server. Click "Manager App" as shown in the figure below.

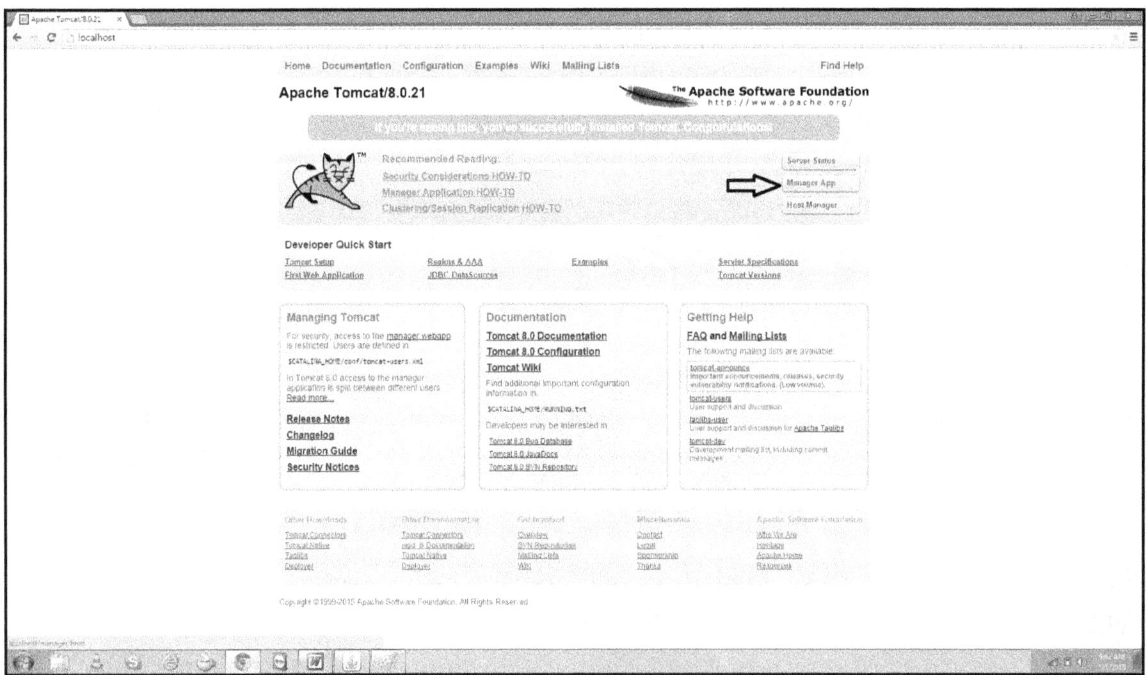

Step 2: The server will challenge you for user/password. Provide the admin user and password to proceed. Upon successful authentication and authorization, you will see the application manager page. Click "Choose File" button below for "Select WAR file to upload" as shown in the figure below.

Deploy

Deploy directory or WAR file located on server

Context Path (required):

XML Configuration file URL:

WAR or Directory URL:

Deploy

WAR file to deploy

Select WAR file to upload | Choose File | No file chosen

Deploy

Step 3: Once you browse the war file, click deploy. The server will now deploy the war file and upon successful deployment it will immediately refresh. Now, you should see deployed application under the list with the running status "true" as shown in the figure below.

Applications

Path	Version	Display Name	Running	Sessions	Commands
/	None specified	Welcome to Tomcat	true	0	Start Stop Reload Undeploy Expire sessions with idle ≥ 30 minutes
/Bis	None specified		true	0	Start Stop Reload Undeploy Expire sessions with idle ≥ 30 minutes
/docs	None specified	Tomcat Documentation	true	0	Start Stop Reload Undeploy Expire sessions with idle ≥ 30 minutes
/examples	None specified	Servlet and JSP Examples	true	0	Start Stop Reload Undeploy Expire sessions with idle ≥ 30 minutes
/host-manager	None specified	Tomcat Host Manager Application	true	0	Start Stop Reload Undeploy Expire sessions with idle ≥ 30 minutes
/manager	None specified	Tomcat Manager Application	true	2	Start Stop Reload Undeploy Expire sessions with idle ≥ 30 minutes

Step 4: Now, open a browser and go to the following url ***http://<host>:<port>/Bis Example: http://localhost/Bis***. This should load the login page of the application.

The other important files that needs to be understood for build and deployment are build.xml, context.xml and log4j.properties. Please refer chapter 21 for description and usage of these files.

18

TESTING

As the name suggests, testing is verifying whether the system built is as per the requirements specification. For our application we need two type of testing, unit testing and system testing.

Unit Testing

The unit testing needs to be performed by the developer for the individual use cases. For example, the developer who builds the manage attendance use case must verify whether this use case is working exactly as per the corresponding requirements specifications. Ideally, the implemented use case must satisfy all the requirements, it should be error free and must not have any bugs. A good developer leaves no stone unturned to make sure that the use case implemented by him/her is 100% bug free and 100% in compliance as per the requirement specifications for that use case.

System Testing

The system testing to be performed by the testing team. Once all the use cases are implemented by the developers, the solutions architect assembles them all and deploys the specific version of complete software solution to the testing environment. This solution is complete and this is the one which goes to the UAT and than to the production. The testing team performs rigorous testing on the testing environment and logs the issues, observations and bugs. This goes back to the development team. The development team fixes these bugs and a new version is deployed to the testing environment. The testing team once again performs all the tests on this version and reports back bug or regressions to the development team. This is a cyclic process and with each cycle the quality of the software improves.

User Acceptance Testing (UAT)

Once an acceptable point is achieved the solution is deployed to the UAT environment for user acceptance testing. In this testing, the client primarily verifies that the software solution is as per their requirements and expectations. Post approval of this the software solution is deployed to the production environment. Upon go-live the solution become usable for the end users and the end users will start using the software solution or web application in our case. Errors may happen even in production if the software lacks premium quality. The support team provides production support and takes care of the issues on the production environment.

19

DEBUGGING

What is a bug?

A bug in software is an error, a malfunction, a flaw, a fault or a failure either with the business logic or with the software code. The bug results in functioning of the software code in an unexpected way or not as per the requirements or expectations.

Steps to resolve a bug

The process of identifying, analyzing, reproducing and fixing a bug is called debugging. Lesser the number of bugs, higher the quality of the software. Lets learn to resolve a bug with a practical example from our sample application.

Describe the bug

While testing the use case update attendance, the sample application is failing to update the attendance.

Reproduce the bug

1. Log in to the BIS-SMS sample web application with the user padma.kulkarni who has BisAdmin rights.

2. Load the student into context whose id is MyFaAsYo12042004.

3. Goto manage attendance page.

4. For semester two, the current value of attendance is 0. Update it to 105 and click submit button.

5. As per the requirements specification, this page should now display 105 as updated attendance for the given student and semester. The page is rather displaying the same old value i.e. 0 instead of 105.

Reproduce the issue on your environment. Make sure that your environment and the client's environment has same version of the application and also the same version and same set of patches. A patch comprises of one or more modified java or other files belonging to the application.

Diagnosis and resolution

After ensuring that there is no discrepancy in version and patches reproduce the issue. Lets assume that the issues is reproduced on the technical support team's environment. Now, it is time to figure out why the attendance is not getting updated in the database table. This is the bug analysis phase. Open the application log file and look for the messages or exceptions related to this use case.

The log file has the following relevant message:

"The update count for attendance update is : 0"

This means that the update operation is failing. Otherwise the update count would have been 1 instead of 0.

Lets now open the java class where the update query is called. This is there in StudentAttendanceService.java. We identified this because we know that in our application the database operations are performed by the service classes. In case of no clue about the exact java file we can use a debugger in the IDE with a break point at a point of suspicion in the code. If not sure where to place the breakpoint, one can set it at the controller servlet level.

Within the updateStudentAttendance method we have this query.

```
UPDATE STUDENT_ATTENDANCE SET ATTENDANCE=? WHERE STUDENT_ID=? AND
SEMESTER=?
```

We will now execute this query with our values at a sql client for the given database and schema. The query to be executed is.

```
UPDATE STUDENT_ATTENDANCE SET ATTENDANCE=105 WHERE
STUDENT_ID='MyFaAsYo12042004' AND SEMESTER=2
```

The sql client now says, 0 rows updated. The most likely cause is that the record pertaining to the where conditions might not be existing in the student attendance table. To verify this lets execute the following query.

```
SELECT * FROM STUDENT_ATTENDANCE WHERESTUDENT_ID='MyFbAsYo12042004'
and SEMESTER=2;
```

This query is now returning zero rows. This confirms that the record for the where conditions is not there in the student attendance database table. The next question is why the page is displaying zero for the attendance when there is no record available in the database table. Analyzing the code reveals that the page displays zero if attendance is not found in the database table.

We now know the reason for the bug. Lets fix this bug now. In order to update the attendance for a given student and semester a record must be existing in the student attendance table. After careful analysis another vital information is revealed that this bug is only happening for the newly added students using add new student use case.

The add new student as of now is inserting records via database transaction to two database tables student details and parent details. For every new student, we need to insert a record to student attendance table with initial value for attendance as zero for each semester.

Write a separate method in AddStudentService.java class called insertNewStudentToSA and include that in the new student creation database transaction.

Verifying the fix

Add a new student using the add new student use case. This now adds two records to the student attendance table for this new student. Now, go to manage attendance page and update the attendance for each semester. The update query will not fail as there are records to be updated for the given where condition. This confirms that the issues is resolved and the bug is fixed.

Applying the patch

Once the bug is fixed we need to patch the client environment. This is done by replacing the modified java files with the existing java files. Identify the jar file to which these files belong. Ship the updated jar file to the client. Once the client replaces the old jar file with the new one. The bug is fixed on that environment.

20
OTHER IMPORTANT TOPICS

AJAX

In many cases when a user interacts with a web page, it is not at all necessary to reload the entire page just to change a view or a value in a small region of the page. In such cases only refreshing a small region of the page will suffice. Refreshing a region has lots of advantages compared to reloading the entire page. It saves time, reduces network traffic, saves internet data consumption, reduces burden on the server etc. The most important advantage is that the user feels as if things are real time.

This programming paradigm in which a web page is partially refreshed based on the user interaction is achieved through a combination of various technologies and it is called AJAX. Ajax stands for Asynchronous javascript and xml.

In AJAX when a user interacts with a web page, a javascript function is invoked on the browser side itself. This javascript function utilizes XMLHttpRequest object to interact with the server via Ajax request. The server returns the response text. This response text for the ajax request is consumed by the javascript call back function. This function in turn uses the response text either for computation or for direct display on the region of the page. The region of the web page is then refreshed enabling the user to see the Ajax response for a particular user interaction.

Hence, Ajax has two parts one on the client side where XMLHttpRequest javascript object is leveraged and two on the server side where the http request is responded with a response text.

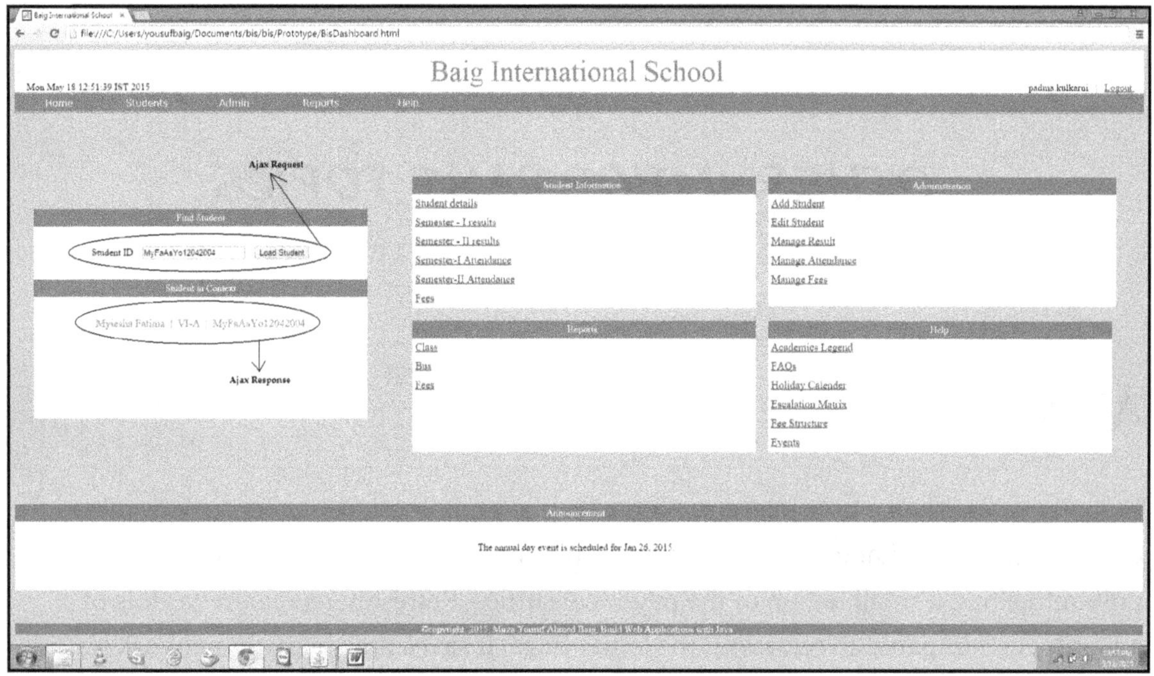

For a detailed implementation with design and working code please refer the use case implementation for *load student* in chapter 15.

Performance tuning and best practices

The following measures help in increasing the performance of the web application:

1. Keep the rendered html/jsp pages as light as possible. The web pages build using ide's generally add lots of redundant and unnecessary html tags. Make sure that the pages have only those tags and attributes which are required.
2. Use Ajax wherever applicable.
3. Apply all the best practices for java code development at the server side.
4. Release/Close resources immediately after the usage.

5. Handle every single exception in the code.
6. Use logging as if you are going to provide technical support to the application after going live.
7. Evolve the database design as much has possible.
8. Clean up unused variables and functions in the javascript (.js) file.
9. Clean up all the unused styles in the cascaded style sheet (.css) file.
10. Use data sources for interaction with databases.
11. In a business critical application perform validation both at the client side as well as the server side.
12. Use page templates wherever possible.
13. Leverage proven architectural and design patterns.
14. Reuse html pages from the prototype for building the actual jsp pages.
15. Optimize the server for performance following recommended practices in the specific server's administrative guide. One such example is increasing the heap memory size for the server.
16. Be complaint with the recommendations for the framework used. This will be helpful for framework upgrades. Otherwise, there will be issues and the upgrade will not be seamless.

Scalability

A software solution that has provisions to easy extend or enhance it for future requirements is called a scalable system. Scalability is an important factor for any software solution design. Rigid systems require lots of human effort, rework, cost, downtime etc whereas scalable systems are flexible to enhance.

For the sample project we built in this book, in case we want to add couple of new use cases we have to just build a jsp view, service class, command processor and beans in compliance with the framework and the new use case becomes pluggable. The sample application along with our framework is scalable. Hence, we can extend or enhance it with ease. We can easily add any number of use cases to our sample application in future because it is designed to be highly scalable. Scalability needs to be kept in mind at the architecture and design stage.

A practical example of scalability is modern day desktop computer's mother board. These motherboards come up with open slots for memory (RAM). Once you purchase a desktop with 4 Gb RAM, it can be later scaled up to 16 or 32 Gb of RAM just by inserting memory cards in the open slots provided. In case of non scalable mother boards, the user has to buy a new mother board or desktop itself with the new requirement for the memory.

21
IMPORTANT FILES

Besides the java classes, jsps, .css and .js files a deployment ready web application has few other important files and folder. In this chapter we will have a closer look at all these important files and folders that are must to have a smooth and error free deployment and execution of the application.

web.xml

Generally, many web applications are deployed to a server. Each web application has its own set of customizations, properties and other JEE configurations. In order to specify these things to the server, each web application is packaged with a deployment descriptor which is nothing but an xml file. This xml file is called web.xml as per Java Servlet specification.

In Java Platform Enterprise Edition, the web.xml file (deployment description) describes how a web application should be deployed to the container. The web.xml resides in the WEB-INF folder of the web application root.

Lets look into the important tags and attributes of the web application deployment descriptor (web.xml). For this lets use the web.xml file of BIS-SMS sample web application.

Describes the controller servlet.

```
<servlet>
      <servlet-name> ControllerServlet </servlet-name>
```

```
        <servlet-class>
              com.bis.servlet.ControllerServlet
        </servlet-class>
  </servlet>
```

Describes the Ajax controller servlet.

```
  <servlet>
        <servlet-name>
              AjaxControllerServlet
        </servlet-name>
        <servlet-class>
              com.bis.servlet.AjaxControllerServlet
        </servlet-class>
  </servlet>
```

Describes the mapping for controller servlet.

```
  <servlet-mapping>
        <servlet-name>
              ControllerServlet
        </servlet-name>
        <url-pattern>
              /BisControllerServlet
        </url-pattern>
  </servlet-mapping>
```

Describes the mapping for Ajax controller servlet.

```
  <servlet-mapping>
        <servlet-name>
              AjaxControllerServlet
        </servlet-name>
        <url-pattern>
              /BisAjaxControllerServlet
        </url-pattern>
  </servlet-mapping>
```

Describes the resource reference for application (BIS) data source.

```
  <resource-ref>
         <description>BIS Datasource</description>
        <res-ref-name>jdbc/bisDataSource</res-ref-name>
        <res-type>javax.sql.DataSource</res-type>
        <res-auth>Container</res-auth>
  </resource-ref>
```

Context.xml

Apache Tomcat servlet container does not provide any GUI to create connection pools and data sources. This is achieved via a resource tag entry in context.xml file.

The context.xml files are application specific as well as at server level. The one at server level is located at $CATALINA_BASE/conf/context.xml. For configuring data source security realm we need to add the data source resource entry to this file. This is detailed in the chapter titled securing application under the configuration heading. And the one specific to application is under the META-INF folder of the subjective application.

We need to add entries to two context descriptors for our application.

One in the server context descriptor located at $CATALINA_BASE/conf/context.xml and other in the application context descriptor located at $CATALINA_BASE/webapps/Bis/META-INF/context.xml

An entry is added to server's context descriptor file for a data source which is used by the container managed security provider. This data source is used for authentication and authorization purpose by the server.

We need to add an entry to the context.xml file belonging to our sample application which is located within the /Bis/META-INF folder. This entry creates a data source to be used in our sample application. The connections returned by this data source will provide us access to our application tables.

```
<Resource
      name="jdbc/bisDataSource" auth="Container" maxActive="20"
      maxIdle="5" maxWait="10000"
      factory="oracle.ucp.jdbc.PoolDataSourceImpl"
      driverClassName="oracle.jdbc.OracleDriver"
      url="jdbc:oracle:thin:bis/bis@127.1.1.0:1521:XE"
      type="oracle.ucp.jdbc.PoolDataSource"
      connectionFactoryClassName="oracle.jdbc.pool.OracleDataSource"
      connectionPoolName="BisPool" validateConnectionOnBorrow="true"
      sqlForValidateConnection="select 1 from DUAL"
/>
```

The above entry in the context.xml file of our application will create a data source called bisDataSource. We perform a JNDI look up for this data source in our application. Please refer the DatabaseService.java class in the components chapter for the actual code to look up this data source.

The driver class name is specified as OracleDriver because we are using Oracle database. The URL points to localhost with the port 1521 where the system identifier for database instance (SID) named XE is running. And "bis" is the database schema name.

22

APPENDIX

Database scripts

Schema: BisSecurityRealm

```
CREATE TABLE USERS      (

      USER_NAME VARCHAR2(15 BYTE) NOT NULL, USER_PASS VARCHAR2(15 BYTE)
      NOT NULL, CONSTRAINT "User_Name_PK" PRIMARY KEY (USER_NAME) ENABLE
)

CREATE TABLE USER_ROLES (

      USER_NAME VARCHAR2(15 BYTE) NOT NULL, ROLE_NAME VARCHAR2(15 BYTE)
      NOT NULL, CONSTRAINT "User_Roles_CPK" PRIMARY KEY  (USER_NAME,
      ROLE_NAME) ENABLE
)

ALTER TABLE USER_ROLES ADD CONSTRAINT USER_NAME_FK FOREIGN KEY
(USER_NAME) REFERENCES USERS (USER_NAME) ENABLE;
```

Schema: Bis

```
CREATE TABLE BIS_CONSTANTS     (

      PROPERTY VARCHAR2(30 BYTE), VALUE VARCHAR2(80 BYTE), REMARKS
      VARCHAR2(60 BYTE)
)

CREATE TABLE CLASS_TEACHER_MAPPING   (
```

```
      EMPLOYEE_ID NUMBER, GRADE VARCHAR2(4 BYTE) NOT NULL, SECTION
      VARCHAR2(1 BYTE) NOT NULL, CONSTRAINT CTM_CPK PRIMARY KEY (GRADE,
      SECTION) ENABLE
)

CREATE TABLE COSCHOLASTIC_RESULTS   (

      STUDENT_ID VARCHAR2(16 BYTE) NOT NULL, SEMESTER VARCHAR2(1 BYTE)
      NOT NULL, CRITICAL_THINKING VARCHAR2(15 BYTE), CREATIVE_THINKING
      VARCHAR2(15 BYTE), COLLAB_LEARNING VARCHAR2(15 BYTE),
      COMMUNICATION_SKILLS VARCHAR2(15 BYTE), COMPREHENSIVE_GROWTH
      VARCHAR2(15 BYTE), INTELLI_QUO VARCHAR2(15 BYTE), EMO_QUO
      VARCHAR2(15 BYTE), SOCIAL_QUO VARCHAR2(15 BYTE), HEALTH_QUO
      VARCHAR2(15 BYTE), COMMUNITY_CONSC VARCHAR2(15 BYTE),
      SCHOLASTICPERFORMANCE_REM VARCHAR2(300 BYTE),
      COSCHOLASTICPERFORMANCE_REM VARCHAR2(300 BYTE), CONSTRAINT CSR_CPK
      PRIMARY KEY (STUDENT_ID, SEMESTER) ENABLE
)

CREATE TABLE EMPLOYEE_DETAILS (

      EMPLOYEE_ID NUMBER NOT NULL, FIRST_NAME VARCHAR2(20 BYTE),
      MIDDLE_NAME VARCHAR2(20 BYTE), LAST_NAME VARCHAR2(20 BYTE),
      DATE_OF_BIRTH DATE, MOBILE_NUMBER VARCHAR2(15 BYTE), DEPARTMENT
      VARCHAR2(20 BYTE), DESIGNATION VARCHAR2(20 BYTE), HIRE_DATE DATE,
      SEX VARCHAR2(1 BYTE), ACTIVE_FLAG VARCHAR2(1 BYTE), ADDRESS
      VARCHAR2(100 BYTE), MANAGER_ID NUMBER, CONSTRAINT EMPLOYEE_ID_PK
      PRIMARY KEY (EMPLOYEE_ID) ENABLE
)

CREATE TABLE PARENT_DETAILS   (

      FATHER_NAME VARCHAR2(30 BYTE), MOTHER_NAME VARCHAR2(30 BYTE),
      GUARDIAN_NAME VARCHAR2(30 BYTE), FATHER_MOBILE VARCHAR2(15 BYTE),
      MOTHER_MOBILE VARCHAR2(15 BYTE), GUARDIAN_MOBILE VARCHAR2(10 BYTE),
      ADDRESS VARCHAR2(100 BYTE), FATHER_QUALIFICATION VARCHAR2(50 BYTE),
      MOTHER_QUALIFICATION VARCHAR2(50 BYTE), ANNUAL_INCOME VARCHAR2(10
      BYTE), STUDENT_ID VARCHAR2(16 BYTE) NOT NULL, CONSTRAINT
      PARENTDETAILSPK PRIMARY KEY (STUDENT_ID) ENABLE
)

CREATE TABLE SCHOLASTIC_RESULTS     (

      STUDENT_ID VARCHAR2(16 BYTE) NOT NULL, SEMESTER VARCHAR2(1 BYTE)
      NOT NULL, ENGLISH_GRADE VARCHAR2(1 BYTE), MATHS_GRADE VARCHAR2(1
      BYTE), SCIENCE_GRADE VARCHAR2(1 BYTE), SOCIAL_GRADE VARCHAR2(1
      BYTE), LANG2_GRADE VARCHAR2(1 BYTE), LANG3_GRADE VARCHAR2(1 BYTE),
      COMPSC_GRADE VARCHAR2(1 BYTE), ARTS_GRADE VARCHAR2(1 BYTE),
      MUSIC_GRADE VARCHAR2(1 BYTE), DANCE_GRADE VARCHAR2(1 BYTE),
```

```
	PHYSICALEDU_GRADE VARCHAR2(1 BYTE), VALUEEDU_GRADE VARCHAR2(1
	BYTE), SCHOOLPROJECT_GRADE VARCHAR2(1 BYTE), ENGLISH_REM
	VARCHAR2(150 BYTE), MATHS_REM VARCHAR2(150 BYTE), SCIENCE_REM
	VARCHAR2(150 BYTE), SOCIAL_REM VARCHAR2(150 BYTE), LANG2_REM
	VARCHAR2(150 BYTE), LANG3_REM VARCHAR2(150 BYTE), COMPSC_REM
	VARCHAR2(150 BYTE), ARTS_REM VARCHAR2(150 BYTE), MUSIC_REM
	VARCHAR2(150 BYTE), DANCE_REM VARCHAR2(150 BYTE), PHYSICALEDU_REM
	VARCHAR2(150 BYTE), VALUEEDU_REM VARCHAR2(150 BYTE),
	SCHOOLPROJECT_REM VARCHAR2(150 BYTE), CONSTRAINT SR_CPK PRIMARY KEY
	(STUDENT_ID, SEMESTER) ENABLE
)

CREATE TABLE STUDENT_ATTENDANCE     (

	STUDENT_ID VARCHAR2(16 BYTE) NOT NULL, ATTENDANCE NUMBER, SEMESTER
	VARCHAR2(1 BYTE) NOT NULL, CONSTRAINT SA_CPK PRIMARY KEY
	(STUDENT_ID, SEMESTER) ENABLE
)

CREATE TABLE STUDENT_DETAILS  (

	ACTIVE_FLAG VARCHAR2(1 BYTE) NOT NULL, FIRST_NAME VARCHAR2(20 BYTE)
	, MIDDLE_NAME VARCHAR2(20 BYTE), LAST_NAME VARCHAR2(20 BYTE),
	GENDER_CODE VARCHAR2(1 BYTE), BIRTH_DATE DATE, BIRTH_CITY_NAME
	VARCHAR2(20 BYTE), BIRTH_STATE_CODE VARCHAR2(2 BYTE),
	BIRTH_COUNTRY_CODE VARCHAR2(2 BYTE), BLOOD_GROUP VARCHAR2(3 BYTE),
	BUS_ID NUMBER, STUDENT_ID VARCHAR2(16 BYTE) NOT NULL, GRADE
	VARCHAR2(4 BYTE), SECTION VARCHAR2(1 BYTE), HEIGHT VARCHAR2(3
	BYTE), WEIGHT VARCHAR2(3 BYTE), SIBLINGS_STUDENT_IDS VARCHAR2(100
	BYTE), CONSTRAINT STUDENTIDPK PRIMARY KEY (STUDENT_ID) ENABLE
)

CREATE TABLE STUDENT_FEES     (

	STUDENT_ID VARCHAR2(16 BYTE) NOT NULL, JAN_ACAD VARCHAR2(1 BYTE),
	FEB_ACAD VARCHAR2(1 BYTE), MAR_ACAD VARCHAR2(1 BYTE), APR_ACAD
	VARCHAR2(1 BYTE), MAY_ACAD VARCHAR2(1 BYTE), JUN_ACAD VARCHAR2(1
	BYTE), JUL_ACAD VARCHAR2(1 BYTE), AUG_ACAD VARCHAR2(1 BYTE),
	SEP_ACAD VARCHAR2(1 BYTE), OCT_ACAD VARCHAR2(1 BYTE), NOV_ACAD
	VARCHAR2(1 BYTE), DEC_ACAD VARCHAR2(1 BYTE), JAN_BUS VARCHAR2(1
	BYTE), FEB_BUS VARCHAR2(1 BYTE), MAR_BUS VARCHAR2(1 BYTE), APR_BUS
	VARCHAR2(1 BYTE), MAY_BUS VARCHAR2(1 BYTE), JUN_BUS VARCHAR2(1
	BYTE), JUL_BUS VARCHAR2(1 BYTE), AUG_BUS VARCHAR2(1 BYTE), SEP_BUS
	VARCHAR2(1 BYTE), OCT_BUS VARCHAR2(1 BYTE), NOV_BUS VARCHAR2(1
	BYTE), DEC_BUS VARCHAR2(1 BYTE), REMARKS VARCHAR2(200 BYTE),
	CONSTRAINT SF_PK PRIMARY KEY (STUDENT_ID) ENABLE
)

CREATE TABLE TRANSPORTATION_DETAILS (
```

```
    BUS_ID NUMBER NOT NULL, TRANSPORTATION_TYPE VARCHAR2(12 BYTE),
    DRIVER_EMPLOYEE_ID NUMBER, BUS_NUMBER VARCHAR2(12 BYTE),
    HELPER_EMPLOYEE_ID NUMBER, CONSTRAINT TD_PK PRIMARY KEY (BUS_ID)
    ENABLE
)

    ALTER TABLE CLASS_TEACHER_MAPPING ADD CONSTRAINT CTM_FK FOREIGN KEY
    (EMPLOYEE_ID) REFERENCES EMPLOYEE_DETAILS (EMPLOYEE_ID) ENABLE;

    ALTER TABLE COSCHOLASTIC_RESULTS ADD CONSTRAINT CSR_FK FOREIGN KEY
    (STUDENT_ID) REFERENCES STUDENT_DETAILS (STUDENT_ID) ENABLE;

    ALTER TABLE PARENT_DETAILS ADD CONSTRAINT STUDENTIDFK FOREIGN KEY
    (STUDENT_ID) REFERENCES STUDENT_DETAILS (STUDENT_ID) ENABLE;

    ALTER TABLE SCHOLASTIC_RESULTS ADD CONSTRAINT SR_FK FOREIGN KEY
    ( STUDENT_ID) REFERENCES STUDENT_DETAILS (STUDENT_ID) ENABLE;

    ALTER TABLE STUDENT_ATTENDANCE ADD CONSTRAINT SA_FK FOREIGN KEY
    (STUDENT_ID) REFERENCES STUDENT_DETAILS (STUDENT_ID) ENABLE;

    ALTER TABLE STUDENT_DETAILS ADD CONSTRAINT SD_FK FOREIGN KEY
    (BUS_ID) REFERENCES TRANSPORTATION_DETAILS (BUS_ID) ENABLE;

    ALTER TABLE STUDENT_FEES ADD CONSTRAINT SF_FK FOREIGN KEY
    (STUDENT_ID) REFERENCES STUDENT_DETAILS (STUDENT_ID) ENABLE;

    ALTER TABLE TRANSPORTATION_DETAILS ADD CONSTRAINT TD_DFK FOREIGN
    KEY (DRIVER_EMPLOYEE_ID) REFERENCES EMPLOYEE_DETAILS (EMPLOYEE_ID)
    ENABLE;

    ALTER TABLE TRANSPORTATION_DETAILS ADD CONSTRAINT TD_HFK FOREIGN
    KEY (HELPER_EMPLOYEE_ID) REFERENCES EMPLOYEE_DETAILS (EMPLOYEE_ID)
    ENABLE;
```

Index

A

Achieve, 317

Add Student, vii, viii, xiii, 45, 67, 140, 153, 277, 280, 291

AddStudent.jsp, xiii, 67, 280, 281, 282, 291

AddStudentCP.java, xiii, 281

AddStudentService.java, xiii, 283, 329

ADF, xvii, 17, 350

Administration, vii, 43, 153

AJAX, xiv, xviii, 159, 160, 161, 162, 331

AjaxControllerServlet.java, xi, 117

Apache, vi, xiii, 6, 23, 24, 26, 97, 101, 105, 112, 142, 144, 145, 148, 256, 311, 314, 318, 321, 322, 337

Application, v, vi, ix, xiii, 2, 26, 34, 84, 317

Architecture, v, ix, 2, 80, 84, 96

artifacts, 4, 119, 162, 172, 267, 281, 301

Assessment, vii, 39, 40, 248, 250

attributes, 31, 34, 107, 313, 332, 335

Authentication, vi, xi, 34, 35, 144

Authorization, vi, xi, 34, 35, 149, 165, 311

B

Baig International School, 1, 34, 113, 138, 147, 149

bean, 98, 126, 128, 171, 182, 187, 206, 207, 217, 222, 238, 246, 272, 273, 281, 288, 289, 290, 291, 304

best practices, xiv, xix, 93, 332

Bis.war, xiii, 317, 318, 321, 322

BisBean.java, xi, 127

BisCommand.java, xi, 121

BisConstants.java, xi, 134

BisCP.java, xi, 121

BisDashboard.jsp, xi, xii, 58, 149, 162, 165

BisFramework, ix, 95, 96

BisHome.jsp, xi, 77, 78, 97, 116, 135, 137, 149, 157, 158, 172, 187, 207, 222, 246, 257, 273, 291, 304

BisLogin.jsp, xi, 57, 145, 314, 315

BisScript.js, viii, xii, 71, 72, 160, 162, 166

BisSecurityRealm, ix, xiv, 87, 311, 312, 313, 339

BisService.java, xi, 124

BIS-SMS, ix, x, xiii, 1, 2, 34, 84, 107, 113, 135, 143, 173, 267, 281, 301, 311, 314, 315, 327, 335

BISStyle.css, viii, 74, 77, 78, 138, 150, 172, 196, 210, 230, 256, 257, 277, 297, 309

Bisutility.java, xi, 128

Blueprint, v, 2

browser, 13, 26, 71, 73, 84, 94, 95, 96, 98, 99, 108, 116, 118, 158, 160, 161, 167, 169, 197, 212, 231, 265, 283, 322, 323, 331

bug, xiv, 101, 325, 326, 327, 328, 329, 330

business, xviii, xix, 3, 81, 84, 97, 101, 121, 122, 142, 160, 169, 171, 197, 212, 231, 256, 265, 279, 299, 327, 333

button, 48, 104, 144, 150, 159, 167, 275, 307, 309, 320, 322, 328

C

Cascaded Style Sheet, viii, 73

CATALINA_HOME, 23, 24

Class, vi, vii, ix, 31, 38, 48, 89, 105, 115, 118, 140, 154, 174, 190, 268, 269, 274, 276, 282, 302

CLIENT, viii, 71

Client Tier, x, 96

code, xviii, 3, 57, 58, 60, 61, 62, 63, 64, 65, 66, 67, 68, 69, 70, 71, 77, 78, 90, 98, 104, 105, 108, 112, 132, 135, 137, 149, 157, 158, 162, 167, 173, 174, 182, 187, 196, 198, 206, 208, 211, 213, 217, 222, 230, 232, 238, 246, 257, 264, 267, 268, 270, 272, 274, 277, 278, 281, 283, 291, 297, 301, 303, 305, 327, 328, 329, 332, 333, 338

Command Pattern, viii, 80

Command Processor, x, 98

Command Processors, xi, 113, 119

complexity, xviii, 350

compliance, 85, 93, 325, 334

Components, v

COMPONENTS, x, 113

Compose, v, 2

computational, 71, 135

Configuring, xiii, 26, 311

connection, 3, 111, 112, 132, 133, 134, 163, 164, 175, 176, 177, 179, 180, 181, 200, 201, 202, 203, 204, 205, 206, 215, 216, 217, 234, 235, 236, 237, 238, 269, 270, 271, 281, 284, 285, 286, 287, 288, 289, 290, 304, 337

connectivity, x, 111

Constants, ix, 90

context, 37, 38, 41, 42, 43, 73, 107, 112, 133, 134, 158, 160, 161, 162, 167, 168, 174, 196, 211, 230, 297, 312, 313, 317, 320, 323, 328, 337

Context, xiv, 132, 150, 320, 337

Context.xml, xiv, 337

Control Flow, x, 98

Controller Layer, ix, x, 94, 97

ControllerServlet.java, x, 115

Criteria, vii, 49

CSS, xviii

D

Dashboard, vii, 58, 149

data, viii, xiii, 26, 55, 69, 81, 84, 88, 94, 97, 99, 111, 112, 131, 133, 134, 143, 159, 171, 172, 181, 217, 266, 267, 271, 272, 281, 288, 301, 311, 312, 313, 314, 331, 333, 336, 337

Data Sources, x, 4

Database, v, vi, x, xiv, 2, 6, 9, 12, 96, 111, 300, 339

DATABASE, ix, x, 87, 111

DatabaseService.java, xi, 112, 132, 172, 196, 210, 230, 256, 277, 297, 309, 338

date, 47

DEBUGGING, xiv, 327

default, 18, 26, 49

dependency injection, 80

Deployment, v, 4, 28, 319

Design, v, vi, viii, ix, 2, 27, 30, 80, 81

DESIGN, ix, 87

developer, 350

Diagnosis, xiv, 328

Diagram, vi, 31

E

Employee, ix, 89

engineering, xvii, xviii, xix, 83, 84, 350

environment, 5, 6, 23, 24, 25, 97, 325, 326, 328, 330

ER-diagram, 87, 88

error, 36, 43, 101, 105, 116, 118, 129, 130, 131, 133, 134, 163, 164, 173, 175, 179, 180, 199, 200, 201, 202, 203, 204, 205, 214, 215, 216, 233, 234, 237, 268, 269, 271, 282, 284, 286, 287, 288, 302, 314, 325, 327, 335

execute method, 81, 98, 99, 116, 117, 118, 119, 121, 160, 161, 163, 167, 169, 170, 173, 174, 197, 198, 199, 212, 213, 214, 231, 232, 233, 265, 266, 267, 268, 279, 280, 281, 282, 299, 300, 301, 302, 303

execution, 81, 98, 101, 142, 158, 335

Executive Summary, vi, 34

explicitly, 108, 281, 288

F

features, 71, 116

Fees Status Page, viii, 65

fields, 30, 45, 46, 47, 81, 124, 126, 144, 182, 206, 217, 238, 272, 277, 291, 305

file, x, xiii, 6, 14, 23, 26, 71, 73, 77, 101, 102, 104, 105, 112, 132, 134, 135, 142, 187, 207, 208, 222, 246, 273, 274, 291, 305, 312, 313, 314, 315, 317, 318, 320, 321, 322, 323, 328, 330, 333, 335, 337

finally, 3, 81, 95, 143, 144, 164, 166, 176, 179, 180, 201, 202, 203, 204, 205, 206, 216, 237, 238, 271, 283, 284, 286, 287, 288, 289, 290, 303, 304, 317

Footer, vii, 50, 54

FORM, 314, 315

Framework, v, ix, 3, 93, 119, 121, 161

FRAMEWORK, ix, 93

G

GetReportByClassCP.java, xiii, 267

GetStudentAcademicsCP.java, xii, 232

GetStudentAttendanceCP.java, xii, 198

GetStudentDetailsCP.java, xii, 172, 173

GetStudentFeesCP.java, xii, 213

governance, 101, 142

H

Hardware, v, 5

Header, vii, 50, 54

Help, vii, viii, xii, 35, 49, 50, 56, 70, 140, 143, 155, 256, 257

High Level Design, v, 2

Home Page, vii, 58

html, 14, 50, 53, 56, 57, 58, 59, 60, 61, 62, 63, 64, 65, 66, 67, 68, 69, 70, 71, 73, 94, 97, 98, 115, 117, 135, 137, 138, 140, 141, 145, 148, 149, 156, 167, 256, 257, 263, 288, 332, 333

HTML5, xviii, 292, 293

Http, x, 108, 161, 199, 214, 233

I

information, 34, 37, 38, 39, 40, 41, 50, 54, 88, 89, 101, 102, 104, 108, 126, 142, 158, 187, 207, 222, 246, 273, 315, 329

Installing, vi, 5, 6, 14, 23

instance, 116, 118, 122, 128, 163, 166, 181, 187, 199, 205, 206, 207, 214, 217, 222, 233, 238, 246, 268, 271, 272, 281, 283, 288, 289, 290, 303, 338 interface, 2, 53, 94, 98, 108, 113, 116, 117, 119, 121, 122, 124, 128, 134, 173, 267, 281, 301

J

Java, i, ii, v, ix, x, xi, xvii, xviii, xix, 3, 23, 30, 93, 94, 95, 98, 111, 113, 115, 124, 135, 141, 148, 320, 335, 350

JavaScript, viii, xviii, 71, 97

jdeveloper, vi, x, 6, 14, 17, 20, 22, 23, 102, 318, 321

jsp, 71, 73, 77, 82, 94, 113, 116, 118, 135, 137, 138, 140, 141, 144, 149, 165, 171, 181, 187, 196, 207, 208, 210, 217, 222, 230, 246, 256, 257, 266, 271, 272, 273, 277, 281, 289, 291, 297, 303, 304, 305, 309, 314, 332, 333

JSP, xviii, 97, 135, 317

Jsp page, 99

L

layout, vii, 53, 54, 105

legend, viii, 50, 56, 70, 257

level, xviii, xix, 3, 53, 73, 80, 82, 83, 84, 101, 105, 158, 328, 337, 350

link, 50, 54, 75, 76, 77, 138, 150, 157, 168, 169, 196, 197, 211, 212, 230, 231, 256, 257, 264, 265, 278, 279, 297, 299, 313

Load Student, vi, vii, xi, 36, 59, 150, 158

LoadStudentCP.java, xi, 162

Log4j, x, xi, 101, 102, 104, 113, 142

log4j.properties, x, 105, 323

logging, x, 101, 102, 104, 105, 142, 333

LOGGING, x, 101

Logging Levels, x, 101

logic, 3, 71, 81, 84, 97, 121, 122, 160, 169, 171, 197, 212, 231, 256, 265, 279, 299, 303, 327

Login, vii, 57, 145, 148, 174, 199, 214, 233, 302

M

Manage Attendance Page, viii, 66

ManageAttendance.jsp, xiii, 66, 300, 301, 303, 304, 305

ManageAttendanceCP.java, xiii, 301

Menu, vii, 50

menu items, 50, 73

method, 3, 98, 104, 114, 116, 117, 118, 119, 121, 122, 124, 131, 132, 134, 145, 146, 150, 160, 161, 163, 164, 167, 169, 170, 171, 173, 174, 175, 181, 187, 197, 198, 199, 200, 202, 205, 212, 213, 214, 215, 216, 217, 231, 232, 233, 234, 238, 246, 265, 266, 267, 268, 271, 274, 279, 280, 281, 282, 283, 288, 289, 290, 291, 299, 300, 301, 303, 304, 305, 314, 315, 329

Middleware, 16, 350

Miscellaneous, vii, 35, 49

Model Layer, ix, x, 94, 97

Module, vi, vii, 35, 36, 43, 48, 49

MVC, viii, ix, xviii, xix, 3, 80, 81, 93, 95, 119, 121

N

navigation, 2, 54, 55, 77, 94, 97, 149, 173, 199, 214, 233, 268, 282, 283, 302, 303

O

Object, vi, ix, 30, 81

OOAD, vi, 27, 30

options, viii, 4, 68

Oracle, vi, xvii, xviii, 6, 9, 14, 16, 22, 23, 96, 315, 338, 350

Outline, v, 2

P

package, 108, 115, 117, 121, 124, 126, 127, 128, 132, 134, 162, 173, 174, 182, 198, 199, 206, 213, 214, 217, 232, 234, 238, 267, 268, 272, 281, 283, 301

Pages, vii, xi, 49, 113, 135

patch, xiv, 328, 330

Patterns, viii, 79, 80

PATTERNS, viii, 79

Performance, vii, xiv, 39, 40, 41, 248, 250, 255, 257, 259, 332

Phase, vi, 33

phases, 27

PL/SQL, xviii

plug and play, 93

pool, 112, 312, 337

presentation, 94, 135

productivity, 93

PROJECT, x, 113

Prototype, v, vii, viii, 2, 57, 58, 59, 60, 61, 62, 63, 64, 65, 66, 67, 68, 69, 70, 144, 149, 158, 167, 196, 211, 230, 256, 264, 277, 297

public, 50, 81, 104, 115, 117, 121, 124, 126, 127, 129, 130, 132, 133, 134, 162, 163, 173, 175, 179, 180, 182, 183, 184, 185, 186, 187, 198, 200, 202, 204, 205, 206, 207, 213, 215, 216, 217, 218, 219, 220, 221, 222, 232, 234, 237, 238, 239, 240, 241, 242, 243, 244, 245, 256, 267, 268, 269, 271, 272, 273, 281, 282, 283, 288, 301

Q

query, 48, 85, 164, 171, 181, 205, 217, 238, 266, 271, 272, 289, 290, 304, 328, 329, 330

R

records, 122, 176, 202, 203, 266, 271, 272, 273, 274, 277, 283, 288, 289, 329, 330

redeploy, 90, 132

Reference, 57, 58, 59, 60, 61, 62, 63, 64, 65, 66, 67, 68, 69, 70, 144, 149, 158, 167, 196, 211, 230, 256, 263, 264, 277, 297

region, 54, 55, 56, 59, 135, 158, 160, 165, 167, 267, 331

Report, vii, viii, xiii, 48, 49, 68, 69, 263, 275, 276

ReportByClass.jsp, xiii, 68, 69, 266, 267, 273, 274

ReportByClassBean.java, xiii, 272

ReportByClassService.java, xiii, 268

Requirements, v, vi, 2, 5, 27, 33, 34, 144, 149, 158, 167, 196, 211, 230, 256, 263, 277, 297

resolution, xiv, 328

response, 84, 98, 99, 114, 115, 116, 117, 118, 119, 121, 160, 162, 163, 164, 165, 167, 169, 173, 197, 198, 212, 213, 231, 232, 265, 268, 282, 301, 331

Results, vii, viii, ix, 49, 61, 62, 90, 139

ResultSet, 132, 133, 163, 174, 175, 177, 180, 181, 200, 201, 202, 203, 214, 215, 217, 234, 269, 271, 272

ResultsLegend.html, xii, 70, 140, 257

Reusability, 93

Roles, ix, xiii, 88, 311, 315, 339

S

scalability, 93, 122, 334

Scalability, xiv, 333, 334

Schema, ix, xiv, xv, 87, 88, 339

SDLC, vi, xviii, xix, 1, 27

Security, xiii, 24, 49, 314

Semester, viii, 39, 40, 61, 62, 63, 64, 151, 152, 157, 204, 209, 247, 306, 308

Sequence, vi, 31

sequence diagrams, 30, 31, 170, 171

Serializable, 124, 127

Service Classes, xi, 113, 122

Servlets, x, 97, 113, 317

Session, x, 107, 108, 129, 131, 174

SESSION, x, 107

setter, 124, 205, 206, 238, 289, 304

SID, 338

side navigation, 55

SOA, 80, 350

software, 350

Software, v, vi, 5, 27

solutions, xvii, xviii, 79, 80, 325, 350

specification, 33, 34, 53, 158, 167, 196, 211, 230, 256, 264, 278, 297, 315, 325, 328, 335

Specification, vi, 34, 57, 58, 59, 60, 61, 62, 63, 64, 65, 66, 67, 68, 69, 70, 144, 149, 158, 167, 196, 211, 230, 256, 263, 277, 297

Specifications, v, vi, 2, 33

standards, 93, 317, 318

static, 31, 50, 55, 56, 104, 115, 117, 129, 130, 132, 133, 134, 135, 162, 173, 175, 187, 198, 200, 208, 213, 215, 222, 232, 234, 246, 256, 267, 269, 273, 282, 283, 301

Student Academics, vii, 38

Student Attendance, vii, viii, ix, xiii, 41, 43, 63, 64, 89, 297, 300

Student Details, vii, viii, ix, 37, 60, 88, 266, 281, 289

Student Fees, vii, ix, 42, 89

StudentAcademics.jsp, xii, 61, 62, 232, 246

StudentAcademicsService.java, xii, 232, 234

StudentAttendance.jsp, xii, 63, 64, 198, 207, 208

StudentAttendanceBean.java, xii, xiii, 198, 206, 301, 304

StudentAttendanceService.java, xii, xiii, 198, 199, 301, 303, 328

StudentBean.java, xi, 126

StudentDetails.jsp, xii, 60, 136, 137, 170, 172, 187

StudentDetailsBean.java, xii, xiii, 172, 182, 281, 291

StudentDetailsService.java, xii, 162, 163, 172, 174

StudentFees.jsp, xii, 65, 213, 222

StudentFeesBean.java, xii, 213, 217

StudentFeesService.java, xii, 213, 214

StudentResultsBean.java, xii, 232, 238

system, ii, 1, 3, 13, 23, 24, 30, 31, 33, 34, 35, 36, 37, 38, 39, 40, 41, 42, 43, 45, 46, 48, 50, 53, 80, 83, 84, 85, 90, 101, 107, 142, 143, 144, 325, 333, 338

T

Table, ix, 88, 89, 90

Teacher, ix, 89, 190

template, vii, 54, 55, 71, 135, 137

Testing, v, xiv, 3, 28, 325, 326

Tier, x, 96, 97

Tomcat, vi, xiii, 6, 23, 24, 26, 97, 105, 112, 144, 145, 148, 256, 311, 314, 318, 321, 322, 337

transaction, 281, 288, 289, 329

Transportation, ix, 38, 89, 195

U

UAT, xiv, 3, 325, 326

UI, 2, 53, 94, 97, 99, 144, 145, 148, 158, 167, 174, 187, 196, 207, 211, 222, 230, 246, 256, 264, 268, 273, 278, 282, 291, 297, 302, 304

UML, vi, xviii, xix, 27, 30, 31, 85, 143

unique, 37, 46, 131

URL, 166, 167, 338

Use Case, vi, xi, xii, xiii, 30, 144, 149, 158, 167, 196, 211, 230, 256, 263, 277, 297

User Roles Table, ix, 88

Users, ix, xiii, 19, 88, 315

Users Table, ix, 88

Utility Classes, xi, 113, 128

V

variable, 24, 25, 73, 104, 121, 166, 280, 290, 300

View Layer, ix, x, 94, 97

W

Web, i, ii, x, xiii, xviii, 6, 97, 141, 148, 317, 320

Web Server, x, 6, 97

web.xml, xiv, 314, 315, 317, 335

Weblogic, 17, 20, 318

wizard, 7, 12, 320

Y

yahoo mail, 107

About the Author

The author Mirza **Yousuf** Ahmed **Baig** holds a Master's degree in Computer Science Engineering from Jawaharlal Nehru Technological University, Hyderabad, India. And a bachelor's degree in electronics and communication engineering from Gulbarga University, India. He has delivered more than 20 corporate trainings on core Java to IT MNCs.

The author has worked as Technical Consultant for Sun Microsystems and Principal Engineer for Oracle India. He has hands on experience of more than one and half decade on Java, JEE and Oracle Fusion Middleware products including Oracle SOA Suite, Oracle AIA, Oracle WebCenter and Oracle ADF. He has been Architecting, Designing, Coding and Supporting software solutions of various complexity and sizes during his entire career. The author has been a direct technological liaison for fortune 500 clients in USA and India.

He has worked in UAE at client site as an Architect for implementing web 2.0 and integration solutions for Abu Dhabi government sector clients.

The author is Sun Certified Java CAPS integrator and Oracle Partner Network (OPN) Certified Specialist for Oracle WebCenter 11g. He is also among the top 10 rank holders in India for ICFAI's GK national level competition. He has been recognized by Computer Sciences Corporation with an outstanding performer award. Altria group, USA has honored him as Field Combat Specialist 1st class for his contributions as a web developer.
Complete profile:
https://in.linkedin.com/in/yousufbaig.

www.ingramcontent.com/pod-product-compliance
Lightning Source LLC
Chambersburg PA
CBHW080548060326
40689CB00021B/4784

* 9 7 8 1 5 1 4 6 6 8 0 7 8 *